Freedom Is Not Enough

Freedom Is Not Enough

T. S. Eliot for Liberation, Resistance, and Hope

Patrick R. Query

Cover credit: Illustration of T. S. Eliot by Summer Pierre. Used with permission.

Published by State University of New York Press, Albany

© 2024 State University of New York

All rights reserved

Printed in the United States of America

No part of this book may be used or reproduced in any manner whatsoever without written permission. No part of this book may be stored in a retrieval system or transmitted in any form or by any means including electronic, electrostatic, magnetic tape, mechanical, photocopying, recording, or otherwise without the prior permission in writing of the publisher.

Links to third-party websites are provided as a convenience and for informational purposes only. They do not constitute an endorsement or an approval of any of the products, services, or opinions of the organization, companies, or individuals. SUNY Press bears no responsibility for the accuracy, legality, or content of a URL, the external website, or for that of subsequent websites.

For information, contact State University of New York Press, Albany, NY
www.sunypress.edu

The views expressed in this book are the author's and do not represent the views of the United States Military Academy, the United States Army, or the Department of Defense.

Library of Congress Cataloging-in-Publication Data

Name: Query, Patrick R., author.
Title: Freedom is not enough : T. S. Eliot for liberation, resistance, and hope / Patrick R. Query.
Description: Albany : State University of New York Press, [2024] | Includes bibliographical references and index.
Identifiers: ISBN 9781438499772 (hardcover : alk. paper) | ISBN 9781438499789 (ebook) | ISBN 9781438499765 (pbk. : alk. paper)
Further information is available at the Library of Congress.

For Michelle
*"But then there are her hands,
and suddenly the only thing that matters
is what she might hold in them."*

Contents

Acknowledgments ix

Abbreviations xi

Introduction: "Always Present" 1

1. Let Us Go: Eliot and Migration 19

2. Eliot and the Anarchist 39

3. Eliot among the Antifascists 55

4. Shantih, War, and *The Waste Land* 71

5. Freedom Is Not Enough: Eliot on Liberation 87

6. Say It Again: *Coriolanus*, *Coriolan*, and Occupy 103

7. Eliot and Radical Hope, 1939 127

Conclusion: "Every Poem an Epitaph" 145

Bibliography 155

Notes 171

Index 179

Acknowledgments

Writing this book was a new kind of challenge, and I wouldn't have been equal to it without the generous help of a special group of friends and colleagues. They have all shown extraordinary generosity and honesty. What an honor it is to have original artwork by my friend Summer Pierre on the cover, and I thank her. I am especially grateful to the following folks who read some or all of the text and offered valuable advice: Casey Andrews, the anonymous readers at SUNY Press, Ria Banerjee, David Chinitz, Dídac Llorens Cubedo, Frances Dickey, Graham Parsons, Anita Patterson, Steve Pinkerton, Matt Seybold, Fabio Vericat, John Whittier-Ferguson, and Craig Woelfel. They gave me confidence to continue and lifted my spirits in ways they may not even have known, as did Chris Castiglia, Tony Cuda, Julia Daniel, Colleen Eils, the Faculty Writing Group at USMA, Sara Fitzgerald, J. Ashley Foster, Henry Robinson Foster, Jeff Gibbons, Nancy Gish, Gabriel Hankins, Ismael Ibáñez Rosales, Hugh Liebert, Rana Liebert, Tony McGowan, Christopher McVey, Fiala Query, Joaquín Query, Megan Quigley, Kevin Rulo, Aaron Seliquini, Jayme Stayer, Sejal Sutaria, Aakanksha Virkar, Enid Zentelis, and, above all, Michelle Query. I thank Ian Webster and all the other students in my seminar on Eliot's late poetry and prose at the 2022 T. S. Eliot International Summer School, where I also received some welcome and timely encouragement from Leonard Diepeveen and Lyndall Gordon. When it came to getting the book published, I benefited enormously from the counsel of Gabrielle McIntire, John Morgenstern, and especially Doug Mao. And in the home stretch, Rebecca Colesworthy and her colleagues at SUNY Press have been a wonderful editorial team.

    A portion of "Eliot among the Antifascists" appeared in the essay "Democracy, Punishment, Banality: Anti-Fascism 1940–2020" in the *T. S.*

Eliot Studies Annual, Volume 3 and is reprinted by permission of Clemson University Press. I am grateful to the T. S. Eliot Estate for permission to quote from the Eliot–Hale letters.

Abbreviations

Eliot–Hale: The Letters of T. S. Eliot to Emily Hale. Ed. John Haffenden. Estate of T. S. Eliot, 2022. https://tseliot.com/the-eliot-hale-letters.

Letters 1–9: The Letters of T. S. Eliot. Vols. 1–8: 1898–1941. Ed. Valerie Eliot, John Haffenden, and Hugh Haughton. London: Faber, 2009–2021.

Poems 1–2: The Poems. Vols. 1–2. Ed. Christopher Ricks and Jim McCue. London/Baltimore: Faber and Faber / Johns Hopkins University Press, 2015.

Prose 1–8: The Complete Prose of T. S. Eliot: The Critical Edition. Vols. 1–8: 1905–1965. Ed. Ronald Schuchard and Jewel Spears Brooker, David E. Chinitz, Anthony Cuda, Frances Dickey, Jennifer Formichelli, Jason Harding, Iman Javadi, and Jayme Stayer. Baltimore: Johns Hopkins University Press, 2014–2019.

Introduction

"Always Present"

Your writings are jokes as long as they touch not on the reality of subjugation or on opposition to it.

—Ōsugi Sakae

Writing is a vanity, unless it's for the friend. Including the friend one doesn't know yet.

—The Invisible Committee

Nothing guarantees that the fascist option won't be preferred to revolution.

—The Invisible Committee

August 2019. In the inaugural US edition of the *Spectator*, the conservative weekly, there were not one but two approving references to T. S. Eliot: one in an essay promoting Adderall, the other denouncing the Mueller investigation into Donald Trump's acceptance of Russian assistance with the 2016 presidential election. There was also an essay calling for restraint in the use of the term *fascist*, just the kind of thing Eliot used to write in the 1920s and 1930s. The *Spectator*, a British magazine, had made its first foray into the American market wrapped in a conservative mantle Eliot had helped to fashion and, apparently, for which he could still suitably stand. A social and political tradition that had initially held Eliot at arm's length, then embraced him, and was ultimately transformed by him, was being exported anew back to the United States from which

Eliot had originally come. Nearly a century had passed since Eliot shed the down of the poetic iconoclast for the full plumage of a self-avowed royalist, classicist, and Anglo-Catholic, and audiences in the United States had long ago seen the rebel that had left their shores return as the very figure of an old establishment. The only real surprise in this latest return was in how late it was. The *Spectator* seemed to be affirming that the same Eliot who had been synonymous with conservatism for most of the twentieth century would do as conservative torchbearer well into the twenty-first. It was as surprising that the *Spectator* hadn't changed as that Eliot hadn't. Apparently his legacy and appeal had not been fiddled with enough by several generations of readers to make Eliot a less comfortable bedfellow for an old British program that in many respects sells out and shortchanges important currents running through Eliot's work. Apparently some more fiddling was needed to keep the *Spectator* crowd from locking down Eliot for good.[1] Because there is another Eliot capable of speaking to the present, and it is one we need.

In certain poems, including famous ones like "The Love Song of J. Alfred Prufrock" and *The Waste Land*, as well as in aspects of his life story, Eliot anticipates the contemporary world of migration both endless and constantly interrupted. One of his longest and most productive friendships was with an anarchist: Herbert Read. In essays, letters, and the poetic sequence *Coriolan*, Eliot turns out to be an underrated antifascist. Although he was no pacifist, he had genuine respect for pacifism so long as it was consistent and pure, and *The Waste Land* makes one of the great poetic cases for peace. In lesser-known works of the 1930s like *Coriolan* and *The Rock*, he experimented with various ways of representing the potential of public assembly as a site of resistance, the power people can create by getting together in the streets. As his own religious faith grew, so did the intensity and complexity of his exploration of hope. As the times grew increasingly desperate, this exploration took a radical turn, and his newly available letters to Emily Hale, the great love of his life, reveal how high the price of radicalism can be. And when he wrote in a 1935 essay that "Freedom is not enough,"[2] it was another indication of a radicalism few have attributed to Eliot. He pursued a lifelong investigation of freedom, in prose as well as poetry, from philosophical and political perspectives, resisting abstractions and insisting on the kind of freedom that has human scale but also cosmic stakes, concrete expression as well as timeless implications. "Freedom is not enough" was not Eliot's way of saying that freedom must be tempered by restraint, responsibility, decorum, etc., but of declaring that ordinary liberal conceptions of freedom do not make people free enough. He wanted himself and others to be not only freer but also more than free.

What Might Be

In the 1944 introduction to a book called *Shakespeare and the Popular Dramatic Tradition*, Eliot reflected on Shakespearean criticism in terms that, eighty years later, help to illuminate his own legacy. Readers may give a grudging respect to textual, biographical, historical, and archaeological criticism, he observed, because such approaches promise an eventual end: "The prospect that the questions will be finally answered is the justification for asking them."[3] But these were not the kinds of criticism Eliot himself practiced or which kept making Shakespeare interesting to new generations. "Of interpretative criticism, which is the relating of historical fact to contemporary consciousness, there is no end," he wrote, "so the reader is tempted to ask, to what purpose is a journey without a terminus?" Among the answers he offers is that in such criticism we discern "the outlines of the consciousness of the critic's age," and he feels "it is possible that one age may miss what a previous age had grasped." The editors of the *Spectator* seem to see in Eliot what previous ages have grasped, but it would also seem they have been unable to find much more than that, as though the journey of reading Eliot did have a terminus. Some outlines of the consciousness of our age are visible in that conservative use of Eliot, but I want to indicate others. Readers of the present age have an opportunity—I would argue even a responsibility—to grasp something different. Eliot himself, in prose and poetry, insists on revisiting and renewing our relationship with past knowledge in light of present needs. The opening lines of his great poem "Burnt Norton" suggest why:

> Time present and time past
> Are both perhaps present in time future,
> And time future contained in time past.
> If all time is eternally present
> All time is unredeemable.
> What might have been is an abstraction
> Remaining a perpetual possibility
> Only in a world of speculation.
> What might have been and what has been
> Point to one end, which is always present.[4]

These lines are their own journey without a terminus, their possible meanings circling round and round one another as time does in the fluid chronology they describe. One of these meanings I hadn't been able to hear until recently but want to retain: against the dead-end of unredeemable time, comprising past, present, and future, a "world of speculation" offers "perpetual possibility." The "abstraction" of "what might have been" is neither irrelevant nor lost because, just as much as "what has been," it points to an end that is not "always *the* present" but "always present." It is a case not of *The present is all we have* but of *The present has all we need*. If what might have been remains a perpetual possibility, then it is the same as what might be. If this is so only in a world of speculation, then interpretative criticism, like literature itself, presents such a world. And that is where I want to set up an encounter with T. S. Eliot: a zone where we see our present as a world he speculated about and in which possibility is perpetual because we are likewise willing to speculate about what might be.

Most people, if they know of Eliot at all, probably know him as the poet of *The Waste Land* or, to judge from my own students' responses, of "The Hollow Men." Some may think of him primarily as a dead, white, conservative writer whose poems are notoriously difficult to understand. A smaller number may know that he is indirectly responsible for *Cats*—perhaps not small enough, given the reviews of the 2019 film version. Fewer still may see him as a useful ally in the broad contemporary fight against reaction, subjugation, and fascism, but I hope to increase that number in what follows. Whatever his utility may continue to be for the editors and readers of the *Spectator*, I believe Eliot has more to offer than we have traditionally imagined to those whose politics point in a different direction.

The essays contained in this slim volume are the product of several years spent wrestling with the question of how an immersion in the study of T. S. Eliot could inform a politics of liberation, resistance, and hope in the present. Eliot studies are changing at an exhilarating pace, and so are the pressures of living a life committed to principles like freedom, equality, hope, nonviolence, the dignity of the poor and marginalized. Yet the pairing between Eliot and a politics of radical liberation is, as the *Spectator* example merely begins to suggest, not a natural or obvious one. It is instead, I admit frankly, the product of an increasingly pressing personal need to bring what I have learned and loved about the work of Eliot to bear on the political and social issues of most concern to me—or, failing this, to leave Eliot alone.

Like many people, I read "The Hollow Men" in high school, "Prufrock" and *The Waste Land* in college, when I also got just a taste of *Four*

Quartets. I also heard for the first time that Eliot was a devoted Christian and may have been gay (he wasn't). In early graduate school, I was introduced, at first via Paul Fussell, to the intimate ways Eliot and his work were connected to the First World War, and I began to read Eliot's essays and letters. I also learned, via Anthony Julius, of the sinister ways Eliot and his work were connected to antisemitism. All of this was well before I committed to studying Eliot long-term. Even as further dark realities emerged—including racism, misogyny, and more antisemitism—I came back to Eliot for the rich access he could provide, via his biography as well as his poetry and prose, to a twentieth-century world I wanted to know better. At every stage, and as my own political and personal views continued to evolve, I kept finding in the figure of Eliot (at times only in the idea of Eliot) a model for rewarding self-inspection and ways of examining my relationship to culture, to politics and society, to loved ones, and to the passage of time.

What happened is that as the world I inhabited began to feel more like Eliot's of the 1930s—familiar freedoms, dignities, and expectations of safety seeming to collapse by the day—I began to feel as though I were being addressed by the framers of the 1937 survey "Authors Take Sides on the Spanish War" who demanded that British and Irish writers choose a side in the contest with fascism. While I don't think I had been quite guilty of "the equivocal attitude, the Ivory Tower, the paradoxical, the ironic detachment" they condemned, I suppose I had felt there was time to see whether and how Eliot fit into the developing picture.[5] At some point in the last decade, though, time seemed to have run out.

Since then, I have found that if I were going to write about Eliot, this is the problem that confronted me. If I were going to continue working on this figure who had meant so much to me, but who, even in the light of insights based on a raft of recently published works, too often seemed unnervingly out of sync with, even hostile to, the politics I wanted to understand better and, indeed, to practice in my own life, I had to find a way to redeem the poet in the light of my own time. If a given investigation into Eliot could not help me answer the questions *How can Eliot help us make the world a freer and more just place? How can his work help us to confront the forces of subjugation that culminate in fascism?* I could not convince myself to pursue it.

In an earlier period, critics of a progressive bent, including Julius, chose to deal with the same problem through a criticism based on negation, on exposure, on what is often called critique. For a time, many such critics made the decision to reject Eliot on the grounds of his supposedly retrograde views, or to devote what attention they gave him to dismantling the architecture of majesty and authority around him. Eliot's use in the battle against reaction was as an exemplar of the ugliness reaction can encompass. Thus readers were forced to contend with the very real legacies of antisemitism, misogyny, racism, and elitism in Eliot's work, from his caution against "any large number of free-thinking Jews"[6] to his obscene Columbo and Bolo poems, and from his alliance with the fascist Ezra Pound to his enthusiasm for class hierarchies and domination of society by "the best people."[7] Eliot's place in the pantheon of greatness was, at the very least, complicated, and in some cases challenged outright. Critical interest in Eliot had hit a low ebb. If the forces of reaction still wanted Eliot, the argument seemed to go, they could have him.

Such deflating approaches served an important role in bringing Eliot into range for an important new kind of criticism that would follow, which could meet Eliot with the aura of majesty or even sanctity removed. But a hermeneutic of diminishment, of attack, is not what I have in mind. What I propose instead is to enlist the aspects of Eliot's art and thought that do bespeak liberatory values, to focus on those techniques, currents, and works upon which the plausible suggestion of a radical politics of liberation, resistance, and hope can be built, and in doing so to argue for a new way in which Eliot can matter for the twenty-first century. My intention is not to try to turn Eliot into a hero for the far left, nor is it to ignore the aspects of his thought and writing that signal oppression more than liberation. Eliot was a stalwart of social and political conservatism throughout almost his entire career, and he remains, for good reason, an eminent figure, a hero even, of the right. The point of this book is not to make this conservative embrace of Eliot less valid. Eliot's defense of conservative positions—social, political, religious, cultural—is too masterful and thoroughgoing to be much diminished by my minor intervention. Even so, I hope to show how those of a less conservative inclination (in some cases much, much less) can also find nourishment in Eliot's work and the story of his life. The same writer who in 1928 described the point of view of his new book of essays as "classicist in literature, royalist in politics, and anglo-catholic in religion"[8] advocated consistently for the freedom of the individual and defended the freedom of speech of British anarchists, to say nothing of the liberatory pathways artists like Virginia Woolf, Allen Ginsberg, Ralph Ellison, and Bob Dylan found in his poetry. Pursuing such pathways myself without resorting to taking Eliot's words recklessly out of context has the potential to keep

Eliot readers on the left curious and engaged and to recommend Eliot to new readers in search of new models and modes for activism. In doing so, I also hope to challenge some of the exclusivity of the far-right claim on Eliot's legacy. White nationalists or those who talk of rooting out the "vermin" of dissent espouse a form of conservatism that is not Eliot's. If, as the anarchist Margaret Killjoy argues, "Fascists can't have nice things," then they can't have Eliot. Or at least not all of him.

A wise colleague reflected recently that, whereas once we tended to ask what counted as art, we now more often ask: *What happens when we consider a given object as art? What is generated in taking that point of view? How productive is it to think of a given object as art?* Such are the kinds of questions with which I respond to my own students' occasional indignation at the more outlandish instances of "what passes for art" (or poetry, or a novel, or whatever). By redirecting the problem from whether a given object fits a given category to questions of possibility and use, a kind of provisional forward momentum is maintained where there might have been nothing more promising than a collision of categories. I might say of my own approach to Eliot that my question is not *Was Eliot actually, say, an anarchist?* but rather *What happens when we read Eliot with a special concern for themes of importance to those, like anarchists, who prize freedom, equality, and hope above all? Is it possible to read such values* through *Eliot instead of against him*?

Fortunately, I am not alone in this endeavor, and I am indeed following in the footsteps of others who have opened the ground, often through painful labor. Megan Quigley has been at the forefront of the effort, leading the discussion of how to read Eliot in the era of #MeToo, for example, out of a conviction that the exigencies of the present not only call for a reevaluation of Eliot's legacy but also open up new opportunities for reading his work and his life productively. With David Chinitz, Quigley has also edited a new collection, *Eliot Now*, addressed specifically to the new moment. My own sense that others were interested in similar new possibilities for approaching Eliot took off around 2013, when I began to read more and more articles concerned with Eliot as what is sometimes called an engaged poet, a term generally reserved for his contemporaries on the left such as W. H. Auden and Stephen Spender, who, along with many others, took their poetry to the streets in the 1930s. Some of these articles focused on Eliot's lesser-known works. For instance, Hazel Atkins and Peter Lowe both highlight *The Rock*, his often-dismissed Christian pageant play, as an example of Eliot's engaged writing. They emphasize, rather than shy away from, Eliot's having been commissioned to write *The Rock* to support the Forty-Five Churches Fund "to build new churches in London's suburbs."⁹ Lowe writes that, in the 1930s and 1940s, "Eliot becomes an advocate not of spiritual withdrawal but of spiritual engagement. Tackling the wrongs of this world becomes a priority, because failing to address the paucity of modern life would be to him a denial of the Christian vision." He emphasizes "Eliot's social vision in [*The Rock*]" and invokes E. Martin Browne, who affirmed "how much [Eliot's] mind was filled with the needs of the workless, the homeless, those who felt themselves excluded."¹⁰

Steven Matthews likewise focuses on Eliot's work of the early 1930s, writing of the unfinished *Coriolan* sequence that it is Eliot's "nearest approach to poetic commentary upon contemporary political ideas" and, further, that the *Coriolan* poems ought to be understood in the context of Eliot's contemporaneous "political engagement" through the vehicle of the *Criterion*, the literary and cultural journal Eliot edited from its 1922 debut to its end in 1939.¹¹ My own encounter with an "activist's Eliot" really began with a reading of *Coriolan* in light of the Occupy movement's vociferations back in 2012, and the ideas of these other scholars helped me see that my own interest in taking Eliot to the streets was perhaps not such an outlier as I had imagined.

The Virtues of Presentism

A natural objection to my approach is to call it presentist. Oxford Languages defines *presentism* as "uncritical adherence to present-day attitudes, especially the tendency to interpret past events in terms of modern values and concepts."¹² Apart from that word *uncritical*, there is a lot in that definition that accurately describes my method, but I would shuffle the last part. My goal is to interpret present events as well as modern values and concepts in terms of past events and the way that similar values and concepts were expressed at that time. Moreover, although it commenced over a century ago, the career of T. S. Eliot is in many ways still part of our present, not only when viewed through a long enough timescale but also when one considers that several of the issues that shaped Eliot's era are shaping ours: polarized politics, anxiety over migration, massive street demonstrations, rising totalitarianism but also interest in anarchism, state power in tension with individual liberty, impending doom necessitating the search for radical hope. Eliot's responses to such things are of course a product of his own historical conditions and horizons of possibility, but using those responses to deepen and improve our own feels to me not so much *presentist* as simply being responsible about the present. It even begins to feel like reckoning with one of Eliot's most treasured concepts: tradition.

Here, too, others have made the case for this kind of approach convincingly, perhaps none more brazenly than Eliot himself, who in "Little Gidding" wrote simply "History is now and England."[13] Fifty years ago, seemingly channeling Eliot, John Berger wrote in *Ways of Seeing*, "The past is never there waiting to be discovered, to be recognized for exactly what it is. History always constitutes the relation between a present and its past. Consequently fear of the present leads to mystification of the past. The past is not for living in; it is a well of conclusions from which we draw in order to act."[14] When we try to cordon it off from present needs, we not only create a false sense of the past's stasis, "the past offers us fewer conclusions to complete in action." Much more recently, in *Interwar Modernism and the Liberal World Order*, Gabriel Hankins shows how we can also travel the other way along this channel linking past and present. Current understandings of economics and politics reveal truths about Eliot's age that we could otherwise cordon off—and frequently have—as features of a world little resembling our own. At the same time, he shows how much the aesthetics of Eliot and his contemporaries were of one substance with the political and economic systems and institutions that shaped their world and that they, in turn, frequently helped to shape. Matthew Seybold makes the case unapologetically for Hankins's approach: "Hankins's book is a reminder that there is no such thing as an anachronistic politics. The Treaty of Versailles can be better understood through present systems of oppression. Claude McKay's poems and Virginia Woolf's novels mobilize current and future activisms."[15] Nor are the "virtues of presentism"[16] Seybold endorses limited to the audacity to read the past as though it were part of the world we occupy; they include gaining the humility to view the present as precedented, to frame and scale our experience using the reference points of the past. Presentism has the virtue of breaking down temporal barriers, and it is often aligned with an imperative to break down barriers of other kinds as well. As Seybold argues, "Creative writing and cultural criticism was then and should again be urgently transportable between academic, activist, commercial, governmental, and public spheres."[17] For me, the urgency of such transporting has as much to do with the pursuit of truth as with the stakes of the fight and the multiplicity of arenas in which it has to be fought.

Outside of the study of Eliot, there is already considerable wind in the sails of such an approach, thanks to critics who have responded to what they perceived as a need to get the activity of reading and responding to literature up and moving in a new, socially engaged way for our explosive era. Rita Felski speaks the mind of many others in being "motivated by a desire to articulate a positive vision for humanistic thought in the face of growing skepticism about its value."[18] I take inspiration from a group of literary critics giving shape to a new approach to the work of criticism itself: Felski, Joseph North, and Christopher Castiglia, for example, have been engaged in articulating practices that can restore to literary criticism the capacity for both meaningful critique of the status quo and the deliberative expression of alternatives based on imagination and idealism. As the literary and political world tilted increasingly toward practices and outlooks that felt unsatisfying and seemed to promise little in the way of liberating growth, such critics made the brave choice to try something new. Their work has energized a way of reading that seemed at one time to have passed away but that feels urgent and indeed essential right now. "A persuasive defense of the humanities," writes Felski, "is hindered rather than helped by an ethos of critique that encourages scholars to pride themselves on their vanguard role and to equate serious thought with a reflexive negativity."[19] North points to the moment, "sometime in the late 1970s or early 1980s," when "the discipline agreed to transform itself into a discipline of observation, tracking developments in the culture without any broader mandate to intervene in it."[20] Prior to this turn, "literary studies . . . at least on paper, proposed detailed and intellectually rigorous methods both for analyzing the culture *and for taking action to change it*."[21] It "help[ed] readers, each from their own specific material situations, to use the aesthetic instruments of literature to cultivate their most useful practical capabilities."[22] Castiglia describes what kind of mindset it would take for literary criticism to do so again:

> Every critique is a determined affirmation, an inverted expression of idealism. In offering critiques, we measure the present or the past against ideals, in comparison to which what is or has been seems inadequate and unjust. Without ideals, there would be no critique. But our ideals are effaced by rituals of professionalization in a discipline that regards articulation of

idealism as a sign of naïveté, triviality, or bad faith, making idealism cause for embarrassment. A critique that states our ideals, in contrast, would make clear what we are for, demonstrating how idealism is the basis for ethical judgment and encouraging the shaping and expression of ideals necessary to social engagement and change. Affirming our ideals, we claim for critique its greatest and most generous social relevance.[23]

In these chapters, I wear my idealism pretty openly, hoping that by doing so I can gain for my own attempts at critique a purchase in the social world while at the same time establishing some new social relevance for Eliot's work. North writes that "what nonspecialist readers are looking for in literature is . . . something to go on with, something that will help them live their lives."[24] From what I am hearing, and as implied by the quotations above, even specialist readers are increasingly looking for something like that, and my essays aim to help specialists and general readers find it in T. S. Eliot.[25]

In the matter of coming out from behind the illusory disinterestedness promised by the "rituals of professionalization," I am also inspired by Erica Lagalisse, not a literary scholar but a social scientist, who introduces her 2019 book by stating frankly: "It is explicit that I come to the historical studies at hand methodologically as both an anthropologist and for the purposes of practical intervention within social movements and politics today . . . purposefully engag[ing] the past from the perspective of the present."[26] Like Lagalisse, I also pursue an "interdisciplinary activity" to which "diverse specialists will hopefully be inspired to add some qualification, and thus lend their own knowledge and methodological strengths to the problem."[27] Most of what I say in this introduction betrays a certain disciplinary insecurity. This is because I have become, like most of us in the field, so accustomed to minding the lane markers of my profession and mindful that I am deliberately choosing to challenge them. But here, too, I take encouragement from North, who writes, "Hitherto, literary scholars on the left have tried merely to interpret the world. We are now entering a new situation. Might there not be a case for a systematic attempt to change it?"[28] And I am bucked up by Lagalisse, who suggests that "maybe when it comes to fighting fascism, every possible strategy is worth trying."[29]

Some strategies may even include making the strangest of alliances and bedfellows. Maia Ramnath, an anarchist, recognized the tension between ideological purity and practical necessity as she waited in line to vote in a New York City election. As she listened to a MAGA hat-wearing man spew "rage and hate" at those in line, she was confirmed in her view that joining forces wherever possible was the way to go, even if it meant seeming to endorse the apparatus of state control by casting a vote. Being an anarchist lining up at a polling place "felt like teaming up, all hands on deck in a desperate emergency, in the way that you wouldn't ask about ideology when trying to put out a fire or turn a car from hurtling over a cliff or stop a gunshot victim from bleeding out."[30] Lines drawn by rage, fear, and hate frequently have the effect of gathering together the people on the other side of them.

This book, then, is a record of my use of the strategy of reading T. S. Eliot to learn, broadly, how to make the world a freer and more just place and, specifically, how to get better at liberation, resistance, and hope. This goal led me to focus on a handful of still more specific areas where I suspected—hoped—Eliot's work might be useful, such as protest and occupation, pacifism, migration, friendship, freedom in unfree times, antifascism, and hope in the face of apparent doom. In most cases, or at least in a sufficient number to keep justifying the effort, I discovered that Eliot's writing could indeed do this work. It proved, not surprisingly, rich, complex, and nuanced enough to support the kind of readings I hoped to pursue without, crucially, violating what I understood of the explicit ideas and ideals Eliot espoused. The specter I envisioned of a square peg being made to fit the round holes never quite materialized. Rather, my critical operation began to feel like one of eschewing pegs in favor of, say, blocks: something to build with.

Instead of *What does a poem mean?* I encourage my own students to ask *What can a poem do? How much of a certain kind of meaning can you build out of the material of a poem, with careful and consistent reference back to it and without contradicting other aspects of it?* My investigation of Eliot in light of the ethics of radical freedom kept revealing that Eliot's work provided more of the right kind of blocks than I had suspected. A responsible reader neither dominates the text nor is dominated by it. She is not indifferent to the text's claims nor obsessed with its essence or being, but is instead in dialogue with it. If such a reader also aspires to a kind of activism, such a dialogue will likely include some knowing appropriation. If the kind of appropriation of Eliot I am engaged in is a transgression of Eliot's own statements and biography, the severity is either mitigated or exacerbated by the fact that I know what I'm doing. The patterns of Eliot's life and ideas are familiar enough to me that, as I select from those patterns the material I can use for the present cause, I know pretty well what I am leaving out, and I can live with the trade-off. If you're going to sin, another wise colleague once advised, the thing is to do so with intention. Eliot himself was sympathetic to certain transgressors, like Baudelaire, whose willful offense is still preferable to indifference; they are at least "men [sic] enough to be damned."[31] I make no claim about my own manliness according to this formula. I only say that, at the very least, the needs of the moment make the risks seem worth it.

I initially thought of titling the book *Why Eliot Matters*, inspired by Christopher Hitchens's *Why Orwell Matters*. But that would have been misleading, about both my purposes and Eliot's current importance. Eliot seems to matter now (and not only to the editors of the *Spectator*) more than at any point since his death, owing to the opening up and gathering together of massive archives of his writing in the past dozen years or so: the publication of the eight-volume *Complete Prose*, the two-volume *Poems*, the nine-volume (and counting) *Letters*, the coming *Plays*, and the newly opened correspondence with Emily Hale. And it all follows on an era in which interest in Eliot was already revivified by new studies of his connections with race, popular culture, gender, war, visual art, music, and more. Eliot matters and is going to go on mattering in all kinds of ways for the foreseeable future. My own more limited interest is in showing how Eliot can matter to a particular kind of liberatory politics and to a kind of literary criticism that wants to come closer to activism, where activism is understood as the pursuit of social change in service to ideals.

All the while, I am trying to remain vigilant about the risks to scholarship attendant upon the movement from ostensible detachment to political engagement. But I have seen in enough new scholarship, some of it mentioned already, that there seems to be a significant interest within Eliot studies in more precisely linking Eliot's poetry with cultural and social praxis—an approach that takes a step beyond even the de-sanitization of Eliot exemplified by Chinitz and others and toward a reading of Eliot's work as socially concerned, as politically engaged, as, if not activist, at least offering raw material for idealistic action. This "activist's Eliot" does not suddenly become the *engagée* W. H. Auden, but he does afford readers a way of trying out the potential leverage of the poetry and ideas of the poet in the political world of the present. He affords readers, too, some license for worrying less about chronology and more about what seems to be happening, or perhaps *needs* to be happening, with the words of the past *now*. Doing so would be a way of practicing what Jack

Halberstam, David Graeber, and others call "low theory, a theory that is appropriate to a politics that needs to do something in the moment, as opposed to build[ing] a large, extensive, long-term, abstract project. Low theory answers to the contingencies of the moment."[32] In a way, all we have are such contingencies. They are what make the present and our experience within it *present*. They are also perpetually opening new ways of looking at the past. If we grant those contingencies a more central place in our reading practice, rather than holding them in abeyance or pretending they don't exist, we can inhabit our world more thoroughly and might even be doing a little better by the future.

The opening lines of "Burnt Norton," cited at the outset, can be read as an invitation to such a mode of reading. As can the lines that immediately follow:

> Footfalls echo in the memory
> Down the passage which we did not take
> Towards the door we never opened
> Into the rose-garden. My words echo
> Thus, in your mind.
>   But to what purpose
> Disturbing the dust on a bowl of rose-leaves
> I do not know.
>   Other echoes
> Inhabit the garden. Shall we follow?[33]

These essays are an attempt to follow some of those other echoes in Eliot's work, to open doors and follow certain passages to the present that would not have been open if not for the present taking its particular forms. Just as the speaker of the first lines of "Burnt Norton" acknowledges that something of what was then the future, our present, was contained in the present of those lines' initial uttering, we know that our own present carries aspects and versions of that other present, our past. Eliot could not foresee just how his words would echo in our minds, decades on from his writing them, to what purpose they would disturb dust in the future, and he was pleased to relinquish control over meaning to the play of time and context. We readers are always reading in that "one end, which is always present," and if we accept the invitation Eliot expresses in "Burnt Norton" and throughout his career, based on a view of time that is reciprocal, cyclical, and mutual, then we allow our world to be filled with light, music, and voices that would otherwise remain unseen and unheard. We can affirm with confidence that we are doing the very best with Eliot that we can and perhaps a little of what we must for our troubled present.

Two final points, on absences. First, certain absences in my table of contents would seem conspicuous if I were not allowed to justify them by stating that some topics—Eliot and ecology, Eliot and patriarchy, Eliot and race, for instance—either have been or are currently being treated substantively by others. I see my own chapter topics as at times more general and portable, at times more narrow, and in any event suited to fill in the spaces around those projects of more depth. Is this an evasion? Yes and no. Considering how foundational ecology is to the human predicament at present—our political and economic initiatives will not matter at all if our societies collapse from climate change—it is virtually impossible to justify leaving it out of any serious intervention on behalf of hope. But the scope and scale of the ecological and environmental crisis render—for this writer, anyway—their adequate treatment in a book of such comparably minor ambitions as this one unworkable. The climatic threat to the continuance of organized human life on Earth is simply of another order of magnitude than the problems I do treat, and I cannot commit the farce of including an essay on this topic as simply one chapter among others.

And there may be no more stark dividing line than antiracism between the forces of reaction and those in pursuit of the world of peace, equality, and freedom I have been sketching. So why not address it here? Simply put, I do not find Eliot all that helpful on the matter. His views on Jewish and Black people seem at best characteristic of the genteel, liberal (to use a word Eliot would hate to hear applied to himself) modes of supposedly benign chauvinism common to his era and at worst as crass and bruising as any expressions of the racist far right, then or now. So he may be a resource in the antiracist fight, but more likely in the negative sense that, again, has been well explored and is not my emphasis here. Readers interested in learning should start with Gabrielle McIntire's *Modernism, Memory, and Desire* (2008) and perhaps finish with Jayme Stayer's *Becoming T. S. Eliot* (2021). To use Eliot to further a politics of liberation in matters of race or ethnicity would be to read that effort against Eliot rather than through him, which is the commitment of my project. So, too, with gender. I do not find enough in Eliot for animating—again, in a positive way—a robust politics of gender equality. The struggle against subjugation ought to be open to all kinds of unexpected alliances and to admit all manner of strange bedfellows. But it nonetheless admits of distinctions and emphases. When it comes to race and gender, I won't cancel Eliot for his sins, but neither will I pretend that he can do much to save us.

Second, all questions eventually culminate for Eliot in the spiritual. It may come as a surprise to those who know Eliot only as the author of his famous early poems, but there is no major poet of the twentieth century for whom Christianity was more central. I affirm unequivocally that seeking to bring his whole self into union with the divine will is the great theme of Eliot's life in writing and the end toward which all of his reflections bend. It is also outside the scope of this book. For one reason, Christianity's claim on Eliot, and vice versa, has already been lovingly, thoroughly, and consistently explored and argued. From an early study like Kristian Smidt's *Poetry and Belief in the Work of T. S. Eliot* (1961) to the more recent *T. S. Eliot and Christian Tradition*, edited by Benjamin Lockerd, and *Mortality and Form in Late Modernist Literature*, by John Whittier-Ferguson (both 2014), Eliot's journey of faith has, in the nearly one hundred years since his Christian conversion, constituted one of the most reliable avenues for investigating the meanings and uses of his work. My own intended audience has been less lavishly served. Those who may or may not share Eliot's Christian faith but who can hear in the skeptical, searching, inquiring voice of Eliot's Christian poetry a potential ally in the real fight for the world of peace, equality, and freedom they know is possible: resources for these folks do not yet fill library shelves, and they may not get more than this book. And if it should turn out that Eliot was right, that his solutions to life's problems will at some point prove incomprehensible to the nonbeliever, then perhaps I'll only have inadvertently helped him to win some souls. For now, though, I propose to "halt at the frontier of metaphysics or mysticism" as Eliot did in his famous essay "Tradition and the Individual Talent."[34] If everything in this book brings a reader right up to the point beyond which lies the spiritual—the point at which my arguments cease to be of much help—I think this is a satisfactory outcome. I would encourage any such readers to take up boldly the spiritual questions that must predominate at that point and to look for another guide. Eliot approved of such restraint in Baudelaire: "It is a proof of his honesty that he went as far as he could honestly go and no further."[35] I believe I can stay within the bounds of honesty by expanding somewhat the earthly material through which the big spiritual questions are foreshadowed, modeled, and prepared, showing it to be broader and more diverse than we have often supposed and, for now, be satisfied with that outcome as well.

In one of his most important books, *Possibilities: Essays on Hierarchy, Rebellion, and Desire* (2007), anarchist anthropologist David Graeber defended an approach to scholarship that is at once idealistic and deeply aware of its limitations, an approach I have tried to adopt in this book. "Of course, the world is not really generated by the descriptions we make of it," he wrote:

> [*Possibilities*], then, is meant to assemble a series of different and sometimes even incommensurable perspectives on a very real world. They are unified, above all, by a commitment to the idea that that world could possibly look very different than it does—but just as much, perhaps, by the belief that, ultimately, the very combination of anger and curiosity, of intellectual play and creative pleasure that goes into crafting any worthwhile piece of critical social theory also itself partakes of something of the powers that could transform that world into something better. What unites them, then, is a utopian ideal.[36]

The chapters that follow try to make productive and unapologetic use of anger, curiosity, intellectual play, and creative pleasure. They are likewise unified by idealism but try to unfold that idealism with an appropriate level of humility in the face of a world that is always outstripping and outliving our descriptions of it. Several of Eliot's own ideas were thus outstripped and outlived by the world he lived in and the one that followed: sometimes for the better, improving the possibilities for human dignity and equality, but sometimes not. Others have come back, and their effect on those possibilities is uncertain, but the times are so desperate that we must identify what, if anything, we need from T. S. Eliot today, as from any writer of the past. This book is an attempt to gather aspects of both "what might have been and what has been" in the legacy of T. S. Eliot and then to suggest what might be of use in a hopeful struggle for liberation and against reaction, coercion, and extinction.

Chapter 1

Let Us Go

Eliot and Migration

Migration. The movement of persons away from their place of usual residence, either across an international border or within a State.

—International Organization for Migration

The first words of the poem that put Eliot on the literary map are words of migration. "Let us go," the thrice-repeated invitation in the first stanza of "The Love Song of J. Alfred Prufrock," is on its surface only an invitation to a walk through city streets, not a journey across geographical frontiers, but the poem is migratory on multiple levels, beginning with its composition. The style was inspired by the French symbolist poet Jules Laforgue, and the first passage Eliot composed was the one about the Danish Prince Hamlet. Begun in Cambridge, Massachusetts, in 1910, when Eliot was a student at Harvard, the poem was continued in Paris and Munich in 1910 and 1911, and revised back at Harvard and then in London, before being first published in Chicago in *Poetry* magazine in 1915.[2] In the process, the poem by a young American had accreted European languages. First it acquired an Italian epigraph—from Dante. By the time of its appearance in the collection *Prufrock and Other Observations* (1917), it was further framed by a dedication, in French, to a Frenchman and an additional Dantean epigraph in Italian. So although the action of the poem never gets beyond the local "half-deserted streets," "Prufrock" is both the product of a migratory process—literal and figurative—and the expression of a young man at the start of a long process of migration.

I say "beyond" those streets, but in a way the action of the poem never gets *to* them: the absence of movement is as central to the poem as its obsession with going somewhere. The Prufrockian push-and-pull with Europe, the plight of a would-be traveler tantalized by the possibilities of cosmopolitanism but who finds more doors closed than open, introduces a theme that Eliot would explore throughout his work: from "Prufrock" to *The Waste Land* and from "Journey of the Magi" to *Four Quartets*. Europe summoned Eliot early in his career, and he responded with enormous imaginative and intellectual energy, but it wasn't long before he discerned that European borders—internal and external, political as well as imaginative—can be cruelly difficult to traverse. It foreshadows a lesson being learned daily by millions of migrants today, with far higher stakes than the development of a literary sensibility.

In 2019, Penguin Random House released the *Penguin Book of Migration Literature*, edited by Dohra Ahmad and introduced by Edwidge Danticat. Unsurprisingly, T. S. Eliot does not appear in it. But in this chapter I want to make a case for Eliot's relevance to the consideration of migration, both in his day and in ours. Certain aspects of his biography and some of his most famous poems speak to the experience of migration in the twenty-first century. I deliberately choose the somewhat vague construction "speak to" because, as will continue to be the case in these chapters, it is not so much a way through the challenge that Eliot offers as a way *to* it. Reading Eliot for migration yields better questions than answers. That they come from an unexpected quarter is as useful a reason for entertaining them as are the increasingly desperate circumstances of the Earth as a place of migration.

Could we see Eliot as a migrant? One way to bring him into a meditation on migration is to listen to a contemporary writer whose experience of migration shares a great deal with Eliot's. Ariel Dorfman, in a review of the Penguin volume, writes that, although as a younger person such terms were available to him, he chose not to "distinguish myself . . . as a refugee, like those festering in camps set up for the famished of Biafra or for displaced Palestinians . . . Nor did I want to cast myself in the prototypical role of migrant," as his grandparents had.[3] Instead, as he moved from Argentina to New York to Chile and back to New York, with stops in California and Europe in between, he decided to think of himself as "an exile, a term that, I thought, would preserve my dignity and freedom, and allow me to take my place in a romantic and heroic tradition." This designation served him well for many years, until after settling down in New York he came to accept that "I am merely someone who has chosen to live elsewhere, more fully, safely, and creatively than if I had remained in my homeland." Although his years as an exile did encompass "trauma and insecurity, it is also true that their painfulness and uncertainty were mitigated by . . . my privileged education and ability to speak perfect English," a "network of solidarity," and "the blessings of a literary vocation."[4] The points on his journeys and the degree of political upheaval prompting his movements are quite different from those of T. S. Eliot the migrant. Otherwise, Dorfman might be describing Eliot's own peregrinations in search of both a home and an identity.

Eliot always saw himself as a kind of migrant. His early history is indeed characterized by migratory movements: east from St. Louis to Boston, then to Paris and London and the long hunkering-down period that followed. "Some day," he wrote to his friend Herbert Read in 1928,

> I want to write an essay about the point of view of an American who wasn't an American, because he was born in the South and went to school in New England as a small boy with a n***** drawl, but who wasn't a southerner in the South because his people were northerners in a border state and looked down on all southerners and Virginians and who so was never anything anywhere and who therefore felt himself to be more a Frenchman than an American and more an Englishman than a Frenchman and yet felt that the U. S. A. up to a hundred years ago was a family extension.[5]

So perhaps less a migrant than a "metic," meaning "resident alien," wherever he was. In the years of writing *The Waste Land* he indeed referred to himself as a metic, and he occasionally signed himself *Metoikos*. "Resident alien" is a rather dreary bureaucratic term primarily used to designate a tax status. It conveys even less "trauma and insecurity" than Dorfman's account of exile becoming plain voluntary expatriation. It might be possible to read the obvious sense of superiority in Eliot's words as the reflection of deep insecurity, but prejudice—sharpest in the racial slur—clearly insulates Eliot from feeling too much trauma over his position. A great distance separates such a position from that of a less privileged migrant or a person who because of race, class, caste, or gender lacks the ability to go anywhere at all. Even so, Eliot's (unrealized) idea for an essay on his own ambivalent "point of view" does convey a profound sense of disjunction, nonbelonging, and the kind of rootlessness that is disorienting rather than empowering.

More trauma and insecurity colors an episode from Eliot's early experience of Europe. Before he settled down in England, he briefly found himself a migrant of a more troubled kind just after the outbreak of the First World War. There is good reason to consider his predicament as an American in wartime Germany that of a refugee, except that virtually every definition of *refugee* indicates that one must be fleeing their *own* home due to persecution or the danger of violence or disaster, not returning from abroad under such circumstances. Eliot, like other British and Americans, was fleeing Germany and nearby countries before international hostilities hardened into closed borders and indefinite detentions. But Eliot hardly sounds like a refugee when biographer Lyndall Gordon writes that in the summer of 1914 "Eliot had barely settled down in Marburg when war broke out. On 3 August he moved, via Rotterdam, to London, and thence, in October, to a new retreat, Oxford, where he remained till June 1915."[6] A closer look at the experience, however, shows that Eliot did have to think and act like a refugee until he reached England.

He recounted the experience in a letter to his mother of August 23, 1914. He writes from London, having had to make his way there from Marburg, Germany, with some adventure but little grave difficulty. At the outbreak of war, he tells her, "We all supposed that after the mobilization, we could (as proved to be the case for those of us who were Americans) slip away without difficulty." Before long he did come to appreciate "the seriousness of our position. We were told it would be impossible to leave for a fortnight; that it would be impossible for the summer course to continue; but that to fill our time during the enforced stay various makeshift courses and conversation groups would be arranged. The director made a speech in which he cautioned us to be very careful, to avoid crowds, and not to talk in foreign languages in the street."[7] His immediate concern was getting word of his safety to his parents, and he spent half his handy German currency to cable them. As for so many refugees, the banal matter of money quickly became one of relentless urgency. "Realising his letters of credit were not being accepted in Marburg," another biographer, Robert Crawford, writes, his hosts, the Happichs, "did not charge him for board. Down to about 40 marks, he worried if he stayed longer he might not have enough cash to reach the frontier. Russian and French summer-school students were detained indefinitely. Foreign nationals faced the poorhouse if their money ran out."[8] It is anxiety rather than immediate danger that characterizes the interval between the declarations of war and his escape to England. "The suspense," he informs his mother, "penned up with no certain communications and no knowledge of when we could get out, and with only imperfect sympathy with the people we were among . . . ; all this made a fortnight seem a month." On August 16, he finally boarded a train for Frankfurt. The adventure gets slightly more intense once he and his friends begin to move: "When we made up our minds to leave, I did not know whether it would be possible to get to England or not . . . and I thought I could throw myself on the consul at Rotterdam, in any case. Anything to get out of the country, even if we had to travel steerage (we were prepared for that). . . . The trip to Frankfurt is ordinarily an hour and a half. It took five hours."[9] Later: "We had taken a chance; it was not certain that we could get through Cologne by train; but the boats down the Rhine would have taken three days, and it was raining . . ." Other hardships included having to sleep in a station, the lack of dining cars being run in the train, "a tedious wait," several changes of train, and being "very uncomfortable" for a time until being merrily waved through at the Dutch frontier. "And that's all," he concludes. "The American pass does anything in Germany."[10]

As a story of migration, it lacks great texture or tension, and we wonder what happened to his Russian and French costudents. It does contain certain features that have been common to—if greatly intensified in—the more desperate situations of millions of migrants: delay, tedium, discomfort, uncertainty about durations, the strategic temporary erasure of national identity, the fixation on passages and borders. And the story of his flight from Germany evokes, in its way, three terms—the migrant, the camp, and the border—that have become crucial to reckoning with a Europe in the midst of its present cultural and political crises of identity: crises based on coming and going by individuals, masses, and nations. Written when he was still experiencing Europe from a position of relative insecurity, his famous early poems capture an unease that may have less to do with migration than with the idea of Europe itself, in which coming and going, then as now, can appear tantalizingly easy and yet be fraught with shadows, "cunning passages," and "contrived corridors."[11]

Eliot made a turn away from European maps and itineraries around the time of his conversion to Christianity and adoption of British citizenship, after which the spatial mechanics of movement into and through Europe fall away almost entirely from his poetry. I would argue that the most useful work for the contemporary migrant or student of migration is the work he did before he settled for good in his own English sanctuary. Later poems are full of wisdom for the spiritual traveler but fewer representations of the migrant who actually has to get somewhere. That kind of migrant, who needs money, shelter, and translation help, is more apt to find something familiar in poems like "The Love Song of J. Alfred Prufrock" and *The Waste Land*.

The United Nations World Migration Report for 2022 estimates that there were over 281 million migrants in the world in 2020, a figure nearly double that of 1990 and amounting to 3.6% of the global population.[12] Within this total are groups of migrants who occupy more narrow categories—refugees, asylum seekers, stateless persons, trafficked persons, migrant workers, separated children—terms that have crucial significance in political and administrative judgments about the status of individuals. Universally accepted definitions of any of the terms, however, are nonexistent; interpretations vary dramatically between locations and according to the amount of pressure migration puts on a given system or boundary. There are migrants, and then there are migrants. Almost a third of the global migrant total comprises "forcibly displaced" persons, a population no one would confuse even with migrant workers or climate refugees, certainly not international students or expatriate poets. The glossary of the UN's International Organization for Migration offers *migrant* as "an umbrella term, not defined under international law, reflecting the common lay understanding of a person who moves away from his or her place of residence, whether within a country or across an international border, temporarily or permanently, and for a variety of reasons."[13]

Under this broad definition, Eliot himself was certainly a migrant at various points in his life, as indeed he claimed to be. He was obviously a different kind of migrant when he came to Europe as an international student in 1910 or even when he briefly became—almost—a refugee in 1914 than the people currently filling the migrant camps of southern Europe, the Middle East, or the United States, whatever their particular status. Eliot's ideas about migration tend to outpace his own somewhat insulated experience of it; however, the poetic use he made of the combination provides one means of coming closer to the experience of a portion of those 281 million.

Eliot was forever interested in the movements of ideas—and, to an extent, people—through Europe. A fascination with the "mind of Europe" is evident in his earliest published poems, central to *The Waste Land* and his groundbreaking essay "Tradition and the Individual Talent," and foundational to the critical program of the journal he cofounded, the *Criterion*. Yet in the first half of his career, terms like *nation* and *geogra-*

phy play a relatively insignificant part in his thinking about the European idea. Especially in the years spanning, say, 1910 and 1927, Eliot's sense of Europe is characterized far more by movement, by moments of contact and intellectual commerce, by the flux and combination attendant upon travel—actual or imaginative—than by a very deep sense of place or a determining sense of boundaries. Globalization as we know it was a long way off, but Eliot's eyes were nonetheless trained on international flows and exchanges, especially of literature, culture, religion, and politics but also of money. From 1917 to 1925, he worked as a clerk in the Colonial and Foreign Department of Lloyds Bank in London. "The business," Crawford notes, "was notably polylingual. Checking and cross-checking banks' reports, evaluating their activities and solvency in wartime, Tom absorbed texts in French, Spanish, German, Portuguese, Danish, Swedish and Norwegian," an exercise that certainly informed the play of languages in *The Waste Land*.[14]

The deep note of locality, of place, would come to sound much more strongly in his writing of the 1930s and beyond, perhaps not coincidentally when European borders, both physical and intellectual, began to ossify. As Atossa Araxia Abrahamian observes, the "emancipatory potential of statelessness" that had glimmered briefly in the interwar period "began to dissipate by the end of the 1930s." Eliot's poetry mirrors a shift in the discourse around states and individual identity. According to Abrahamian, "Abstract academic and legal debates—about whether states make a people or vice versa, about whether individuals or nations were subject to international law, about the boundaries of national sovereignty and territory and whether legal personhood existed outside the state—revealed themselves as morally insufficient in the face of the political realities of totalitarianism and the real-life suffering experienced by so many people during the 1930s and 1940s."[15] Those who could save themselves through the assertion of nationality, of citizenship, had little choice but to do so. Those who were denied or stripped of such an identity were usually the first to be cast aside or crushed by the machinery of the new order—the Jews and Romani of Germany and neighboring countries constituting the most devastating examples. Eliot's settling into Englishness was not undertaken as a defense against similar horrors, but it is in keeping with the mood of a time when stability and strong state—or at least national—ties were generally prized above cosmopolitanism.[16]

In the earlier part of his life, what he later lamented as the "closing of the mental frontiers of Europe"[17] had not yet set in, notwithstanding the temporary locking down of physical frontiers in the First World War. The birth of the *Criterion* reflects the interest during the immediate postwar years in dislodging identity from citizenship, of multiplying the possibilities for at least an imaginative or critical statelessness. Much as his later work reflects the widespread retraction of such limbs, the Europe evoked in Eliot's early poems stirs with the energy of crossed borders and even "nonstate political orders" of the earlier period.[18] And yet, for all its exploratory internationalism, this poetic Europe is hardly an ideal borderless Schengen Area. For all the imaginative investment Eliot, especially in his prose, places in Europe as a shared tradition, a field for the circulation of culture, his poetry also consistently confounds that vision, showing this European idea to be doomed, apparently by a quality within itself. In this way, Eliot's early writing anticipates the contemporary European scene: enamored of diversity, open borders, and the free exchange of ideas; and yet, in practice, always tripping over and entangling itself upon the invisible border mechanisms that don't so much surround Europe or its constituent parts as form the essence of what Europe means.

Writing about the crisis of migration in contemporary Europe, Etienne Balibar quickly arrives at the question of borders: "Europe conceived itself as developing borders of its own," he writes, "but in reality it *has no borders*, rather *it is itself a complex 'border'*: at once one and many, fixed and mobile, internal and external. To say it in plainer English, Europe is a *Borderland*." From this observation, he derives two key implications: "Firstly, that Europe is not a space where borders exist alongside one another but rather *on top of one another* without really being able to merge into one another. Secondly, that Europe forms a space within which borders *multiply* and *move* incessantly, 'chased' from one spot to the other by an unreachable imperative of closure, which leads to its 'governance' resembling a permanent state of emergency."[19] He cites as examples the efforts of northern European countries to close their doors to Syrian refugees not at their own borders but at those of their southern European counterparts (especially Italy and Greece), and the proliferation of impromptu borders around temporary zones of encampment for migrants. These are only the latest manifestations of what Balibar sees as a fundamental paradox of European identity: the simultaneous assertion of territorial integrity—for states and the collective—and the insistence upon political boundaries fluid enough to keep in, or out, particular peoples at particular times.

The mention of encampment is, of course, freighted with terrible resonance in the European context. Giorgio Agamben argues that the camp is the representative modern formation—as opposed to the city or even the state—for understanding human life on Earth after the Second World War. And he does indeed take as his starting point the Nazi concentration camps, which introduced new frames of reference for considering the human condition, namely *bare life* (*zoe*) and *qualified life* (*bios*). It is important to note that the contemporary migrant camp is a profoundly different institution (if it can be called that) than the Nazi labor and extermination camps. Yet the operations of bare life and qualified life nonetheless inform how we understand contemporary migrant experience, particularly in the camp. To oversimplify, *qualified life* is political and social, life experienced as speech, action, and interaction; whereas *bare life* is what is left when such agency and engagement are stripped away and life is reduced to little more than a biological function.[20] In a migrant camp, however humane, bare life predominates. In a zone rigidly marked off from the established machinery for political life in Europe, one's meaningful existence—again, from the European political perspective—is as a body, a number, a bare life.

Camp-bound migrants, of course, are not the only people whose lived experience falls somehow outside the available frameworks for purposive engagement in political Europe. "Gypsies, Roma and Travellers," writes Becky Taylor, "are some of the most marginalized and vilified people in society. They are rarely seen as having a place in a country, either geographically or socially, no matter where they live or what they do."[21] "The state," writes James C. Scott, "has nearly always been the implacable enemy of mobile peoples."[22] The notion that today's migrants from Africa and the Middle East represent a violation of or a threat to established European identity is undermined by the fact that Europe has for centuries been home to large populations of people for whom traveling is a way of life. "Their history," Taylor argues, "is as intimately tied to the broader sweep of history as the rest of society's. Understanding their history is to take in the founding and contraction of empires, Reformation and Counter-Reformation, wars, the expansion of law and order and of states, the Enlightenment and the increasing regulation of the world."[23] To put it another way, there have been Romani in Europe for as long as there has been an idea of Europe at all. The "legitimacy of their presence" has always been "highly contested," even though they predate and frequently outlast the institutions, hierarchies, and nation-states against which their own mobile, heterogeneous identities are measured.[24] They have always presented "a profound threat to social hierarchy, as they opened up the possibility of another way of being."[25] Although they "remain unwelcome" in most of modern Europe, Roma, Gypsies, and Travellers have persisted in the mobility that defines them even as it frequently disqualifies them from full belonging in an orthodox European political vision.[26]

Such peoples resemble the *nomad*, theorized by Gilles Deleuze and Félix Guattari, whose independence and power derive from mobility, from remaining outside or alongside the apparatus of state control, from being a citizen of nowhere. But Deleuze and Guattari make a crucial distinction between two kinds of mobility. They write in *A Thousand Plateaus*:

> The nomad has a territory; follows customary paths; he goes from one point to another; he is not ignorant of points (water points, dwelling points, assembly points, etc.). But the question is what in nomad life is a principle and what in nomad life is only a consequence. To begin with, although the points determine paths, they are strictly subordinated to the paths they determine, the reverse of what happens with the sedentary. The water point is reached only in order to be left behind; every point is a relay and exists only as a relay. A path is always between two points, but the in-between has taken on all the consistency and enjoys both an autonomy and a direction of its own. The life of the nomad is the intermezzo. Even the elements of his dwelling are conceived in terms of the trajectory that is forever mobilizing them. *The nomad is not at all the same as the migrant; for the migrant goes principally from one point to another, even if the second point is uncertain, unforeseen, or not well localized. But the nomad goes from point to point only as a consequence and as a factual necessity; in principle, points for him are relays along a trajectory. Nomads and migrants can mix in many ways, or form a common aggregate; their causes and conditions are no less distinct for that* (for example, those who joined Mohammed at Medina had a choice between a nomadic or Bedouin pledge, and a pledge of hegira or emigration).[27]

The nomad, that is, is not reduced to bare life, unlike the migrant moving from boat to camp to train to camp to boat on the way to some envisioned point where further migration will be unnecessary and qualified life might return.

There are also European travelers who retain the full measure of qualified life and political belonging even though they are always on the move. One brief meditation from Balibar is likewise alive to both the overlapping qualities and grim distinctions between the kinds of people in Europe who do a lot of moving around:

> On the one hand there are those who practically "live" on planes, airports, *shopping centres*, conference halls, and on the other hand those who travel by foot or on trucks on the roads of exile, carrying a child in their arms and a backpack on their shoulders—the only things that they still own. But between these two extremes are also masses of more or less "precarious" migrants and non-migrants. Somewhere in the middle of the Mediterranean gigantic container ships coming from the now enlarged Suez canal and the decaying dinghies of human smugglers crammed with migrants meet one another (do they actually "meet"?).[28]

Obviously this landscape of movement—planes, airports, shopping centers, conference halls, container ships—is not that of Eliot's Europe of the 1910s and 1920s. Yet Eliot's writing from that period does capture the paradoxes of movement described here by Balibar. The famous opening invitation of "The Love Song of J. Alfred Prufrock," "Let us go," is a vexed one—confident, ironic, ultimately doomed—and in it one can hear the young Eliot, via Prufrock, expressing a chronic trouble in the mind of Europe, one that has hardly abated—even if it has changed shape—since 1914.

Prufrock, it might be said, is like a nomad whose territory defeats him. It frustrates his attempt at movement. "Let us go" remains an invitation only, one that immediately runs up against territory it cannot navigate, obstacles it cannot overcome. Prufrock wants to be a nomad but is promptly snagged by place, by what Deleuze would call "points." "Let us go," he calls three times in the opening stanza of the "Love Song," concluding, as everyone knows, "Oh, do not ask, 'What is it?' / Let us go and make our visit."[29] That is the invitation of the nomad. And what greets him—what greets us—once he sets out on the nomadic path? A room. Then a city, full of the particulars of place. And movement is stopped dead. There is no more going, only regret, second-guessing, stasis, and drowning. So what went wrong? In Agamben's terms, Prufrock experiences mostly bare life (expressed as disarticulated anatomy: arms, legs, hair), and his attempts at qualified life—social and political life—end with the first stanza, after which they are hypothetical only ("And should I then presume? / And how should I begin?").[30] He is stateless but no refugee, a nomad for whom the points subordinate the path; he lives a kind of genteel bare life in a very real place, presumably Boston but with elements of St. Louis, where he has arrived but that he cannot—or will not—fully access, and where, in any case, the women who "come and go" are talking about a Europe even more remote.

Why does Prufrock seem to reject qualified life at this stage when it appears everywhere around him? One possibility is that he does so as a means of resistance. Antje Ellermann discusses the fascinating situation whereby migrants, for example, sometimes destroy their identification documents so as to maintain their existence in what Agamben calls the "state of exception."[31] There can also be provisional safety in bare life, as the director knew who told Eliot and his peers "not to talk in foreign languages in the street." Prufrock in a sense exists as do the deliberately undocumented: placeless in order to avoid punishment or repatriation but also kept from belonging or further movement. Like Eliot's, his is a privileged placelessness, of course, and it would be a stretch to say Prufrock is a migrant. The culture he perceives of shallow conformity and salon surfaces, where "the women come and go / Talking of Michelangelo," is one to which he may not want to belong.[32] And yet he is not quite a nomad. Like Eliot, he is "never anything anywhere." He occupies a tortured Schengen Area of the imagination: inside by virtue of his bare life and body, outside in every meaningful social regard.

If Prufrock the would-be nomad is defeated by his territory, *The Waste Land* is a further exploration of the kind of territory that, eliminating many borders, nonetheless renders free movement impossible. *The Waste Land* is a catalog of obstacles mapped onto the European landscape, physical and cultural. The dominant speaker in "What the Thunder Said" might be a Syrian or Palestinian refugee, grinding her way to Alexandria, Athens, Vienna, London (though presumably not Jerusalem) and finding them Unreal. Listen to the way the lines describe the plight of a migrant both in the fundamentals of inhospitable landscape—road, rock, and not enough water—and in the weird ambiguity typical of European border dynamics:

> Here there is no water but only rock
> Rock and no water and the sandy road
> The road winding above among the mountains
> Which are mountains of rock without water
> If there were water we should stop and drink
> Amongst the rock one cannot stop or think
> Sweat is dry and feet are in the sand
> If there were only water amongst the rock
> Dead mountain mouth of carious teeth that cannot spit
> Here one can neither stand nor lie nor sit
> There is not even silence in the mountains
> But dry sterile thunder without rain
> There is not even solitude in the mountains
> But red sullen faces sneer and snarl
> From doors of mudcracked houses[33]

In some ways *The Waste Land* reads like an abortive European Union. In light of Agamben's ideas, however, the possibility emerges that the abortive quality is inherent in the European promise itself, just as it is in the poem—the way that borders are not peripheral to Europe but enmeshed in its very political terrain. In the way it mixes and flows between languages, traditions, and historical periods, *The Waste Land* makes manifest Eliot's desire for Europe to exist as a mind in which ideas may freely move. But what actually moves in the poem? As in "Prufrock," the first migratory suggestion is quickly undercut by the barbed particulars of the local: "In the mountains, there you feel free. / I read, much of the night, and go south in the winter. / / What are the roots that clutch, what branches grow / Out of this stony rubbish?"[34] Read the poem for suggestions of movement between places and see where they lead. Who moves anywhere in the poem's European landscape? Only the Dantean "crowd flow[ing] over London Bridge,"[35] undone by death, and "hooded hordes swarming / Over endless plains."[36]

Instances of generative travel are precious few in the poems preceding Eliot's Christian conversion in 1927. Gerontion in his "sleepy corner" does not move, nor apparently has he ever: "I was neither at the hot gates," he confesses, "Nor fought in the warm rain / Nor knee deep in the salt marsh, heaving a cutlass, / Bitten by flies, fought."[37] His landlord has traveled, but this is taken as a sign of contamination, and Eliot uses his depiction as the occasion for some awful antisemitism: "My house is a decayed house, / And the Jew squats on the window sill, the owner, / Spawned in some estaminet of Antwerp, / Blistered in Brussels, patched and peeled in London."[38] This is only another iteration of the wandering Jew myth, with travel figured not as cosmopolitanism or adventure but as exile and sterile rootlessness. The triad of European place names signals not a shared identity but a miscellany and a dead-end. Similarly, the cast of international characters who appear later in the poem—Mr. Silvero, Hakagawa, Madame de Tornquist, Fräulein von Kulp—call up not a fruitful heterogeneity but rather anxiety about the incapacity for collective engagement with a shared tradition. This stance recalls that of another American expatriate writer, Henry James, who wrote of "the cosmopolite" that "there comes a time when one set of customs, wherever it may be found, grows to seem to you about as provincial as another."[39]

A distinct change occurs and people do get moving productively in "Journey of the Magi," published the same year Eliot joined the Anglican church. At the same time, European place names fall away from his poetry, and Eliot appears to make a choice to forego historical and geographical particulars in favor of a vision of migration as a spiritual experience, not a physical one. This poetic choice corresponds to a biographical one, as it coincides with Eliot's transformation from an American migrant in England to an Englishman on a spiritual journey. In the same year that he joined the Church of England, 1927, he became a British citizen. In "Journey of the Magi," Eliot is not much interested in the particulars of geography, which in any event he gets all wrong, according to Horace M. Kallen, who (coming close to the imagery of *The Waste Land* himself) wrote to Eliot: "There is no way that men traveling with horse and camel can pass from snowline to vegetation over-night and reach Bethlehem. That sink lies in the arid Judean hills, which stick up sharp and nude all around. They slope eastward to the waste lands of the Dead Sea, south to the Desert. There is no snow nearer than Hermon, to the north, several camel journeys away."[40] Eliot was unruffled by this bit of pedantry, replying, "I am much interested to hear your criticism of my geographical ignorance. Theoretically I believe one ought to make verse as watertight as prose on such points. On the other hand, if I had bothered about the topography and archaeology of Asia Minor, I should have had to omit a good deal of detail which really is meant to be symbolical."[41] As an imaginative evocation of hard travel in the Levant, however, the poem does respectable work, particularly in its gritty opening verse paragraph: "A cold coming we had of it, / Just the worst time of the year / For a journey, and such a long journey."⁴² Eliot's Magi travel by camel and horse rather than by truck, boat, or train, but other aspects of their ordeal would be familiar to migrants two millennia later:

> The ways deep and the weather sharp [. . .]
> Then the camel men cursing and grumbling
> And running away, and wanting their liquor and women,
> And the night-fires going out, and the lack of shelters,
> And the cities hostile and the towns unfriendly
> And the villages dirty and charging high prices:
> A hard time we had of it.
> At the end we preferred to travel all night,
> Sleeping in snatches,
> With the voices singing in our ears, saying
> That this was all folly.⁴³

It could be the narrative of Moroccan refugees trying to make their way to Europe, the camel men *Muharriboo al-Bashar*.⁴⁴ But it would be folly, too, to pretend that such superficial commonality connotes an equivalent experience. As Eliot said, his concern in the poem is with symbolism, not realism. That the Magi's journey is as much symbolic as physical, as well as their planned return to their point of origin, marks them as travelers of another privileged kind: pilgrims. In their fixation on an envisioned point, they are more migrants than nomads, but the divine sanction of their journey as well as its predetermined circularity makes it a pilgrimage, one of the oldest and most honored forms of travel in the Christian world, as in other religious traditions.

Far from the reduction to bare life threatened by migration, their journey imbues them, even before their encounter with the newborn Christ, with a form of glory. Their traveling, even more than that encounter, which is described only as "satisfactory," ennobles the Magi, and it leaves them changed, as it was intended to do:

> We returned to our places, these Kingdoms,
> But no longer at ease here, in the old dispensation,
> With an alien people clutching their gods.
> I should be glad of another death.⁴⁵

Previously understood terms like "Birth" and "Death" have been mixed and enriched. Proximity to the divine has altered the Magi's relation to the known, physical world. Transformation under the sign of a journey is the ideal of pilgrimage and would seem to suggest the need for a third term beyond *bare life* and *qualified life* to name the pilgrim's existential status. Perhaps *numinous life* is a better designation for the life of a pilgrim, the bodily and political dimensions of whose movements between points are illuminated by the sacred.

This was a territory Eliot began to plumb only after he became an Anglican. "Journey of the Magi" opens the way, and by the time he writes *Four Quartets*, he is speaking of voyagers, travelers, and explorers with a resolution absent in his early work. People are moving in trains, on ships, on foot down country lanes, down city streets, alone and in pairs, not as hordes swarming or crowds flowing but as real people going somewhere. And yet stronger still than the movement of people in *Four Quartets* is the imperative of stillness. Place supersedes movement, which is invoked in the poems primarily to abolish it, to liberate the audience from the idea of traveling at all. The idea of Europe shrinks to the size of "a winter's afternoon, in a secluded chapel." Indeed, "History is now and England."[46] The "still point of the turning world" introduced in "Burnt Norton" becomes a celestial body the gravity of which pulls in every thought of motion through space or time, even the idea of stasis, which depends for its meaning on the opposing idea of movement: "Neither from nor towards; at the still point, there the dance is, / But neither arrest nor movement. And do not call it fixity, / Where past and future are gathered. Neither movement from nor towards, / Neither ascent nor decline."[47] The work of this still point is so colossal in the *Quartets* that it renders all humbler points—the kind required by migrants, nomads, pilgrims, and tube commuters—unreal. In one magisterial work, Eliot writes as powerfully as he ever would about human travel and relegates travel to the realm of illusion. Meanwhile, the political boundaries of Europe vanish.

In "East Coker," Eliot paradoxically settles down into locality and introduces a type of traveler new to his work: the explorer. Many have found inspiration in the idea that "Old men ought to be explorers," in spite of—or perhaps because of—the poem's explorers being explorers not of the actual physical world.[48] These intrepid old men are interior explorers only, as the lines immediately preceding and following make clear: "Love is most nearly itself / When here and now cease to matter. / Old men ought to be explorers / Here or there does not matter / We must be still and still moving / Into another intensity / For a further union, a deeper communion."[49] At the time he published "East Coker," March 1940, Eliot's own traveling days weren't exactly behind him, but another world war had closed not only mental but all manner of physical frontiers. And it might be said that the traveling he would do in the remainder of his life now lacked the restlessness or zeal of earlier years. Herbert Read relates that Eliot was not a natural traveler, preferring the orderly life of routine in a familiar setting, more often the town than the country. "He might enjoy a holiday in the south of France or, in his later years, in the West Indies," wrote Read, "but he was not a traveller by choice and often reproved me for my cultural peregrinations."[50] At fifty-one he wasn't yet an old man, but the appeal and importance of interior journeys had begun to supersede those between points on the earth. He had long before ceased to be a migrant or even a metic, and the change is reflected in the poetry.

Thus in "The Dry Salvages," Eliot invests ordinary passengers on a train and an ocean liner with metaphysical import but omits any details about where they are coming from or where they are going: "Fare forward, travellers! not escaping from the past / Into different lives, or into any future."[51] The lines carefully delineate the character and contours of their spiritual journey. Origin and destination, past and future, and forward motion are erased, and the specifics of transport—the "station," "the narrowing rails," "the deck of the drumming liner," "the furrow that widens behind you"—become insubstantial.[52] The centrality of the spiritual banishes the physical almost entirely. The "hither and farther shore" are not points but constructs for the consideration of the spiritual. "Fare forward, voyagers" is a call not to migrant, nomad, or even pilgrim, but to the contemplative, who is released from the sequence of past, present, and future, who is not even to "think of the fruit of action."[53]

The traveler in "Little Gidding" is another pilgrim, but at first only a hypothetical one: "If you came this way, / Taking the route you would be likely to take / From the place you would be likely to come from."[54] The hypothetical traveler becomes actual, and the hypothetical pilgrimage gains a known point of destination toward the end of the first section: "You are not here to verify, / Instruct yourself, or inform curiosity / Or carry report. You are here to kneel / Where prayer has been valid."[55] In the final section of "Little Gidding," Eliot returns to his new favored type of traveler, the explorer, and it is an explorer whose journey bends inward: "We shall not cease from exploration / And the end of all our exploring / Will be to arrive where we started / And know the place for the first time [. . .] When the last of earth left to discover / Is that which was the beginning."[56] It is a profoundly comforting idea for those with the detachment or the security to contemplate it. That Eliot composed most of *Four Quartets* while millions of Europeans were being forcibly deprived of those conditions, migrating for their lives or being forcibly detained in camps, is neither an indictment of the project nor any sign of his indifference. It is, however, powerful evidence that the gates of Europe, when they close, do not shut with equal violence or permanence on all alike.

The consolations of the kind of interior migration described in *Four Quartets* are perhaps beyond measure, which is part of the problem. The costs and rewards of actual migration, including into and across Europe, are measured in hard distances, border crossings, cash payments, calculations of safety or danger, and time spent in camps. To achieve the serenity of the pilgrim or the contemplative, who are forever traveling but without restlessness or anxiety, would seem to require either the disregard or the nonexistence of actual places, or at least no urgent need to move physically between them. The migrant contending with actual geographies is more likely to rattle and throb from point to point, to fear death by water or lack of it, and to wait without patience. Only in belonging, perhaps even in citizenship, it appears, can one be freed from the European predicament in which a person can't stand, lie, or sit but also can't seem to get anywhere.

As I have suggested, both the migrations and locations in Eliot's early poetry appear as traces only, as snatches and combinations, neither as three-dimensional figures nor as the points that serve only as indicators of the nomad's path. It is a poetry neither of staying nor going, a poetry of the borderland in a voice that nonetheless imagines, indeed longs for, the stabilizing frame of either journey or residence. For contrast, consider the lines of the late mestiza poet Gloria Anzaldúa in her book *Borderlands/La Frontera*: "Now let us go. / *Tihueque, tihueque.* / Vámonos, vámonos" . . . "We have," she writes of Chicana people like her, "a tradition of migration, a tradition of long walks."[57] That is one tradition Eliot does not command. And not until 1927, or perhaps not until he began *Four Quartets* in 1935, did he begin to command the other tradition of rootedness.

The kinds of strained journey Eliot briefly endured in 1914, when sustained or repeated, can change a person, indeed are changing millions of people in Central and North America, Africa, the Middle East, and Europe as I write. Multiplied by those numbers, they change societies as well. There are projected to be 150 to 200 million climate refugees alone by the year 2050. There is little in Eliot's 1914 account to suggest the hellish emergency status that would come to typify Europe at other moments, including the present one.[58] And yet Eliot's major early poems seem to partake of Balibar's reasoning, that, do what it might with or at its ostensibly official borders, Europe is better understood as a borderland itself, a territory better expressed in a poetry of fragments than on any map. The serene still point where there are no real borders, distances, dangers, or camps doesn't seem very European at all.

Chapter 2

Eliot and the Anarchist

Eliot was not always a good friend. When he married Valerie Fletcher in 1957, he didn't bother to tell his closest friend, Mary Trevelyan, until just prior, via telegram; or John Hayward, his confidante, literary advisor, and longtime flatmate, until after the fact. Nor did either of these decades-long friendships survive the new marriage. Eliot could be devoted, but Lyndall Gordon writes of those closest to him "that after years of knowing Eliot you found, suddenly, that you did not know him. He could leave relationships and pass on."[1] In the latter part of his life, his deepening spiritual examination of himself often meant leaving even intimate friends out in the cold. As Gordon first noted, and as I will discuss in chapter 7, when it came to Emily Hale this pattern was tied up with Eliot's ideas of penitence and renunciation on a journey to beatitude. Whether impelled by the mystical or the mundane, "full awareness of one's effect on others" eluded him.[2] "He can't help hurting us," Mary once wrote to John.[3] One problem was that Eliot needed things from Trevelyan, Hayward, and Hale: care, companionship, spiritual company, protection, literary advice, an image of ideal womanhood. When the need was gone, so was the devotion. His friendship with Herbert Read was of a different kind: less intimate, less needy, more equal, and longer lasting. It registers lower on the scale of emotional intensity, but it also registers a powerful connection between the personal and the political. Eliot and Read were actually ill-matched politically as well as spiritually, but neither of them ever abandoned the relationship, and their mutual commitment is full of hope as well as political potency.

In his chapter "Friendship as Resistance," Todd May writes about how key features of friendship—relations of equality, voluntary choice, a shedding of certain borders between individuals—can "be both a model for and a route into a democratic politics. They are a model for such politics because they show what it can look like," and they "[train] . . . participants in the mode of political solidarity required by democratic movements."[4] May is most interested in how friendship can function as an alternative and a challenge to the kinds of social relationships preferred and enforced by neoliberalism, especially "the consumer and the entrepreneur." At the level of "the formation of individuals in neoliberalism," he sees "friendship offering the possibility of political resistance."[5]

Another point of view, however, holds that while friendship may retain such revolutionary potential, it is nonetheless "the modern relationship *par excellence*" under neoliberalism, fully assimilable and commodifiable by neoliberal logic.[6] Friendship, writes Simon Wallace, is "the flipside to the erosion of the family as the basic economic relationship" and "reaches its apex with neoliberalism."[7] We need only think of the Facebook verb to *friend* someone and the way the number and visible signifiers of friendships have been coopted as part of a "profile" to be produced, consumed, and frequently monetized. Wallace even suggests how susceptible to exploitation by neoliberalism are some of the characteristics of friendship that might otherwise seem most disruptive of it. May argues that anti-neoliberal friendships are "relations of equality" and "a 'voluntary choice,'"[8] but Wallace points out that "equipped with the ultimate power to choose, the liberal subject is encouraged to select their 'social networks' . . . The neoliberal friend is a conscious and intentional creation . . . In contrast to familial relationships based on obligations of 'unconditional' love (or hate), contemporary friendships affirm people's individual agency," a celebrated value of the neoliberal order and its central type, the consumer.[9] Friendships are motivated less and less by "the desire to interact with like-minded people" and more by "the desire to advertise the 'profile' choices we make about the company . . . we keep."[10] Under such a regime, friendships are merely commodities.

These are entirely pertinent perspectives to bring to bear on the friendships in our historical present. However, the friendship between Eliot and Herbert Read is not best understood as a result of or as a response to neoliberalism. Their era was not ours. Their society was busy with particular pressures that would only be released by the global cataclysm of World War II, which itself would clear the way for the eventual rise of the neoliberal order we know. But some of the ways in which friendship can serve as a node of resistance to domination are nonetheless evident in Eliot and Read. They were products of an era inhospitable to genuine friendship in ways different from ours but still instructive. Technologies of commodification had not degraded human relationships to anything like the degree familiar to us, but Eliot and Read knew ruthless political polarization as well as we do. We often think of friendship as something that happens outside the sphere of political action; it is what is there (if we are lucky) when we stop working, stop struggling, when we don't want to trouble about politics anymore. But not only does friendship act as a consolation during the long wait for a world conducive to values of equality, choice, peace, and dignity, it prefigures that world. The friendship of Eliot and Read serves as a reminder that even as we struggle toward goals we likely will never reach, we don't have to wait to experience something of their fulfillment.

Herbert Read was an anarchist. But he was T. S. Eliot's kind of anarchist. Read accepted a knighthood in 1953 for "services to literature" and was roughly condemned by the anarchist community for doing so. He was the kind of anarchist who could write: "The work of art . . . is a product of the relationship . . . between an individual and a society, and no great art is possible unless you have as corresponding and contemporary activities the spontaneous freedom of the individual and the passive coherence of a society. To escape from society (if that were possible) is to escape from the only soil fertile enough to nourish art,"[11] which echoes more than a little certain formulations of Eliot's, were it not for that "spontaneous freedom of the individual." As Dana Ward writes, "In the annals of anarchy it is not at all rare that noblemen evolve into anarchists," and he gives Kropotkin and Bakunin as examples. "The reverse journey from anarchism to nobility," he writes, "is an exceedingly rare route, rarer still if the anarchism remains securely packed in the accompanying baggage. Yet such was Herbert Read's experience."[12] He was an anarchist who embraced the classicism of Eliot and T. E. Hulme, who was in the 1930s accused of fascist sympathies, and who talked affirmatively of "the voice of God" and "the rule of God."[13]

Just as it was in Read's day, it is still necessary to make clear the distinction between the popular sense of the term "anarchy" and the much more nuanced characteristics of the political ideal that goes by that name. Try as they might, anarchists have still not convinced the broad public that "anarchy" does not mean "chaos," at least not to them. It means, rather, the desired end-state of a politics committed fully to freedom and equality. Anarchists from William Godwin to Kropotkin to Emma Goldman to Read hold up the ideals of nonhierarchical relations, freedom of association, noncoercion, spontaneity, and mutual aid as central to their ideal society. Such principles, far from aiming at the obliteration of order, aim to secure the most abiding—because most natural—kind of order, one entirely nondependent on artificial structures and institutions to guard or sustain it. According to Ward, "Anarchy is inconceivable in the absence of order, and, most importantly, vice versa."[14] A father of anarchism, Pierre Josef Proudhon, declared "Liberty" to be "not the daughter but the mother of order."[15] That which is most chaotic in modern society, most anarchic in the vulgar sense—war, crime, poverty, and so on—is viewed by anarchists as symptomatic of a capitalist system based on coercion and inequality that guarantees it will persist. Anarchism seeks to eliminate such disorder by endorsing only the kinds of action that tend to give rise to its opposite.

It is a libertarian politics but distinguished from the right-wing variety by that commitment to equality. "I am truly free," wrote Bakunin, "only when all human beings, men and women, are equally free."[16] Beyond such broad commitments, anarchism has always refused to be made orthodox. Freedom, change, and the criticism of all established structures are not principles that lend themselves easily to institutionalization or codification. The modes and language through which individual anarchists and groups of anarchists have pursued the same ends for the past two hundred years vary dramatically. But such variety is a characteristic anarchist value. As Žiga Vodovnik explains, "Anarchist thought cannot be reduced to one single dimension as, despite its unshakeable basic premises, it is full of internal contradictions, its own criticism and, consequently, redefined positions."[17] It is not "a coherent and completed system, but a set of ideas which addresses important questions but leaves many of them unanswered; it is a set of inquiries and researches without final results."[18] It is true that an anarchist who accepts a knighthood places almost unbearable strain on the concept of anarchism itself, but then anarchists have tolerated the chasm that would appear to divide the violent, propaganda-of-the-deed version of Bakunin or Alexander Berkman and the pacifist one of Dorothy Day and, indeed, Herbert Read. Anarchism throughout its history has been a broad tent.

But it doesn't shelter everyone. And certainly not T. S. Eliot. There are anarchists who believe in and worship God, even anarchists like Read who are also somehow royalists, but Eliot is not one of them. Indeed, Eliot was not ambivalent in his condemnation, or more often dismissal, of anarchism in the 1920s and 1930s, the years during which he worked most closely with Read as fellow editors of the *Criterion*. During the *Criterion* years, "the years of *l'entre deux guerres*," Eliot's understanding of anarchism was considerably deeper than the purely popular one that equates it with chaos.[19] Still, the majority of his references to anarchy in the 1920s and 1930s are in that vein. He most often seems to be echoing Matthew Arnold's use of the term in *Culture and Anarchy*, a text from the late 1860s he invokes fairly regularly. He generally associates "anarchy" with decay, dissolution, and as in his famous essay on James Joyce's *Ulysses*, futility. Joyce's method, he wrote, "is simply a way of controlling, of ordering, of giving a shape and a significance to the immense panorama of futility and anarchy which is contemporary history."[20] His references to anarch*ism* (as opposed to anarch*y*) generally emphasize its egoistic or solipsistic shadings. It is the equally wrong opposite of communism, he argues, because it stresses only the value of the individual.

And yet he could muster a fair amount of benign tolerance when it came to those thinkers of whom he approved. In a letter to Stephen Spender in 1947, he wrote that *anarchism* was usually used as a scary word to characterize ordinary liberals, a word intended to alarm those without great intelligence.[21] Such tolerance, at a minimum, would have been required to keep him working so consistently and so well with Read and vice versa. The closeness of this relationship shows us something of how, in politically perilous and divided times, people of goodwill who hold wildly divergent political ideas manage not only to coexist but to produce work together. Indeed the *Criterion*, for all its ostensible ideological uniformity, was one of the places where such waters met between the wars. Jason Harding, Gayle Rogers, and others have helped to establish just how heterogeneous a set of voices the *Criterion* actually supported. As Harding demonstrates, "The journal did not attempt to express a single editorial 'line' or to reflect the impress of one person's point of view."[22] And this was true even though the *Criterion* did consistently reflect "Eliot's foundational desire to stitch together into some kind of unity the Latin-Christian elements of the otherwise diverse cultures of Western Europe"[23]

In the *Criterion*, Eliot presided over one of the most influential English-language journals of politics and culture of the era, and he did so with Read as what Harding calls his "unofficial assistant editor," his "anarchist aide-de-camp."[24] "There is little doubt," Harding writes, "that Read's social and political opinions during the 1930s were anathema to Eliot, and vice versa."[25] Still, the two men stuck out the 1930s together and remained devoted to one another until their deaths. They were more than colleagues; they were, to put it simply, friends. But when it comes to challenging structures that would limit human flourishing and meaningful contact, friendship is not simple at all. In the one between Eliot and Read, one condition in particular, which could be part of a definition of friendship itself, can point the way to other liberating, truly democratic relationships and even societies. If we pull back to consider the broad pattern in the carpet made by the two men's careers, we discern a feature that is subtle, durable, and hard to represent falsely over the course of a public career, what might be called a habit of hope: a commitment to continued engagement as the means to its own end. In the friendship of Eliot and Read we can recognize the possibility of creating another world within the shell of a less hospitable one.

Born in Yorkshire, Read was five years Eliot's junior. He started out as a Christian and a Tory but lost both convictions by the time he went to university at Leeds in 1911. He fought in the First World War and published early poems about the experience, going on to associate himself with the Imagists and other avant-garde artists of London. He published a single novel, *The Green Child*, in 1935 but earned his greatest fame as a critic of art and literature. Like Eliot, he preferred to think of art in terms of its social function; one of his most important books was *Education through Art*, which had a lasting impact on education in Britain through its empirically based advocacy of art in schools. Its impact on anarchism may have been even greater. "Anarchism . . . is fundamental to the schemes proposed" in the book, writes biographer James King.[26] Read "advocated a reformation of the sense which could lead to a gradual, peaceful transformation of society."[27] George Woodcock writes that *Education through Art* made it "impossible for anarchists in the future to neglect the role of education as a powerful weapon in the advance towards a free society."[28] Eliot was restrained in his criticisms of the book, which with its Jungian and surrealist insights he was bound to find unpersuasive. Read later wrote that he and Eliot had never "exchanged anything but . . . pedantic criticisms of each other's work," a somewhat remarkable feat considering how much of each other's work they read and how far apart its philosophies usually were.[29]

There is much debate in anarchist circles about when precisely Read became an anarchist and whether his admitted "temporiz[ing] with other measures of political action," his "open[ness] to a charge of having wavered in my allegiance to the truth" ought to be taken as indicators of an essential inconsistency or as the natural, and ultimately inconsequential, divagations of a highly tuned mind actively engaging with a turbulent political landscape.[30] All such debate, though, comes to little in light of Read's own self-assessment, which includes the concessions above about temporizing and wavering. In 1968, the year of his death, he avowed that "my own anarchist convictions . . . have now lasted for more than 50 years" and that he could trace his initial turn toward libertarian thought to "1911 or 1912."[31] David Goodway's assessment is that "Read's anarchism was not peripheral to his other, varied activities. Rather it was—knighthood and all—at the core of how he viewed the world in general."[32] Harding writes that Read "declar[ed] for anarchism" publicly in 1937 in the *Authors Take Sides on the Spanish War* questionnaire, and then in an article for the *Adelphi*. In 1938 he did so on the opening page of his book *Poetry and Anarchism*, which Faber published on Eliot's recommendation, albeit one made "without enthusiasm," according to Harding.[33]

Eliot and Read met in 1917 when Read (with his colleague Frank Rutter) invited Eliot to write for their new magazine *Art and Letters*. Each man was somewhat intimidated by the other, Read by Eliot for his refined manner and growing literary reputation, Eliot by Read for his decorated war service. Eliot would go on to publish several early essays and poems in *Art and Letters*, and in 1922 he first asked Read to write something for his own new journal, the *Criterion*. In the postwar years, Read wrote, their "acquaintance . . . ripened to a friendship slowly but surely."[34] He and Eliot attended the same parties, dined together regularly, and Read "would sometimes spend the night at Chester Terrace" with Eliot and his first wife Vivien.[35] They closely witnessed the disintegration of one another's first marriages, under painfully similar circumstances. "Literature aside," they "habitually talked of taxes, death duties and, especially, cheese."[36] Their written correspondence is voluminous. "My dear Read" becomes "Dear Herbert" around 1927. As a poet, Read "knew . . . that I had some measure of [Eliot's] esteem—after all, he sponsored the publication of my poems with Faber's."[37]

The friendship was not characterized by great intimacy or what we might today call vulnerability. "From the beginning," Read wrote after Eliot's death, "there was a withholding of emotion, a refusal to reveal the inner man."[38] Despite their decades of closeness, Read found him "inaccessible."[39] He could detect, for instance, that during the marriage to Vivien "Eliot's sufferings . . . were acute, but only once did he unburden himself to me," in a letter Eliot may have asked him to destroy.[40] Read himself leaned toward reticence and knew better than to misjudge it. "I know that my own reserved nature," he reflected, ". . . is often mistaken for an absence of feeling or sympathy."[41] He was not afraid to use the word "love" to describe their bond. The note of restraint in their friendship, rather than suggesting an absence of passion, trust, or warmth, is instead evidence that the devotion, loyalty, and indeed love the two had for one another flowed from something other than emotional intensity.

The differences of opinion between Eliot and Read—on art, on psychology, on politics, on religion—persisted and widened over the life of the *Criterion*. Between the lines of the journal is written the story of a sometimes contentious relationship that nonetheless survived the contentious interwar years intact. And after that time, with the organ of their formal working relationship dissolved, the devotion remained, seemingly sustained by a positive force of its own. Even at the time of their first meeting, Read's burgeoning pacifism, which would "become a deep conviction" for him, had divided his views from Eliot's. "But neither this issue," he declared, "nor the many issues bound up with it (the whole complex of humanism and romanticism) ever threatened our devotion to one another."[42] When Eliot declared publicly in 1928 "that he was a classicist in literature, a royalist in politics, and an anglo-catholic in religion," he meant it, and Read "could only retort that I was a romanticist in literature, an anarchist in politics, and an agnostic in religion."[43] Their convictions did not come gradually into closer alignment, but in part because of their understanding and experience of one another, both Eliot and Read were able to broaden their capacity for forbearance regarding points of view they did not share. On its own, it would be a tepid basis for a friendship, but it marks a starting point for describing a feature that can make a friendship durable.

With both fascism and communism ascendant in Europe, and growing agnosticism in Britain matched by a renewed attraction to orthodox religion among writers, the interwar years were a period bent on dividing people into camps. That 1937 questionnaire, *Authors Take Sides*, initiated by Nancy Cunard and signed by a dozen writers including W. H. Auden, Heinrich Mann, and Pablo Neruda and returned by 148 others, put it severely: "Are you for, or against, the legal Government and the People of Republican Spain? Are you for, or against, Franco and Fascism? For it is impossible any longer to take no side."[44] And deep investment was part of Read's makeup. In *Poetry and Anarchism* he would write:

No man in his sense can contemplate the existing contrasts with complacency. No one can measure the disparity between poverty and riches, between purchasing power and productive capacity, between plan and performance, between chaos and order, between ugliness and beauty, between all the sin and savagery of the existing system and any decent code of social existence (Christian or moral or scientific)—no man can measure these disparities and remain indifferent. Our civilization is a scandal and until it is remade all our intellectual activities are vain.[45]

If his reply to *Authors Take Sides* didn't quite "declare for anarchism," it certainly sounded like that of an anarchist: "In Spain, and almost only in Spain, there still lives a spirit to resist the bureaucratic tyranny of the State and the intellectual intolerance of all doctrinaires. For that reason all poets must follow the course of this struggle with open and passionate partisanship."[46] For his part, Eliot refused to be drawn in, writing "While I am naturally sympathetic, I still feel convinced that it is best that at least a few men of letters should remain isolated, and take no part in these collective activities."[47] Even before the questionnaire reached him, he had written in a *Criterion* "Commentary" that the danger of the Spanish Civil War for non-Spaniards was "rather a deterioration of political thinking, with a pressure on everyone, which has to be stubbornly resisted, to accept one extreme philosophy or another . . . that the precarious balance of ideas in our heads may be upset by one or the other extreme view."[48] Views didn't get much more extreme than anarchism to a person of Eliot's convictions and persuasion, and yet Read's stark divergence from his own on the question of Spain didn't strain the relationship to breaking.

During the Second World War, writes Read's biographer King, "since the very existence of poetry was under siege, Eliot and Read," as publishers of poetry, "acted as fifth-column conspirators in the same cause."[49] With Eliot at Faber and Read at Routledge, but Faber the publisher of Read's books and the relationship between Eliot and Read strong, the two could collaborate to get new poetry published despite difficulties of both supply and demand. And the alliance was not only editorial. After the anarchist publisher Freedom Press was raided and four of its members arrested in November 1944 under Defence Regulation 39A, Eliot extended himself to add his name to a letter, drafted by Read and fellow anarchist George

Woodcock, protesting "arbitrary police action and . . . other means of indirect coercion . . . against Freedom Press."[50] Besides the *New Statesman and Nation*, the letter also ran in several other publications, including *Peace News* and, notably, the *Spectator* (albeit "edited and reduced").[51] "Most of us do not subscribe to the political theories held by Freedom Press," the letter read, "and have no connection with the anarchist movement, but we respect their right to propagate opinions, and regard any attempt to curtail their freedom of speech and writing as a general threat against those liberties."[52] That Eliot "stood by the protest" was "a fact," Woodcock later wrote, "which I am always happy to quote against those who describe him as a reactionary."[53]

The reactionary label was obstinate, however, and a few years later Read would have the opportunity to return the favor. "In some friendships," writes May, "there may be an orientation toward the friend that, we might say, pulls us off the centre of ourselves, allowing us to expend ourselves . . . on behalf of the friend."[54] In 1950, despite being "obviously unsympathetic to his old friend's anti-democratic tendencies," Read could be found defending Eliot against charges of antisemitism.[55] Later still, Read appraised Eliot's play *The Confidential Clerk* in terms of honesty and respect, ones that resonate rather nicely with the voices of Eliot's later works: "an intricate comedy, smooth on the ear, 'but one can only ask why a man of his intelligence should spend his time on such trivialities. . . . I think he tries to compensate for fading fires, of emotion and inspiration, but that too is a form of heroism.'"[56] They sound like the words of a true friend.

Mere tolerance of unappealing views or indulgence of another's foibles, however, could never be enough to animate a working relationship or friendship as rich as Eliot and Read's. There is a great deal of positive content to it, and there are many areas in which to look for and find overlap in the two men's thinking: their shared enthusiasm for classical Greek and medieval European culture, their 1930s equation of the twin totalitarianisms of fascism and communism, their poetic and critical attempts to reconcile romanticism and classicism, their sensitivity to the most promising currents of artistic modernism, their love of order, their love of mystery novels, their love of good cheese. But friendship is more than the overlapping regions in a Venn diagram of two persons' ideas. Eliot and Read met all the conditions for friendship laid out by Elizabeth Telfer in her famous 1970 essay, "Friendship": "shared activities, the passions of friendship, and acknowledgment of the fulfillment of the first two conditions."[57] In the case of Eliot and Read, I would expand on that first condition, "shared activities," by adding to it the idea of the forms of their thought; Eliot and Read thought alike. The two men's minds tended to describe certain similar patterns as they moved around ideas of any kind.

Dana Ward claims that Read's anarchism underpins his commitment to "organic form," but adds, significantly, that "what distinguishes Read's contribution to anarchy is that free association, mutual aid, and equality are also tempered by a sense of proportionality, symmetry, texture, balance, and the summary term, 'form.'"[58] These tempering qualities, he argues, flow from universal values inherent in the laws of nature, what Read calls "the plan of nature." "A realistic rationalism," writes Read, "establishes a universal order of thought, which is a necessary order of thought because it is the order of the real world; and because it is necessary and real, it is not man-imposed, but natural; and each man finding this order finds his freedom. Modern anarchism is a reaffirmation of this natural freedom, of this direct communion with universal truth."[59] Deriving aesthetic values from patterns in nature is obviously not unique to anarchists, and it is interesting to note the increasing extent to which Eliot did so in his poetry. The *Four Quartets* indeed provide an immersion in such patterns, and often in his early work Eliot used the subversion of natural patterns for his signature effects, itself a measure of the centrality of nature to his aesthetic. But of course Eliot would never speak of universals in nature, or in much else. In his doctoral dissertation he had declared, "What is subjective is the whole world" and "All significant truths are private truths,"[60] ideas that even after conversion he never truly relinquished and that, moreover, sound far more anarchist than classicist. To anarchist ears it sounds distinctly un-anarchist to talk of "universal truth," but there is in Read's careful balancing of freedom and structure, or rather locating freedom within order, quite a lot of T. S. Eliot's aesthetics as well as his theology.

On this count it is actually Eliot, with his abiding commitment to historicity, cultural specificity, and points of view, who sounds the more truly anarchistic. Daniel Colson writes that "anarchist theory 'is above all an ethical project which directly engages, in its least practice, in judging the value of relations and situations.'"[61] "For anarchists," writes Jesse Cohn, "treating literature as 'autonomous' from the social means failing to think autonomy in social terms; ergo, questions of literature must always be situated in a wider social context, with the aim of determining what kind of relationships the text offers to bring about between ourselves and one another, between ourselves and the world."[62] All the best recent

Eliot scholarship has shown his critical views to be deeply situational, contextual, and historically contingent, as the old talk of New Critical detachment fades away.

But this train of thought, while tantalizing and at times productive, is not, in the end, the one I feel is actually the most useful in understanding the relationship between Eliot and Read. One could multiply examples like the above in great number—cases where Eliot's ideas sound a note consonant with anarchist principles, or where Read's anarchism is expressed in a language very close to Eliot's classicism. And there are seeds of sympathy in the poetry itself, a shared aesthetic language transcending the expressed political views of either man. But I question whether simply sharing enough of the same views, checking enough of the same boxes in the survey of preferences and positions, even of thinking in similar ways or learning tolerance for another's uncongenial ideas, is enough to keep people working, by choice, in close quarters in times as intensely politically divided as the 1930s. I confess that I am not finding it to be sufficient at present. And shared views are no guarantee at all of friendship. "When a person begins to share activities with another, we would generally be reluctant to call the relationship with that other a friendship," writes May. "There could be a spark there, as when two people recognize mutual interests, or enthusiasms, or a common way of seeing things. However the friendship itself develops over time. It is a temporal thickness of shared activity that creates a friendship."[63] Eliot and Read certainly had that thickness in their friendship of almost fifty years. Moreover, their shared interests and activities amounted to the work of a lifetime, and they thought alike, in formal if not ideological terms. But even this doesn't particularize their friendship among many others, and it doesn't pinpoint what we might adopt from it for ourselves.

Eliot and Read model a friendship based on freedom, equality, and hope: freedom to pursue their own ideas and courses, equality in the absence of instrumentalism (one needing something consistently from the other), and hope evident in the simple fact of their continuing to work together despite major differences of outlook. Such qualities may have been possible in part because friendships are not movements. Some of the power of friendship as resistance is in its narrow scope. As Wallace observes, "Partly as a riposte to the large, centralized movements of the nineteenth and twentieth century that tended to turn people into 'masses,' friend and family are appreciated in this formulation for their smallness, localness, and personal authenticity."[64] Even Eliot and Read, for all the singularity they have ensured for themselves through writing, are still subject to a kind of massification in the way that they were and are so often thought of—and as I have in part represented them here—as the categories that describe them: royalist, anarchist, elitist, conservative, radical, reactionary, etc. Their "profiles," as it were, are complicated by their friendship with one another, and in this way demonstrate a special potential of friendship to confound and circumvent structures and expectations that would limit human connection to categorizable, commodifiable, governable terms. In the early and middle decades of the twentieth century, if neoliberalism was not yet triumphant, no less a power than global political totalitarianism was at work managing the possibilities for human affiliation. In its particularity and low profile, a friendship like Eliot and Read's evades such management by being too local to appear on the radar of such totalizing forces.

Smallness may not only be an advantage, however, as Wallace points out. The consolation it provides may also foster a kind of political quietism: "We do not command a movement, we do not belong to mass parties, the ruling classes do not tremble at our utterances, we are without an institutional base—still, we will always have our friends."[65] It would be nearly impossible not to admire the friendship between Eliot and Read for the boundaries it seems to break. But whatever they gained through tolerance and compromise, they may have lost of resolve and fierce devotion to their respective causes. What they gained personally within the intimate sphere of their friendship they may have sacrificed in large-order impact. They had their friends, as it were, but neither of their political positions shook the world.

In a way, their friendship embodies the taking of a side in the eternal debate between compromise and coalition-building on the one hand and ideological purity on the other. Both men chose to work with and for their ideological opposites. The question of whether more world-building was gained or lost in that choice is ultimately answerable only according to the observer's own ideological predilection. The anarchists, for their part, have a pretty strong claim on victory in such cases. No less a radical body than the Invisible Committee sees in the friendships that outlast insurrections the realization in miniature of the desired revolution: "Strategic intelligence comes from the heart and not the brain, and the problem with ideology is precisely that it forms a screen between thinking and the heart. To put this differently: we're obliged to force open a door to a space we already occupy. The only party to be built is the one that is already there."[66]

It would be trite as well as false to claim that through their friendship Read and Eliot showed the way past the ideological impasses or limits to human freedom of the large portion of the twentieth century they shared. If they found a tolerable way to live through oppressive times, it was not a way available to millions of others for reasons of background, education, race, class, gender, ability, or locale. Both men, it must be acknowledged, were among the British elite in ways both informal and formal. Moreover, neither man was an old-time liberal, and so neither could have been satisfied with an order in which mutual acceptance, co-existence, and mild good will are the highest aims. Both had their sights set on much more glorious possibilities. Neither man lived to see his ideal world realized nor, indeed, could have envisioned its realization in any near future. And yet, to risk triteness, who does? Who ever has done more than strive to strive towards such things?

Read and Eliot both left legacies in writing with the potential to change the world. But the more humble activities of caring for one another and working together over time may be their more immediately applicable legacy in an age like ours, when so much work seems to have come to nothing and when the shifting weather of disaster necessitates the constant reappraisal of ends and means. Every day presents a new catastrophe and invites renewed consideration of whether our friendships are refuges from life or the answer we've been looking for all along. Casting aside the risk of triteness, it was Eliot and Read's shared capacity for change, for honest wrestling with the contingencies and pressures particular to the day, and for resisting the allure of complacency and indifference, that made such politically disparate characters so compatible professionally and personally. To go one step further, it was their abiding *hope* that did that work, where hope is understood as the good-faith willingness to engage and reengage with stubborn problems, to plunge anew into changed circumstances in the belief that doing so is not only sufficient to the day but required of it, and, moreover, that the effort is not only its own reward but promises a reward for the commonweal. Both Eliot and Read spent a lifetime trying to reconcile aesthetics and politics and trying it with all kinds of tools—the tools of verse, of fiction, of drama, of literary and art criticism, of philosophical and psychological theorizing, of political and cultural critique, of education and economics. If at any point they embraced systems of thought, they did so provisionally enough to admit of needful adjustment. *Classicist, royalist, Anglo-Catholic* sounds plenty doctrinaire, but, thanks to revelations like the publication of the *Complete Prose* and the Hale letters, readers are coming to see how intricate and multiple were the currents running below such apparently decisive terms.

A central and profoundly influential tenet of anarchist thought is the commensurability of ends and means, sometimes expressed as—or in—"prefigurative politics." This is the idea that in pursuing a given end you should actually practice it in your means: no wars for peace, no hierarchy on the way to equality, no coercion as a precursor to liberty. Occupy Wall Street quickly became known for such an anarchist-inflected approach to protest. "For many Occupy activists," writes Christian Scholl, "social change was *immanent to the process* unfolding in the encampments. By locating the goal within the action itself, means and ends melted together."[67] The idea of prefigurative politics is a potentially inspiring way to think about friendship: "Most of us would find it a better world in which we could trust one another a little more, feel a little less in competition with one another, and feel less a means to others' ends. By modelling such relationships, friendship can not only offer the preparation for political solidarity; it can not only show us, in the intimacy of our particular worlds, what a better world looks like; it can also motivate us to achieve such a world."[68] The principle of prefigurative politics often means that instead of awaiting a future in which ideals of liberation or equality are realized, or even preparing for such a future, one should focus instead on what already exists of that future in the present. Žiga Vodovnik speaks of "Bakunin's idea that the seeds of future society must be sown in the existing social system and thus create 'not only the ideas but the facts of the future itself.'"[69] If friendships are such facts, it suggests that when we judge Read and Eliot we ought to look not (or at least not only) at what they say but at what they do. And their detours and departures, their lack of adherence to programs or systems, for which they are at times taken to task by the doctrinaire, are the demonstration of their shared ethic of hope.

The best lines in which each man expressed this capacity, this conviction, actually speak in the language of anarchism, but the labels are less important than the spirit. This is Eliot, in "The Dry Salvages": "For most of us, this is the aim / Never to be realised; / Who are only undefeated / Because we have gone on trying."[70]

And this is his friend Herbert Read: "I have striven for change, even for revolution. My understanding of the history of culture has convinced me that the ideal society is a point on a receding horizon. We move steadily towards it but can never reach it. Nevertheless we must engage with passion in the immediate strife—such is the nature of things and if defeat is inevitable (as it is) we are not excused."[71]

Chapter 3

Eliot among the Antifascists

So consistent has the overlap been between fascism and antisemitism for the century of fascism's institutional existence that the two -isms are frequently used almost interchangeably. That the most total expression of fascist ideology in world history concentrated its energy on the eradication of a Jewish population is not in any sense coincidental. More recently, the polo-shirt-wearing fascists of Unite the Right inaugurated their wild rumpus by chanting "Jews will not replace us" as they marched with their tiki torches through Charlottesville, Virginia. Fascism and antisemitism are not synonymous, however. There is such a thing as Jewish fascism. And even anarchists, the best antifascists of all, include among their leading historical lights the antisemitic Bakunin alongside the Jewish Emma Goldman and Alexander Berkman.[1]

With the opening of the Emily Hale letters, there can remain little doubt that Eliot was, at least for a good portion of his life, an antisemite. In those letters, Eliot's casual antisemitism is visible in an unguarded and frequently repulsive form (although not a fascist one), and it isn't difficult to perceive in it a way in which Eliot's reputation has benefited by the correspondence's remaining sealed for so long. He omits no reference to a Jewish person's identity as such, he occasionally uses "Jew" as an adjective ("Jew tailor," "little German Jew economist"), and he often takes the time to distinguish desirable Jews from undesirable ones: "Karl Mannheim . . . being a Jew (though an extremely nice one)"; "a young American Jew . . . rather quiet and likeable"; "he . . . has, especially considering that he is a Jew, a lovely voice and an attractive personality."[2] However, there can remain similarly little doubt that he was an antifascist.

His long friendship with Ezra Pound is the most often cited evidence to the contrary, but as the previous chapter suggested, Eliot's friendships were not always based on ideological symmetry. Eliot saw through Mussolini early and through Pound eventually, admitting to Mary Trevelyan that Pound was "never really sane. Oh yes, as a young man, I swallowed him whole . . . I think he has become gradually, increasingly, insane through a long period of years."[3] Still, he remained devoted to Pound, one of the most notorious and outspoken American fascists of all time, to the end. The fact that both positions, antifascist and antisemite, are complicated and even challenged by evidence elsewhere in Eliot's writing need not preclude stating with confidence what the preponderance and timing of Eliot's words on both subjects make clear.

Thanks to the opening of the Hale archive, a great deal of new ink is going to be spilled exploring the historical and contextual niceties of everything Eliot had to say therein on everything Jewish and fascist. But not by me in this chapter. Given the particular needs of the moment and the specific aims of this book, it will hopefully be enough to say that Eliot makes a better antifascist than a philo-Semite and to move on to a consideration of what in Eliot's writing can expand the resources of those working to fight fascism today.[4] I will focus on a couple of little-known writings by Eliot and then compare Eliot's brand of antifascism to those of three of his contemporaries—Rebecca West, George Orwell, and Hannah Arendt—all of whom share Eliot's tendency to attack fascism with less sound and fury than probing and patience, and to signify more as a result. When Eliot wrote at the end of "Little Gidding," "And all shall be well and / All manner of thing shall be well / By the purification of the motive / In the ground of our beseeching," he was invoking the mystic Julian of Norwich as a guide for the contemporary spiritual seeker.[5] But "purification of the motive" is also a prominent theme running through Eliot's reflections on fascism in and after the interwar years. These reflections suggest that when it comes to fighting fascism, painful self-searching by individuals and nations, more than condemnation of others, is the only means by which "all shall be well," a view shared by West, Orwell, and Arendt: less religious writers but much more famous antifascists.

A widely circulated tweet in late 2016 expressed some incredulity that, so far into the twenty-first century, anyone in the United States actually felt the need to declare oneself antifascist. "You're *supposed* to be against that shit," is the only line I remember precisely. The writer Natasha Lennard argues that the mistake liberal Americans made in the years preceding the recent resurgence of overtly fascist movements was believing that whatever they had been doing was antifascist enough, that merely, say, having come of age after 1945 implied an adequate antifascist position.[6] Since 2016, antifascism, organized and otherwise, has become a more common, visible, and vocal public stance not only in the United States but also in Canada, Europe, Latin America, and elsewhere, even as the presumption that antifascism is virtually automatic has become less tenable. An article by Douglas Murray in that inaugural US issue of the *Spectator* makes a case very similar to one T. S. Eliot, Evelyn Waugh, and other conservatives used to make in the 1920s and 1930s. Its title is "Far Wrong: If Everyone Is a Fascist, Then Nobody Is."[7] Such efforts at nuance provide good evidence that fascism is back, or rather that it never left. Eliot, West, Orwell, and Arendt all observed that fascism, once it moves past the haircuts-and-torches phase, has a way of hiding in plain sight.

Like anarchism, fascism is not so much a set of policies or dogmas as a grouping of characteristic actions. The debates about definitions of fascism or which regimes qualify as truly fascist tend to be less productive than analyses of practices. When Walter Benjamin long ago defined fascism as the aestheticization of politics, it was one way of saying that, to a significant extent, fascism is as fascism does. Likewise, Susan Sontag's famous 1975 essay "Fascinating Fascism" condemns Leni Riefenstahl as a lifelong fascist almost entirely through analysis of Riefenstahl's aesthetics as a filmmaker and photographer. We feel that we know fascism through works like *Triumph of the Will* and *The Last of the Nuba* because fascism speaks and indeed has its being through its aesthetic objects and its choreography of actions. So it is not surprising that what we observe as aesthetic properties of such works are indeed values close to the core of fascist ideology: Sontag emphasizes the celebration of strength, power, and purity as against balance or complexity; the focus on men and myth rather than women or history; the elevation of joy and unity over the critical spirit, ambivalence, or plurality.[8] Robert Paxton's *The Anatomy of Fascism* remains eminently useful for identifying fascism past and present: "Fascism may be defined as a form of political behavior marked by obsessive preoccupation with community decline, humiliation, or victimhood and by compensatory cults of unity, energy, and purity, in which a mass-based party of committed nationalist militants, working in uneasy but effective collaboration with traditional elites, abandons democratic liberties and pursues with redemptive violence and without ethical or legal restraints goals of internal cleansing and external expansion."[9] It is an admirably thorough definition, although it works poorly as a soundbite.[10] Roger Griffin's formulation both captures the ideological (as opposed to structural or historical) nature of fascism and is helpfully memorable, but it requires an additional task of defining (*palingenetic*: new birth, re-creation, or regeneration): "Fascism is a political ideology whose mythic core in its various permutations is a palingenetic form of populist ultra-nationalism."[11] I have found Shane Burley's recent definition "inequality through mythological and essentialized identity" highly useful and portable.[12] In a single phrase it crystallizes an essential feature of fascism—inequality—and distinguishes the fascist version from many others.

Like fascism and antisemitism, fascism and totalitarianism are often uncritically used as synonyms, but the distinction is important for clarifying our thinking about both the post–World War II era and the present one. A fascist movement isn't always totalitarian, nor is a totalitarian regime always fascist. At its core, "the fascist project," writes Burley, "is not about achieving totalitarianism, it is about reclaiming the mythological identity and order, and if totalitarian means are the way to get there then so be it."[13] In the mid-twentieth century, Hitler and Stalin were as frequently and accurately lumped together under the totalitarian label as Hitler, Mussolini, and Franco were under the fascist. And the critical consensus is that the bands of rune-and-shield bigots rallying in city streets these days, although they have very little power over any territory or body of people, are nonetheless authentically fascist insofar as they embrace the values enumerated above and look back as well as forward to historical regimes with much more power of that kind. Fascism is brought into being through its performances, a condition upon which Antifa bases its relentless commitment to oppose every fascist or would-be fascist march, demonstration, rally, or speaker.

Mentioning Antifa and its enemies plunges us right into the present (although Antifa dates to the regimes of Mussolini and Hitler). Why hide the fact that it is the public resurgence of both fascism and antifascism in the past few years in the United States and Europe that motivates my interest in looking back at an earlier version of the same contest? Enough people returned to Orwell after the US election of 2016 to return *1984* to the bestseller list, and I am among a sizeable number to have returned to Arendt at the same moment. Fewer people, no doubt, picked up Rebecca West, and fewer still T. S. Eliot. But my hope is to suggest some ways in which all four—Eliot, West, Orwell, and Arendt—amplify and complete one another's analyses of an era in which fascism had indeed become totalizing. I focus on their writings after WWII had begun, which is to say after the period in which fascism was ascendant and might have been terrifying but its ultimate trajectories unknown. We will never again be as innocent as it was possible to be in the 1920s and 1930s, so we would do well to look at what an earlier generation decided must be done once they knew in full what a failure to act sooner had cost.

There was a time when it was fashionable to call T. S. Eliot a fascist or proto-fascist, but that time appears to have passed. However resistant he was to the kinds of statements and stances that would have aligned him neatly with the most vocal antifascist movements in England, his prose reveals a consistent and resolute antifascism, whatever it may also reveal of elitism, intolerance (including the indefensible expressions of antisemitism), and an at-times consuming passion for order. The confounding thing for his critics has been that he refused to accept the ordinary political triangulation of the day wherein Stalinism, Nazism, and liberal democracy are set against one another and divide the world between them. None of these ideologies was a satisfactory option for Eliot because all lacked the Christian foundation he required of a fully realized society.

He wrote a good deal about fascism throughout the 1920s and 1930s, the decades of its fearsome ascendancy in Europe. When he did so, although he criticized the programs of Hitler and Mussolini for their cultural superficiality and spiritual artificiality, he was as often urging clarity of terminology, criticizing communism as well, or taking a none-of-the-above approach, and the overall effect has left many, if not most, observers unsatisfied. He came to realize that fascism presented a genuine threat but so did the uncritical application of the term *fascist* to what often seemed to him an unlimited array of circumstances, points of view, or persons. The power of words and ideas, not the programs of particular regimes, drew the bulk of his attention, which explains in part why his interwar antifascism can sound tepid at times: "I am not concerned with the feasibility of fascism as a working programme for Italy. What matters is the spread of the fascist idea."[14] In December 1928, in "The Literature of Fascism," he wrote: "What I am concerned with is . . . the possible influence on the public mind of the *idea*, or rather the vague sentiment of approval excited by the word, of fascism . . . People get emotional excitement out of political words, as they do out of other words; the words 'Democracy,' 'Communism,' 'Fascism,' 'Monarchy,' 'Republicanism,' 'Empire,' . . . there are very few of us who do not respond with the proper jerk to one or another of these words."[15] An era when one could employ such forbearance in the face of a rising fascist threat or refer to the "vague sentiment of *approval*" excited by the mention of fascism seems very distant indeed, and yet Eliot's approach is not quaint. This review-essay is his most substantial engagement in the debate over fascism in the interwar years, and while it may disappoint as a piece of political flag planting, its seeming indirection exemplifies a brand of independent thinking that may prove to be a more useful antifascist instrument today.

His primary criticism of the Mussolini regime, in "The Literature of Fascism" and elsewhere, is the poverty of its ideas: "The singularity of the Italian revolution seems to be this, that it began with no 'ideas' at all . . . and proved itself capable of transforming itself as occasions required, and of assimilating ideas as required."[16] It may not sound a very strident critique of fascism, but to anyone who has detected a similar vacuity in the motto "Make America Great Again," its relevance should be apparent. And Eliot's recommendation for diligent scrutiny remains sound, even if it would seem to outstrip the ideational capacity of most fascist movements as it is now possible to see them: "If we are to judge the 'idea' of fascism, then, we must speculate where its 'ideas' came from, how they cohere, and whether they are not still in the process of formation."[17] Almost a century on, most of the answers (most of them disappointing) to such questions are well known, but posing them in 1928, even in the teeth of a headlong rush to take sides, was not unreasonable.

There *is* quaintness in Eliot's folding together of fascists with Christian Socialists and Rotarians, as he had in a *Criterion* "Commentary" of the same year: "We assert strongly that . . . we do not impugn the motives, or question the good works of Rotary . . . or of the British Fascists . . . or of the Christian Socialists . . . but merely put forward the claims of impartial criticism; so that foundations should everywhere be as solid as possible."[18] His commitment to those foundations would remain a signature of his approach, particularly when considering how far political tendencies in Britain, even well after the war, resembled fascist ones. He was at times at pains to distinguish the fascism of Italy from what might be possible in Britain: "It is not our business to criticize fascism, as an Italian regime for Italians, a product of the Italian mind."[19] This scruple, however, subtly receded from his reflections as the European crisis deepened and communism and fascism threatened to squeeze out the positions he preferred to occupy. In July 1929 he wrote in the *Criterion* that "both fascism and communism" exhibit "a combination of statements with unexamined enthusiasms . . . Both fascism and communism seem to me to be well-meaning revolts against 'capitalism,' but revolts which do not appear to get to the bottom of the matter."[20] In the same "Commentary," he came as close as he ever would to an endorsement of fascism, far too close for most bona fide antifascists, and yet not really very close at all when read in context: "The objections of fascists and communists to each other are mostly quite irrational. I confess to a preference for fascism in practice, which I dare say most of my readers share; and I will not admit that this preference is itself wholly irrational. I believe the fascist form of unreason is less remote from my own than is that of the communists, but that my form is a more reasonable form of unreason."[21] That he was willing to risk such a statement, far from revealing a latent or crypto-fascism, actually hints at how far he was willing to go to identify and confront the true evil of fascism, apart from any of its temporary manifestations. If he could identify in himself the string that the idea of fascism caused to vibrate, however embarrassingly, and admit to it publicly, he could eliminate the possibility of any further innocence on the matter. He could remove himself from the millions who found (and find) it easy to denounce an institution but difficult to root out the habits of mind that allow coercion, domination, and unreason to flourish unlabeled and unannounced.

As the years and fascism's record accumulated, his criticism of fascism grew more acute, though it never quite rose to the level of unqualified denunciation. Nor did Eliot give up his preference for linking fascism and communism as nearly equivalent evils or for viewing both through the lens of Christianity. For instance, in a January 1935 lecture, his position, although clear and strong, is expressed in a way unlikely to appease strident antifascists then or now. That it invokes his most cherished and unshakeable ideological frame, Christianity, ought to mark it as decisive: "Can [the Christian] accept the present regime? Can he accept Communism? Can he accept Fascism? The answer to all three of these questions, I think, must be, No . . . The Christian cannot accept either the present state of affairs, or the alternatives offered by fascism and communism."[22] There is underappreciated radicalism in that refusal to "accept the present regime" or "present state of affairs." At a minimum, it casts some doubt on the label, so easily applied to Eliot, of old-fashioned conservative.

Once we stop trying to fix Eliot on one side or the other of a fascist divide and begin to accept that he is answering a different question than was being asked most volubly, we can perceive the genius and the real utility in his writing on fascism. Two remarks from Eliot's public work, one in a lecture and the other in a radio broadcast, amount to his most important statements on the matter of fascism between the wars, precisely because they refuse the terms usually offered for debate. In the 1935 lecture, he declared: "I do not propose to take up the rest of my time by denouncing Fascism and Communism," a task that "has been more ably performed by others, and the conclusions may be taken for granted. By pursuing this charge, I might obtain from you a kind of approval that I do not want."[23] In the radio broadcast, he suggested, "instead of merely condemning Fascism and Communism . . . we might do well to consider that we also live in a mass-civilisation following many wrong ambitions and wrong desires" (wrong, that is, vis-à-vis the Christianity that he believed ought to undergird and determine the right kind of civilization).[24] The "kind of approval" Eliot did not want was and is powerfully attractive to most folks in a time of fascist threat because it insulates one from the most likely and hurting accusations. To refuse to seek it requires considerable strength of purpose. Eliot refuses the kinds of bromides that might have secured the approval of other antifascists because they can serve to mask the "wrong ambitions and wrong desires" that implicate one's own society in the march toward cruelty, state violence, and unfreedom.

Just as its antisemitism is less varnished, the antifascism of his private writing is more decisive. He writes to Hale in 1934 that "as I have said so much about communism . . . I thought it was time I attacked fascism too."[25] In the same year he declares that "Douglas Jerrold," the British journalist, "is a fool. He might become a fascist." He did. "I have got these beastly fascists on the brain at present."[26] Two years later, as militarism solidifies its grip on Europe, he laments "the gloom of contemporary politics . . . It's not so great a strain, mentally, for those who can wholeheartedly believe in communism or fascism, or for those who can complacently accept the kind of disguised fascism or oligarchical, centralized control of everything that we are likely to get: but it's a hard world for those who cannot accept any of the secular alternatives of the time."[27] In November of the same year, in a surprising letter about the Spanish Civil War, he writes what might be his most direct denunciation: "I think that fascism is as great an enemy, because more insidious, to Christianity as communism."[28]

I want to argue, though, that the apparently straightforward pronouncement, however well it satisfies a demand for political side-taking, often cuts less deeply as a weapon of the antfascist than a formulation of the more nuanced kind. I believe Eliot's antifascist credentials are sound, but they would not translate well into a bumper-sticker slogan. Even well into the war, once the monstrous potentialities of fascism had become actual, he was still arguing for precision around the relevant terms. One case, previously unknown, in which he did so is a preface he wrote to a book called *Apel (Roll Call)*, a 1944 Polish account of horrors at the Auschwitz concentration camp. This preface was never published, in English or in Polish translation. In it, Eliot writes that "we are persistently prone . . . to deceive ourselves with names."[29] "If the keepers of the camp were of our own party," the camps "would certainly be called by some other name—'colonies of protective custody,' perhaps, or 'reconditioning centres'—[and] we should be convinced that we had to do with something quite different." But such renaming would be symptomatic of our delusion. The "process of deception" obtains as well on a grander scale. "We all profess devotion to 'democracy,'" he writes. "But democracy has to mean our own notion of democracy. Everything that fails to conform to our own notion of democracy is not only evil, but all the same kind of evil, which is 'fascism.'"[30] Such quibbling at the late hour of 1944 might indicate a failure, to use a phrase much employed nowadays, to read the room. However, Eliot's concern is not to diminish the reality of the fascist threat but, rather, to refuse to let his non-Nazi audience off the hook by quarantining its horror within a cell with the name *fascism* on the door. As with concentration camps, so with political morals. "We need," he writes, "to distinguish between the essence and the attributes of the concentration camp. We should see it as essentially the same evil, whether the conduct of it is more, or less humane. The evil lies in treating any group of human beings, whether foreign or domestic factionaries, whether a nation or a class, as something less than human, as merely pawns or pests."[31] We may neither console ourselves with the term "democracy" nor excuse ourselves by applying the term "fascism." Knowing the evil that underlies every form of dehumanization is the harder undertaking. Only by acknowledging "the terrible congruity" of Auschwitz "to the modern world" can we begin to get free of the forces underlying all manner of official and unofficial dehumanization and apparatuses of state oppression, including camps under any name.

It is a principle he returns to in an essay on (not surprisingly) antisemitism nearly a decade later. In 1953, Dr. William Kolodney, educational director at New York's 92nd Street Young Men's and Young Women's Hebrew Association (where Eliot had read at the Poetry Center in 1950), wrote to Eliot requesting some words on antisemitism in Russia for a pamphlet he was producing. His reply is full of the same incisive attention to primary causes that characterized his *Apel* preface:

> The only striking difference between the present anti-Semitism in Russia, and the anti-Semitism of Hitler's Germany, seems to me this: that the Russians have learned from the mistakes of the Germans, and are much shrewder propagandists. The Nazis persecuted Jews for being Jews, and thereby incurred at once the antipathy of all civilized people. The Russians refrain from any overt doctrine of racial superiority, which would too flatly contradict their supposed principles . . . Just as they have condemned and destroyed their more important Christian victims, not on the ground of their being Christians, but always on some pretext of treason or civil crime, so the Jews who are condemned to death—or worse—are condemned on some other ground, than that of being Jews. But it comes to the same thing in the end.[32]

The danger is not limited to regimes that are unapologetically fascist and thus can easily marry racial or religious prejudice to a program of oppression or murder. The logic of Eliot's linkage of Soviet to Nazi antisemitism carries through to any number of more or less liberal regimes that would try to evade the fact that the victims of their policies—at borders, by policing, through the limitation of access to resources—just tend to be united by a darker skin color, a minority religion, the failure to conform to expectations of gender or sexuality, or some other social distinction. There is always "some pretext" for persecuting or destroying such people other than an "overt doctrine of superiority." But it comes to the same thing in the end.

Taking the fight beyond the condemnation of regimes that wear the badge of fascism openly is Eliot's approach to antifascism. Fascist ideology, he knew, need not present itself with the brazenness of a Hitler or a Mussolini to be just as destructive, under any name, whether in the Soviet Union, the United Kingdom, or the United States. Resisting those movements that fly the flag of fascism may scratch a moral itch, but failing to "distinguish between the essence and the attributes" of fascism will ensure that the evil goes on. Sir Oswald Mosley led the British Union of Fascists on marches through London, but this threat troubled Eliot less than the insidious one that can make fascism a reality even where the label is absent. Likewise, in our time, the tiki-torch boys surely need to be fought, but they are not the ones pulling the levers of state power. Their rallies are easier to confront and their slogans easier to condemn than state pretexts for "treating any group of human beings . . . as something less than human," but that should not delude the antifascist into thinking that it is always possible to judge fascism from a position well outside of it. We are all neck-deep in "a mass civilisation following many wrong ambitions and wrong desires," and it is from that spot, too, that we have to fight.[33]

Eliot's antisemitism is an obvious reason he is not usually part of conversations on the trials of Nazi leaders at Nuremberg. However, his contemporary Rebecca West, who was there, writes of the tribunal with a self-searching force matching Eliot's, on her way to comparable but even stronger conclusions about unclean hands. Judgment on an international scale is the subject of Greenhouse with Cyclamens, the series of essays West wrote on the trials she attended at Nuremberg that ran from November 1945 to October 1946. West and everyone else knew that at the end of these trials must be a death, and so there was, indeed eleven deaths by hanging. Despite the stark inadequacy even of using what West calls "the least dignified form of death" to punish these eleven Nazis for their crimes against humanity, someone inevitably had to die.[34] West writes devastatingly on both the reasons why hanging is the only acceptable form of capital punishment and the way it soils and entangles those who observe, employ, or even countenance it. "There was never a lawful occasion," she admits, "which smelled so strongly of the unlawful."[35] Her words describing the climactic moment at which the lawful system set up to deal with Nazi atrocities acts finally to punish their unlawfulness is loaded with the anxiety of implication that neither she, Arendt, Orwell, nor Eliot denies:

> When the Nuremberg tribunal came to deal with these delicate matters it proved to be as zanyish as we had feared it might be. It undertook the task of hanging eleven men with a dreadful innocence which made the reports of the journalists who witnessed the executions not nearly so unlike the testimony concerning Nazi atrocities which had brought these men to the gallows as one might have hoped. The hangman was an American sergeant who meant no harm but had not fully benefitted by the researches of Marwood and Berry.[36] The ten men slowly choked to death. Ribbentrop struggled in the air for twenty minutes. Yet it would be treachery against truth not to concede that justice had been done. Each one of these men who had been hanged had committed crimes for which he would have had to give his life under German law; and it

would have then been an axe that killed him. But there are stenches which not the name of justice or reason or the public good, or any other fair word, can turn to sweetness.[37]

This is not evasion. It is, rather, exemplary of precisely the kind of critical thought, of ambivalence, of acceptance of reality based on fact all the way down to human excreta that fascism seeks to banish. Another celebrated British antifascist, George Orwell, wrote of hanging in similarly anguished terms in a 1931 essay republished the same year as West's: "It is curious, but till that moment I had never realized what it means to destroy a healthy, conscious man. When I saw the prisoner step aside to avoid the puddle, I saw the mystery, the unspeakable wrongness, of cutting a life short when it is in full tide."[38]

At the end of 1945, when subjects like "war guilt trials" and "punishment of war criminals" were in the air, Orwell had contended with the same questions as West in equally fundamental terms. Visiting a prison holding Nazis, Orwell watches as a "little Jew" kicks an imprisoned SS officer "right on the bulge of one of his deformed feet" and taunts "Get up, you swine!"[39] Orwell knows that

> it is absurd to blame any German or Austrian Jew for getting his own back on the Nazis . . . But what this scene, and much else that I saw in Germany, brought home to me was that the whole idea of revenge and punishment is a childish daydream. Properly speaking, there is no such thing as revenge. Revenge is an act which you want to commit when you are powerless and because you are powerless: as soon as the sense of impotence is removed, the desire evaporates also.[40]

He goes on to name Goering, Ribbentrop, and company and admits: "Somehow the punishment of these monsters ceases to seem attractive when it becomes possible: indeed, once under lock and key, they almost cease to be monsters."[41] With a humility reminiscent of Eliot's, he puts England, too, in the dock: "In so far as the big public in this country is responsible for the monstrous peace settlement now being forced on Germany, it is because of a failure to see in advance that punishing an enemy brings no satisfaction." What is true of kicking a chained man is true also of the most official and most organized tribunal the world had ever seen.

For West, the Nuremberg trials of 1945 turned out to be a non-event. Or, rather, to invoke the distinction she employs throughout the Greenhouse with Cyclamens series: "It was one of the events which do not become an experience."[42] At every turn, the meaning that the Allied powers thought the proceedings could hold kept leaking out, as the form proved incapable of matching or expressing the unprecedented content. After much writing and long reflection she concludes: "The Nuremberg trial must be admitted as a betrayal of the hopes that it engendered. Its makers devised it as well as the times allowed. Conducted by officials sick with the weariness left by a great war, attended by only a handful of spectators, inadequately reported, constantly misinterpreted, it was an unshapely event, a defective composition, stamping no clear image on the mind of the people it had been designed to impress."[43] Punishment there had been, even justice, but not the kind of experience that transforms. West walked away from the tribunal as unconvinced as anyone that fascism had died on the gallows with the Nazis.

Nine years after West completed her Nuremberg essay, Hannah Arendt writes in "Eichmann in Jerusalem" that "no punishment has ever possessed enough power of deterrence to prevent the commission of crimes."[44] This sweeping pronouncement is true in the case of the Nazis not only because of the impossible-to-bridge difference in scale between the crime—the murder of millions of innocent people—and any punishment inflicted on one or a handful of leaders. The tribunals, first at Nuremberg and then at Jerusalem, were doomed to futility because of the courts' lack of "a clear recognition of the criminal who commits this crime," that is, a crime against humanity. Arendt's use of the term *banality* to describe the fundamental characteristic of Eichmann and his cohort caused no end of controversy. But, like the interventions of Eliot, Orwell, and West, the term is Arendt's way of casting a wider net of responsibility than any narrow "antifascism." "The trouble with Eichmann," she writes, "was precisely that so many were like him, and that the many were neither perverted nor sadistic, that they were, and still are, terribly and terrifyingly normal."[45] It was bureaucracy, not anything with a living spirit, that gave meaning to Eichmann's life as a Nazi: "Eichmann was not Iago and not Macbeth . . . Except for an extraordinary diligence in looking out for his own personal advancement, he had no motives at all."[46] Far from ignoring the severity of Nazi crimes, Arendt forces her audience to reckon with the extent to which the disease behind those crimes has already infected all manner of institutions and patterns of life.

Besides *banality*, she also uses the word *thoughtlessness* to name what made it possible for Eichmann to have no awareness of the severity of his actions, and it is this term, *thoughtlessness*, that is perhaps the most germane as we look out on a world in which fascism is thumping with life and has even made significant inroads into institutions but has not yet become total. Today's noisy fascists are animated and idealistic in a way that Eichmann and company, in the end, were not. They present ready targets for antifascist action by all people of goodwill because they are not yet thoughtless. They broadcast their thought, such as it is, at every opportunity, as they try to actualize their beliefs through performing them. Such is an appropriate—though not sufficient—ground for challenging fascism before it becomes truly institutionalized. Once it does, the targets for resistance begin to recede from view, as demagogues and ideologues turn into functionaries and bureaucrats. American author and former white nationalist Christian Picciolini was a firsthand observer of the movement's intentional boots-to-suits strategy as the twentieth century turned into the twenty-first. "I never thought we would have a political climate that really kind of brought it to the foreground," he confesses. "Because it's starting to seem less like a fringe ideology and more like a mainstream ideology."[47] In a far advanced state, Arendt recognized, there is hardly anyone there to punish. Ironically, the more entrenched the fascism, and the more efficient and automatic the atrocities—or, to put it another way, the more the camps, by whatever name, become part of the background of ordinary life—the harder it becomes to know the evil for what it is and to find an authentic footing from which to resist it.

But as Herbert Read said, "We are not excused." It is easy, after Nazism, to look back at interwar writings like the ones in which Eliot focused on terminology and view them as pedantic, misguided, or at least inadequate to the threat. Arendt's ideas, however, force us to consider the possibility that the failure to condemn fascist regimes strongly enough is less grievous than the failure to detect and combat fascist ideas and procedures *wherever they occur and under whatever name*. They do the most damage, she argues, when they carry hardly a whiff of outright evil. In making so much of Eliot's at times maddeningly noncommittal public statements on fascism as a way of buffing up a sense of our own antifascist acuity and rigor, we may have missed the urgent wisdom hidden in his approach. It is an understandable turn to have taken, as accepting that fascism may do its most awful work not under the banners and torches but within the systems to which we have explicitly or implicitly consented, or have just been thoughtless about, puts us in the dock as well.

In a century, then, fascism has remained unconquered by democracy or punishment and vanished into banality precisely when it seems most exposed for an outright confrontation. It amounts to a lot of failure, a lot of inadequacy, a lot of loss and little to show for it, a poor balance between acts and consequences; it's easily enough to leave one despondent. Fully alive to this possibility, however, neither Eliot, West, Orwell, nor Arendt gave in to despair. West in the end salvages hope by conceiving of the antifascist predicament as analogous to a writing challenge. In 1954 she wrote that the Nuremberg trial was a "defective composition." She ends Greenhouse with Cyclamens with this magisterial paragraph:

> But destiny cares nothing about the orderly presentation of its material. Drunken with an exhilaration often hard to understand, it likes to hold its cornucopia upside down and wave it while its contents drop anywhere they like over time and space. Brave are our human attempts to counteract this sluttish habit. Brave were the economists who met together and tried to set the world's leaders straight;[48] brave the Western Germans who inscribed the neat pattern of industry on a patch of earth known to be specially unstable;[49] brave the Berliners and East Germans who set about understanding the problem of the state when international action had wrecked the state to which they naturally belonged;[50] brave the mediocre Fritzsche who tried to put down how happenings looked to people who have never quite known what was happening;[51] and brave the men who, in making the Nuremberg trial, tried to force a huge and sprawling historical event to become comprehensible. It is only by making such efforts that we survive.[52]

It sounds much like the words written years earlier by her contemporary Eliot, about the challenges and elusive rewards of both writing and living. The words of "East Coker" gave solace to British people staring death, defeat, and fascism in the face during the war years and, I suggest, might do so for us, as we again contend with a fascism we might have imagined to have been vanquished had we not read Eliot, West, Orwell, and Arendt or endured the past several years in the Western democracies that were meant to save us:

> There is only the fight to recover what has been lost
> And found and lost again and again: and now, under conditions
> That seem unpropitious. But perhaps neither gain nor loss.
> For us, there is only the trying. The rest is not our business.[53]

Chapter 4

Shantih, War, and *The Waste Land*

The idea that war and communication are opposites has been expressed in many different ways, perhaps most memorably in a quotation frequently attributed to Margaret Atwood: "War is what happens when language fails." The final eight lines of *The Waste Land*, from "London Bridge is falling down falling down falling down" to "Shantih Shantih Shantih," make the sound of language failing, or at least failing to communicate, which amounts to the same thing.

> London Bridge is falling down falling down falling down
> *Poi s'ascose nel foco che gli affina*
> *Quando fiam uti chelidon*—O swallow swallow
> *Le Prince d'Aquitaine à la tour abolie*
> These fragments I have shored against my ruins
> Why then Ile fit you. Hieronymo's mad againe.
> Datta. Dayadhvam. Damyata.
>   Shantih   shantih   shantih[1]

Although individually the lines are articulate and, moreover, drawn from rich veins of veritable literary tradition, any reader not conversant in all of the half-dozen languages represented will experience language as failure. From its first appearance in the pages of the October 1922 *Criterion*, this babel has been, like every part of the poem, subject to intensive interpretation, to understate the matter wildly. The effort to make the passage (and the poem) cohere was underwritten early by the addition of Eliot's own Notes to *The Waste Land* for its December 1922 publication in book form.

Reading between and behind these lines has yielded a century's worth of interpretative rewards, formidable as well as dubious. And of course even on their surface, failing to communicate is not all these lines do. In their strangeness they also beckon toward not-yet-understood realms, and through pure sound, rhythm, and juxtaposition they connect with meaning centers other than the intelligence. But ask any reader new to the poem how much coherence they hear in this sequence of lines. If war is what happens when language fails, then war is what one could reasonably expect to fill the space where this poem ends. And yet it ends with a word for peace.

One way this sequence might be said to cohere and not cohere at once is as scraps of a humanities curriculum. Every line but one is a fragment of another text, including nursery song, epic, lyric poem, religious mantra, popular drama, and classical mythology, and they are drawn from several thousand years of history. The only original line is "These fragments I have shored against my ruins," as though the speaker were at once acknowledging the dissolution of this humanities tradition and trying to salvage it, doing so in the teeth of the failure of language that dooms the effort. These, then, are the two strands I would like to draw together in this chapter: on the one hand war as the failure of language, and on the other the humanities, which have also been doing a lot of failing. As the final lines show in miniature, *The Waste Land* is the right poem for the job.

Rumors of the demise of the academic humanities, those disciplines concerned with the endeavors that make human life unique and worth living—languages and literature, philosophy, art, history, religion—appear not to have been exaggerated. While it is true that the field has survived a good thirty years or more of an always impending extinction, the evidence of its diminished stature and power is unmistakable: required classes eliminated, shrinking majors, whole disciplines and departments cut. Most of the time, this fate is attributed to the ascendancy of business culture: the way that capitalism will eventually identify and either monetize or squeeze out any aspect of life whose service to profit is not immediately apparent. Universities have invested in attractive new facilities and amenities, grown business and technical programs, and cut faculty, especially in the humanities, in the interest of competition, material and fiscal growth, and profit margins. A vexing irony of the situation is that as culture is increasingly wracked by issues requiring deep humanistic understanding—movements for racial, ethnic, and gender justice; a reckoning with painful histories and their representation in public life; contests over the human dignity and rights of immigrants; the narrowing prospects for rich living in a world adding extinction to extinction—the disciplines most invested in them are starved, marginalized, or ignored.

Where they continue to exist, the humanities are deeply enmeshed in the cultural and social currents of the day, as they are intended to be, which has drawn the attention and ire of observers who prefer that academia prepare citizens for dutiful service to capital and the state and stay politely silent otherwise. If the field is to hang on, or one day do more than that, it will have to contend successfully with both business culture and the voices of reaction. I would like to argue, though, that even if the humanities should somehow win such battles, returning, say, to the cultural standing they enjoyed a century ago, they will remain marginal so long as they don't confront war, the force with perhaps the greatest power to restrict the horizons of the human.

That such a confrontation has thus far been avoided is not surprising, considering the astonishing degree to which war is tolerated as a part of the rhythm and texture of human life in the twenty-first century. Tolerated or even excused: In the *New York Times Book Review* in November 2020, Dexter Filkins wrote: "But war is not merely a negative force; it's an engine of change and creativity. It helped create the modern bureaucracy, and it made rulers more democratic because they needed healthy, educated people to fight. War helped liberate women, not just on the home front but even on the battlefield, where increasingly they fought; and war forced artists—like the Cubists and the Vorticists—to look at the world in new ways."[2] Apart from the liberation of women, which has been achieved in countless more effective and less destructive ways, the rest of those gifts of war are laughable. It is like arguing that American slavery produced some good things, too, like a distinctive Southern cuisine and important musical forms, which comes close to the approach currently favored by the US state of Florida in its education protocols. Without wishing to oversimplify Filkins's views, his observations do call to mind a remark A. A. Milne made (with some oversimplification) of T. S. Eliot in 1935: "I do not even know if he would be glad to wake tomorrow into a warless world."[3] Would Filkins be glad to give up all that "change and creativity" for peace? He is obviously not alone in celebrating the virtues of war, but the glibness of his formulation—war's devastation in exchange for enlarged government and some innovative avant-garde painting—is singularly impressive. As a decorated war reporter, he should know better.

Eliot, who did his most lasting work *entre deux guerres*, was never glib about war. It is true that he was no pacifist. It was another matter on which his views did not line up with those of his friend Herbert Read. And yet his skepticism about war as a positive force or "an engine of change and creativity" was profound. As he wrote to Emily Hale in 1936, "The more militarised the world becomes the less freedom and civilisation"[4]: not a statement amounting to a pacifist position by any means, but, as it contrasts war with two of his most cherished values, still an unequivocal accounting of relative goodness. Another is his comment to Milne, "I object as much to the killing of men as of women and children."[5] Profound, too, was his admiration for pacifists who met his standard of consistency and clear thinking. Looking back in 1935 on the First World War, he declared of those who "objected because they believed war to be always and everywhere wrong . . . for these I have only respect."[6] This "small body of people who believe that no war is ever right, the few genuine believers in passive resistance: people who have remained perfectly consistent, whose belief is tenable, and who cannot be refuted" maintained his respect through the 1930s and the Second World War. When he quarreled with pacifists, it was not with these but with those whose positions were more relative or more worldly. Again writing to Hale in 1936, he complained: "Pacifism, not necessarily wrong in principle, tends to become wrong in fact, because it tends to assemble people who object to war for quite different reasons, not all of which can be right; and therefore tends to be degraded to the lowest motive."[7] What he desired above all was clarity and consistency, in language and in reasoning. In a July 1936 *Criterion* "Commentary" he wrote: "There would seem to be no subject today on which more words can more easily be expended to less purpose that that of the ethics of War and Peace."[8] He generally only added his own voice to the "waves of discussion" in order to call for order, precision, and ethical grounding. As with his antifascism, his meticulousness about the words and ways of pacifism can smack of fussiness, with the situation so dire and the clamor all for the stark drawing of lines. Again, though, it is precisely in indirection that Eliot makes his most valuable contributions to the cause.

Eliot's words about pacifism are vanishingly few until the mid-1930s, when he engaged in a number of written debates and extensive formulations of his own, culminating in *The Idea of a Christian Society* (1939). The defining feature of his position in these discussions is his Christian point of view. Christianity clearly afforded him a foundation from which to engage pacifism and pacifists with rigor and care. All kinds of tolerance and even respect for differing views are available to the liberal humanist, which Eliot was not. The dignity he afforded those pacifists whose positions he did not share, and his critique of them when needed, were explicitly those of the Christian. So he writes, for instance, in 1935 that "pacifism like that of Mr. Milne is not a very *Christian* pacifism"[9] and that "no pacifism that is not Christian pacifism is genuine. For it is the pacifists who pinned their faith on the League of Nations who are now most bellicose."[10] For Eliot, liberal positions would not do, and indeed make things worse. In 1939 he feels confirmed in his view "that Liberalism . . . is something which leads . . . to modern totalitarianism."[11] Christian pacifism, on the other hand, he wrote in a 1936 *Criterion* "Commentary," is not subject to such sinister mutations:

> There seems to be only one group of pacifists occupying an impregnable position, and that is the smallest. Those who believe that the word of God revealed to man is uncompromisingly and without exception opposed to the taking of human life may be wrong, but they cannot be confuted. They hold a respectable position, in that they oppose, not the incidental evils of war, but war in itself as an evil; they do not maintain that it is dreadful to be killed, but that it is a deadly sin to kill.[12]

The clarity of his position is bracing, if, for the nonbeliever, unwelcoming. Indeed there were even limits to the warmth of his embrace of Christian pacifists, who were to be tolerated, not necessarily emulated. He concluded in *The Idea of a Christian Society* rather disappointingly only that in such a society "it would be the duty of the Christian who was not a pacifist to treat the pacifist with consideration and respect." Further, "it would be the duty of the State to treat him with consideration and respect, having assured itself of his sincerity."[13] The very "idea of a Christian society seems incompatible with the idea of absolute pacifism" not because of any innate bellicosity in Christianity but rather the reverse: "For pacifism can only continue to flourish so long as the majority of persons forming a society are not pacifists; just as sectarianism can only flourish against the background of orthodoxy."[14] It stands to reason that peace, not pacifism, would predominate in a theocratic society with the Prince of Peace as its inspiration, but it seems a pedantic way to make the point.

Overall, Eliot was on the side of peace, not war, and not at all in the vacuous way that is as easy to apply to the munitions manufacturer as the conscientious objector. It is an understatement, although true, to say that while Eliot was no pacifist, still less was he a jingo or a hawk. Neither his attempts to enlist in the First World War nor his active support of the Allied cause in the Second World War undermine that fact. As is the case throughout this book, however, my interest is not ultimately in naming categories but in setting up new affiliations and solidarities. There is a productive sympathy to be formed between Eliot and a strain of peace people who want to make pacifism more rigorous, more resilient, and less subject to circumstance. There is certainly a great deal in Eliot's prose to benefit would-be pacifists whose ethics need stiffening. But the more surprising and potentially more powerful affiliation I want to explore is the one between *The Waste Land* and a fundamental criticism of war that might be pulsing beneath its fragments.

I would like to carve out a provisional space for thinking about literature and pacifism in an unordinary way, focusing on *The Waste Land* as a response to the First World War. When it comes to thinking about pacifism and the First World War, mine is not the most meticulous or historically grounded way, both of which belong to the book *Writing Against War* (2017), by Charles Andrews. My approach is brazenly idealistic in that it is less concerned with the question of precisely what *was* than with questions of what might have been and what might be. I make no attempt to argue that Eliot was a pacifist; instead, I ask what happens if we read a poem like *The Waste Land* as if *we* were. Reading for peace (I borrow the phrase from Australian scholar Shady Cosgrove) is something we need to do more of, both out of a responsibility to the humanities and out of a refusal to settle for the world of perpetual war we inhabit. Anarchists, anti-capitalists, ecological activists, and other idealists are often motivated by the saying, "Another world is possible." What world might have been possible if people thought in a radically different way about the relationship between poetry and war? What kind of world would be possible, even within the narrow sphere of the humanities, if we tried reading like pacifists?

A certain kind of antiwar poem invites no other kind of reading. In 2003, Eliot's old employer, Faber and Faber, published *101 Poems Against War*. In a review for *The Guardian*, David Wheatley wrinkled his nose at what he perceived as the anthology's "earnestly admonitory" tone, one shared by any number of others in the "boom industry" of antiwar volumes and utterances that greeted the beginning of the invasion of Iraq by the United States and its allies.[15] Wheatley sneers at the "campaigners in poetry's war on war" and asks "Is it the writer's business to understand war better than other people, why it happens and how to stop it?" In his skepticism, he sounds a good deal like George Orwell, who, owing to his relentlessly critical mind and neck-deep firsthand experience of war, would tolerate neither pacifism nor jingoism from writers who never saw combat. Nor would Orwell ever countenance the notion that literature possesses some automatic allegiance to justice or moral rectitude. "The sombre truth," writes Wheatley, "which *101 Poems Against War* never entirely confronts, is that writing about conflict is at its most honest when it does not assume that literature will automatically be on the humanely right side, which is to say 'our' side, no matter who 'we' happen to be."[16] Wheatley complains that Paul Keegan and Matthew Hollis, the editors of *101 Poems*, place their chosen poets "in a position of vatic moral authority, from which to pronounce their 'common plea for humanity.'" He disapproves of what he sees as the assumption that "everything decent and noble in human nature is on the editors' side." He sees too much "self-congratulatory crassness" in the anthology's selections and not enough ambivalence, too much moral certainty and not enough doubt and second-guessing, "too much method and not enough madness."[17] It begins to sound nearly as though he wished Keegan and Hollis had included *The Waste Land*.

Interestingly, in the same year *The Waste Land* appeared, Eliot voiced his own critique of a type of antiwar poem he found too neat and self-congratulatory. In the April 1922 "London Letter," he offered that "the popularity of certain war poems was due . . . to the fact that they appeared to represent a revolt against something that was very unpleasant, and really paid a tribute to all the nicest feelings of the upper-middle class British public school boy."[18] He was presumably referring more to Rupert Brooke than to Wilfred Owen, but he might also have been thinking of Siegfried Sassoon. In any case, he wanted something more out of (anti)war poetry.

If the complexity prized by Wheatley and Eliot has a place in antiwar poetry, then *The Waste Land* might have made an appropriate, though wildly unexpected, addition to *101 Poems Against War*. Because *The Waste Land* works with a subtle, surprising power as an antiwar poem. But along with complexity, including *The Waste Land* would have brought with it a powerful challenge to another of Wheatley's ideas. Reading *The Waste*

Land as an antiwar poem requires the adoption of an idealistic, activist stance that ostensibly more pragmatic readers like Wheatley cannot abide. Particularly when it comes to war, those possible worlds alluded to above are essential to a criticism based in hope, but they are given little thought in a reading of war poetry that privileges above all else the accurate representation of "the full intensity of things as they are in these dark times, never mind the alternative world of 'as it should be.'"[19] Significantly, the words "as it should be" are drawn by Wheatley from a Derek Mahon poem where they describe a world in which the murder (the execution, as Wheatley would probably prefer) of a "mad bastard" has resulted in peace and order. It isn't peace or justice to which Wheatley objects. It is, rather, the suggestion that endorsing war never has a place on the side of the right, in the pursuit of peace, or in an ethical war poetry. For now, I would like to risk taking up only a part of that suggestion, the last part.

My inspiration for taking such a plunge comes fairly directly from Australian scholar R. S. White, who proposes that "war is always a direct threat not only to human beings themselves but also to the Humanities since its function is to undermine the human values and rational methodologies that are at the centre of our disciplines."[20] White qualifies his point only very slightly (though still more than Filkins) by writing: "Conflict is an inescapable part of human society and often even a creative part leading to new developments, but war as state-sanctioned and institutionalised mass murder, is not natural human behaviour and never creative."[21] All I propose to do at present is to take White's suggestion seriously, as I think is its due, to entertain the idea that a fundamental antagonism, even incompatibility, exists between war and the humanities, and to consider the implications of such a stance for the work of literary criticism, particularly on the poetry of Eliot.

One possible implication is that we ought not to confine a study of pacifism to explicitly activist writing. Perhaps even if a poem is not patently anti-war, our critical reading of it ought to be. Reading for peace—like reading for gender, reading for race, reading for class, reading for ecology, and reading for war—provides a motivating impulse as well as a critical framework, ones that, if White is correct, ought to be so foundational as to supersede even that list of other major socially interested approaches. There are a number of things humanities scholars generally consider unacceptable: bigotry, hate speech, undocumented research, argument unsupported by evidence. At times the list might also include a-historicism, too much collusion with state or market power, unfamiliarity with tradition, and inattention to form or to inequities of gender, race, or class. Somehow, though, the humanities have maintained a surprisingly high capacity for the toleration of war, which looms behind and around their work like dark matter. War—or more precisely its end—has been like the ominous card in the deck of Madame Sosostris following "the one-eyed merchant . . . Which is blank." It is "something he carries on his back, / Which I am forbidden to see."[22]

Eliot composed *The Waste Land* primarily in the years just after the First World War, and for a century, critics have (besides a thousand other things) turned over the relationship between the poem and the war that preceded it. Writing to one of these critics, E. M. Forster, in 1929, Eliot himself downplayed the relationship, suggesting that "the *Waste Land* might have been just the same without the War."[23] It was only one of several handwaving remarks he made over the years about the poem and its significance, and it can be tabled for two reasons: In the activist approach, authorial intention comes a distant second to readerly interest, and, for readers, *The Waste Land* has never been and can never be "without the War," which along with the rest of history has created the conditions of possibility for the poem's interpretation. We only choose which of these conditions to emphasize. Indeed, Forster replied to Eliot that "but for the war, I shouldn't myself have had any preparation for the poem."[24]

In terms of close readings that emphasize *The Waste Land* as a war poem, some of the most incisive are those focusing on the imagery of the poem's opening and closing. Michael Levenson argues that the first voice in the poem is of the war dead themselves, whom winter kept warm and spring stirs up.[25] Carl Krockel adds that "spring is only cruel to the speaker, lying under the earth, because he is a buried corpse, perhaps of the war, as a soldier or a representative way of life before the war."[26] Likewise the blasted landscapes at the poem's end are often cited as figuring the war's devastation: "the grass is singing / Over the tumbled graves, about the chapel / There is the empty chapel, only the wind's home. / It has no windows, and the door swings."[27] The invocation of London Bridge "falling down falling down falling down" suggests not only destruction but possibly the addled speech characteristic of shell shock.[28] The famous fragments, "shored against my ruins," speak all too well of physical, political, and cultural worlds reduced to fragments by war on a scale never witnessed before. The poem is full of rats, which plagued the trenches (and corpses) of the war, and names "rats' alley," a direct reference to "a trench in the Somme sector."[29] And back in London there is tension about what will ensue on the home front when "Lil's husband" is "demobbed [demobilized]."³⁰

Another strain of criticism sees the poem as infused with mourning for a very particular French soldier, Eliot's friend Jean Verdenal, the dedicatee of *Prufrock and Other Observations*, who drowned in the mud at Gallipoli. This relationship has been much rehearsed and contested over the years, with some readers seeing the ghost of Verdenal in the encounter in the hyacinth garden, the drowned Phoenician sailor, "My friend, blood shaking my heart," and even the "broken Coriolanus."³¹ The dedication of *Prufrock and Other Observations*, Krockel writes, "reflects how [Eliot] longed to compensate for the loss of Verdenal. He did so through an intense process of identification with him . . . *The Waste Land* expresses how, as a figure which fails to be integrated into a speaker's integrated identity and remains an object of insatiable desire, Verdenal as the object of Eliot's identification also marks the persistence of his traumatic loss."³²

So persistent are war's echoes in the poem that most recent criticism takes the war connection for granted, asking not whether *The Waste Land* is a war poem but what it says *about* war. Many of today's readers have begun pressing *The Waste Land* to speak more decisively about the war with which it has been associated in so many ways for so long. Sarah Cole argues that *The Waste Land* "ruthlessly disenchants its own origins" in violence and in "the waste of war."³³ Ezekiel Black draws a fascinating linkage between *The Waste Land*'s obsession with ineffability, that which cannot be expressed in words, and the several forms of speechlessness enforced by the war: by military culture, by censorship, by shell-shock, by the disconnect between home and frontlines, and by physical mouth trauma. "Voice," he writes, "should be listed alongside the dead as a victim of the war."³⁴ Black is quite right that Eliot did possess a direct personal link to the war in the person of Jean Verdenal. He is also right to point out that key parts of *The Waste Land* "illustrate the dilemma of World War I poetry, that speechlessness is not always subject to physical mouthlessness."³⁵ Krockel links the two with the powerful assertion: "Verdenal and the dead of war form the ordering silence of *The Waste Land*."³⁶

Martin Lockerd links Eliot and *The Waste Land* to perhaps the most famous poet of the war, Rupert Brooke, through the two men's shared preoccupation with decadence, specifically with what Lockerd calls "the inevitable decay of the body personal and the body politic."³⁷ One might say Brooke and Eliot bracket the war, representing on the one hand what it destroyed and on the other what it engendered. Brooke thought that societal and physical decay might be arrested and reversed by the war, whereas Eliot in *The Waste Land* confronted the question of what to do with the decay and wreckage the war had in fact wrought. "The chapel in 'What the Thunder Said,'" writes Lockerd, "contains no grail that might magically cure the Fisher King's decayed body and cleanse the body politic"[38] It is an image of the vacancy of myth and of story. He quotes Levenson who likewise notes the poem's ultimate flight from humanistic solutions: "In the last lines of the poem, the images from Western literature are images of disintegration."

While some readers feel that art acts as a compensatory and reanimating framework in *The Waste Land*, and Levenson's observation notwithstanding, the degree to which *The Waste Land* suggests that poetic structure is capable of reordering or reanimating what war has decimated is, I think, usually overstated. Jack Dudley concurs. Dudley's marvelous essay "Transcendence and the End of Modernist Aesthetics" follows a pattern established in *The Waste Land* through to David Jones's even more massive *In Parenthesis* (which Eliot published at Faber and to which he wrote the Preface) and concludes that not only did "the experience of war [exhaust] the domestic and urban images Eliot constructed" but also that *In Parenthesis* "show[s] up the inability of the modernist idiom to cohere an experience like the war."[39] Poems like *In Parenthesis* and *The Waste Land* "show that a modernist idiom could not finally understand, cohere, or control the chaos of war into poetic order." He records "the failure of parataxis," the mode of fractured utterance that dominates both poems, "to generate larger self-sustaining meanings in the face of war."[40] The soldiers who fill Jones's poem—and, I would argue, the speakers who populate Eliot's—"do not participate in a larger, meaningful poetic structure that validates the war, as Fussell and the coherence reading of Jones claims, but in a structure undercut by a modern terrain of blindness, chaos, and death, navigated alone and without a guide."[41] For *The Waste Land*, I would add to these negatives speechlessness and even thoughtlessness:

"Speak to me. Why do you never speak. Speak.
"What are you thinking of? What thinking? What?
"I never know what you are thinking. Think."

> I think we are in rats' alley
> Where the dead men lost their bones.
> [. . .]
>   "Do
> "You know nothing? Do you see nothing? Do you remember
> "Nothing?"
>   I remember
> Those are pearls that were his eyes.
> "Are you alive or not? Is there nothing in your head?"[42]

Language is only one of the things that fails here. This "modern terrain" is devoid of the consolations of myth, pattern, effective communication, and human insight. What better way to describe an atmosphere actively opposed to the ordering structures that constitute the humanities?

Dudley's argument runs directly counter, as he indicates, to that of Paul Fussell and "coherence readings" of modernist poetry, those that emphasize poetic order and control. Significantly, both readings have a pacifist inflection: Fussell arguing that, by presuming to order the war, *In Parenthesis* isn't anti-war enough, Dudley that the poem cannot order the war and thus reveals modernist poetry's fundamental incommensurability with it. The debate is a worthy one, and both readings respond effectively to the pressing need for frameworks to understand these immense, highly difficult modernist poems written in response to war. Perhaps more importantly, both readings respond to our other pressing need, to bring about a world in which those humanities values can flourish.

Lockerd argues, a bit too breezily as I see it, that Eliot moves directly from a sense of poetry's failure to make war cohere to an embrace of spiritual solutions, thus underscoring the dead-end of humanistic ones. Black, too, in his focus on ineffability, and Dudley with his on war's unrepresentability, have all found compelling ways to undermine the commonly held view of Eliot's poem as making claims for poetry's capacity to forge order where war has made disorder, to communicate meaning where war has enforced silence, or even to understand what war has thrown into confusion. I am inclined to agree with their collective assessment that war, in the poem, has already won, and that Eliot's lines walk readers through the wreckage. Importantly, Eliot's "fragments" are "shored" not *against my ruin* (i.e., to fend off my ruin), but "against my ruins," that is, the broken remains of what is already destroyed. What has been shattered is more than poetic structure, but the very rational values, the tools, the ordering principles and modes at the core of what we call the humanities: communicative speech, coherence, shared understanding, ordered memory, cultural archives, historical pattern. What has shattered them is war.

There is sufficient evidence, it seems, for an anti-war reading of *The Waste Land*. But a more fundamental opposition beckons. One need not look far in British poetry for affirmation that the First World War was a bad war, indeed the worst. *101 Poems* would be a good place to start. But, given its range and scope, the encyclopedic *Waste Land* suggests that a broader tradition, namely the humanities tradition, to which it is heir is threatened by war itself, confirming White's thesis that "war is always a direct threat . . . to the Humanities." The poem is a complex compendium of humanities material—religion, myth, modern and ancient languages, popular and high culture, literary history, philosophy, music, and more—and, in its generic position somewhere between lyric and epic, between dramatic monologue and religious incantation, with its speech registers spanning the mundane and the magisterial, seems to stretch beyond poetry to invoke a field much broader.

I want to tread carefully so as not to conflate the creative work of the artist with the critical work of the humanities scholar, but I do want to suggest, as have many others before me, that *The Waste Land* is more than a poem. It is, rather, a self-critical work that records the degradation of its own material, which is the material of poetry but also of any number of other humanistic projects. As poetry, the best that it can do (as Dudley affirms of *In Parenthesis*), is to proceed along the lines of a negative aesthetic and describe by surrounding with fragments the empty space where meaning might have resided, like a play or novel by Samuel Beckett (who picked up a good deal of his aesthetic from Eliot). It describes the space that might have been occupied by an intact field of human cultural and experiential relations, relations shouldered away by war's relentless dislocations.

The nagging irony, of course, is that *The Waste Land* has long occupied a privileged place in the humanities landscape. Eliot's poem and his contemporaneous literary criticism indeed provided foundations for the modern conception of academic humanities, particularly the study of literature. Which is to say, the prominence and fertility of *The Waste Land* within the modern humanities would seem to give the lie to any notion that war poses a grave threat to the humanities themselves. People like me have made careers (such as they are) on the backs of just this poem and the ways in which it relates to war. War makes the wastelands that can become poetry (as Dexter Filkins reminds us), and interpreting that poetry has been for countless people the rewarding work of a lifetime. I would venture to say, however, that it might have been infinitely better otherwise.

Activist criticism requires something like such a perspective shift. We have come to take for granted a world in which, in Eliot's words "I can connect / Nothing with nothing," in Jones's "What brought him to this type of place [. . .] you simply can't conceive," or in Pound's "I cannot make it cohere," but other worlds are possible.⁴³ Or, at least, to proceed in hope as a literary critic is to work under the conviction that other worlds are possible. The one that the modernists affirm crippled intellectual and expressive capacities may be laid largely if not entirely at the feet of the First World War. Aware of but undeterred by the risk of sentimentalism, I ask: What if we allowed ourselves to imagine what connections, conceptions, and coherences might have arisen in minds such as these in a Europe free a while longer from war's choking antihuman energies? Put another way, imagine what broken whole is implied by Eliot's fragments. The ethical critic reads poems as action in Hannah Arendt's sense, as if they matter to history, as if they are entries in a dialogue the terms of which they do not control. To the extent that *The Waste Land* is a poem registering the destruction, alienation, and waste wrought by war, what if we choose to say *no* to that vision as a self-sufficient representation and *yes* to the poem as a protest against it? What if we read the poem as moving beyond representation to dissuasion?

The Waste Land, of course, does not end with war, but with a Sanskrit word for peace. K. Narayana Chandran argues that the "Shantih shantih shantih" ending of *The Waste Land*, omitting the "Om" with which it is traditionally paired in benediction, "is not so much wished as wished for. Eliot's translation of 'shantih' (which, incidentally, he calls 'feeble' in his note to the first edition of the poem) as 'peace which passeth [all] understanding' therefore assumes an ominously literal meaning"⁴⁴ She continues: "The vanity of uttering 'shantih' in *The Waste Land*, in other words, compares with that of the wise men of Judah whom the Lord rebukes for 'having healed the hurt of the daughter of my people slightly saying Peace, peace; when there is no peace.'"⁴⁵ *Peace*, as the poem's final word, is also its ultimate gesture toward an absent condition, or perhaps a condition of absence. Thrice repeated and unpunctuated, it may be read as the statement of a desire but possessing as little substance in reality as an echo or a dying breath. Franco "Bifo" Berardi's discussion of *mantra* underscores the point. "*Mantra*," he writes,

> . . . is the impulse that creates a mental image, the power to change mental states . . . With sound, it calls forth its content into a state of immediate reality. Mantra is power, not merely speech, which the mind can contradict or evade. What mantra expresses by its sound exists, comes to pass. It is the peculiarity of the true poet that his word creates actuality, calls forth and unveils something real. Mantra is a force able to evoke images, to create and transmit mental states.[46]

There is every reason to consider Eliot a true poet, even by this lofty standard. The *shantih*s with which he closes his most famous poem do indeed call forth and unveil something real, but it isn't peace. As fragments of a mantra, they are at best a marker, in feeble translation, upon the spot where peace might have been.

In 1939, with a second world war just underway, Eliot encouraged a recalibration of the values we ascribe to winning wars: "In the sense in which war is something that starts with the fighting and ends when the fighting stops, we may quite well win this war without ideas. But in that event the statement 'we won the war' must be countered with the question, 'who are we, now that we have won it?'"[47] The humanities are charged not only with ensuring that we are not without ideas but also with safeguarding, challenging, and refining them. Their still more primary function is to answer the question of who we are. One job of the ethical reader is to suggest who we might be. If *The Waste Land* shows us who we are not and who we could have been, it may be the job of such a reader to get more active in healing the hurt by picking up where the poem leaves off and doing more than *saying* "peace, peace" when there is no peace.

The Waste Land is a broken poem, one materially linked to a particular war; however, by virtue of the tradition it invokes, it forces us to ask whether war itself is the wasteland that lies beyond the point where the humanities end. White argues that war's "function is to undermine the human values and rational methodologies that are at the centre of our disciplines." In that way, war is not alone among the threats to the life of the humanities, as academics everywhere know who spend as much time these days defending the humanities as practicing them. But, forced as we have been for the entirety of our century to consider the value of what we do in light—or rather, in the darkness—of war without end, the time might be right to consider whether our disciplines ought to take a less accommodating stance toward a threat that has undermined our interests for so long and so blatantly. As science knows its opposite in mysticism, as inclusion knows its opposite in bigotry, what plainer opposite can there be but war for a profession ostensibly devoted to connection and to the arts of the human?

Chapter 5

Freedom Is Not Enough

Eliot on Liberation

Anyone inclined to write about freedom can be grateful to Maggie Nelson for clearing the decks and establishing compelling new reasons for another discussion of the term. In *On Freedom: Four Songs of Care and Constraint* (2021), she begins by reckoning with its impossibly multiple and conflicting meanings. "Can you think of a more depleted, imprecise or weaponized word?" she asks her reader and herself. "And yet, I still couldn't quit it."[1] Neither could T. S. Eliot. Indeed, without mentioning him, Nelson frames her book on freedom by drawing out some of the points that were key for Eliot, too. She cites "Wittgenstein's famous edict, *the meaning of a word is its use*" and resolves to go on writing about freedom bolstered by Wittgenstein's position: "that the meaning of a word is its use is no cause for paralysis or lament. It can instead act as an incitement to track *which language-game is being played*."[2] Just so, Eliot never fled from a word rather than try to wrestle its imprecision into order, fleeting as any victory might be, and he built his writing career on the idea that the *uses* of language are the poet's real business and, indeed, all any of us really have when it comes to orienting ourselves to others and the world.

Eliot was no believer in "absolute" freedom, and neither is Nelson. She invokes Foucault's important "distinction between liberation (conceived of as a momentary act) and practices of freedom (conceived of as ongoing)" and is energized rather than turned off by Foucault's declaration that "liberation paves the way for new power relationships, which must be controlled by practices of freedom."[3] The mention of "power relationships" may discourage a certain kind of freedom seeker but not the kind for whom freedom is just as real when conceived of in relation to forces and needs beyond the solipsistic self. Neither she nor Foucault needed to have thought about Eliot in this connection, but Eliot's ideas about the inevitability and indeed desirability of constraints on freedom make the connection a tantalizing one.

Nelson finished her book during the COVID-19 pandemic, which provides an urgent, though unplanned, context for her analysis. The pandemic put much of Earth's human population in mind of freedom: how much we missed it, when it would return, whether we were really free before the world went into lockdown, how our personal freedom relates to our social responsibilities. " 'Your freedom is killing me!' read the signs of protestors in the middle of a pandemic," Nelson observes; "Your health is not more important than my liberty!' maskless others shout back."[4] Is the freedom to decide whether to wear a mask outweighed by a responsibility to protect others, or by their freedom from fear of infection by their maskless neighbors? Am I more or less free if I follow state rules about how to conduct myself in public? Regardless of one's position on such questions, the truth was everywhere visible that great swaths of what we used to take for freedom—doing what we wanted whenever we wanted to do it—retracted like the available beach space at high tide. Sometimes this retraction was the result of state intervention: actual closed beaches, parks, stores, and restaurants; cancelled events; limitations on the size of social gatherings. At other times it was the result of people simply choosing not to expose themselves and others to a greater risk of infection: For months I refrained from hugging my own friends and even parents. We stood poised in front of one another like Eliot and the "familiar compound ghost" of "Little Gidding": fixing upon each other with our eyes over our masks "That pointed scrutiny with which we challenge / The first-met stranger in the waning dusk . . . 'What! are *you* here?' "[5] A time of promptly, drastically, but imperfectly curtailed freedoms seems the right one for reflecting on what we could have been doing with freedom before all this and might do now that it has—for the time being—returned.

In this chapter, I am interested in what T. S. Eliot had to say about freedom during the 1930s and 1940s—an era, like our own, of ascendant totalitarianism, reaction, suspicion, and a widespread sense of impending (and present) catastrophe. Eliot's most famous, though not necessarily clearest, articulations of his sense of freedom appear in his poetry and drama, where freedom takes an important place among the themes of interest to him: albeit a distinctly secondary place to themes like love, desire, memory, death, and time. Secondary as well as somewhat obscure. In Eliot's poetry and plays from this period, freedom, rather like migration, is almost always a spiritual or psychological matter. It is often interiorized, mixed with concepts like memory and desire. Even when he seems to invite the historical and political, these quickly become only steps on the way to a higher plane. Eliot's creative work contains many magnificent passages for those who would become spiritually free, but it is comparatively arid when it comes to raw material for use in the work of political, economic, or social liberation. In some lesser-known prose writings, however, Eliot engages with freedom in terms far more enmeshed in the historico-political reality of his day, terms that are, I think, more germane to our own.

Freedom of the Spirit

Eliot's poetry, including dramatic verse, often asks how the spirit or soul can become free. *Murder in the Cathedral*, Eliot's first completed play, was written largely in verse. It was created for and first performed at the 1935 Canterbury Festival and tells the story of the martyrdom of Thomas à Becket, the twelfth-century Archbishop of Canterbury. Although questions of will, choice, and fate figure prominently in the play, "freedom" appears only once, in Becket's declaration of the paradoxical freedom of the Christian: a martyr, he preaches in the Interlude, "is he who has become the instrument of God, who has lost his will in the will of God, not lost it but found it, for he has found freedom in submission to God."[6] The play refers to "liberty" twice, with an effect that likewise diminishes its individual or earthly import. One Tempter speaks of the "fight for liberty" in which "Church favour would be an advantage," and Becket goes to his death hopeful "that His Church may have peace and liberty"—the combination clearly suggesting that worldly freedom is something to be valued only by the worldly.[7]

In *Four Quartets*, Eliot treats the theme of freedom in some memorable but distinctly nonpolitical passages. For instance, in the lines from "Dry Salvages" V, "When there is distress of nations and perplexity / Whether on the shores of Asia, or in the Edgware Road," the *When* and *Whether* disconnect the references to political history from actuality.[8] Even the brief Arendtian ring in the first half of the sentence "And right action is freedom" is undone by the second half: "from past and future also."⁹ Action in Arendt's formulation commits one to the social world and to time. Right or wrong, it promises not freedom from past and future but an obligation to others who exist within the temporal. The results of action may be unknown, but they will unfold in time, not out of it.¹⁰

Eliot returns to the relation of freedom, action, past, and future in a majestic passage in "Little Gidding." Though undeniably beautiful, and even spiritually instructive, it similarly resists, indeed rejects, the pull of the worldly:

> This is the use of memory:
> For liberation—not less of love but expanding
> Of love beyond desire, and so liberation
> From the future as well as the past. Thus, love of a country
> Begins as attachment to our own field of action
> And comes to find that action of little importance
> Though never indifferent. History may be servitude,
> History may be freedom. See, now they vanish,
> The faces and places, with the self which, as it could, loved them,
> To become renewed, transfigured, in another pattern.¹¹

All the particulars of living—servitude, freedom, "faces and places," even "love of a country" and "one's own field of action"—are useful to the spiritual seeker not in themselves but as hints or precursors of truths yet to come. And they vanish in the ascent toward perfect detachment and transcendent fulfillment.

In Eliot's 1939 play *The Family Reunion*, freedom itself is cordoned off in the future—"There is more to understand: hold fast to that / As the way to freedom"—and the past—"one's only memory of freedom."¹² As an experience in the present, "Liberty is a different kind of pain from prison."¹³ Harry, the protagonist, suffers from "a private puzzle" that keeps him spinning in this state of vexed uncertainty about whether freedom, or liberation, is even possible and what it might mean. To his Aunt Agatha he admits, "I have thought of you as the completely strong, / The liberated from the human wheel. / So I looked to you for strength. Now I think it is / A common pursuit of liberation."¹⁴ At times, Harry seems to appreciate that the human wheel is not something to be liberated from but might in fact be the instrument of liberation, but his thoughts are erratic, he is possessed by the past, and he is obtuse about how his own freedom might relate to that of others or, indeed, the physical world.

The Human Wheel

While I don't discount the value of explorations like these, in which freedom is a matter of mystical significance, I think Eliot's nonfiction prose contains ideas that better address the need for, and paths toward, the more workaday kinds of freedom under threat from so many quarters at present. Some of this prose can sharpen our thinking about the questions of freedom we face, but it can also make us better readers of Eliot's creative work. As I have done in other chapters, I will also try to show how Eliot's ideas bring him into the orbit of unexpected others who have felt a similar urgency about understanding a theme—here, freedom—and whom we might otherwise suppose share little if any of Eliot's outlook, people like Walt Whitman and Henry David Thoreau, and more surprisingly still, anarchists like Bakunin, Goldman, Paul Goodman, and Sean Swain. I will focus especially on Eliot's writings contained in volumes 4, 5, and 6 of the *Complete Prose*, which together cover the years 1930 to 1946. For economic and political reasons, these were years of straitened opportunity for most of Britain and the United States, the closest conditions in Eliot's life to the ones we have recently lived through—or are still living in. Substitute the marked pedestrian crossings for "Mask or Facial Covering Required" signs, and what he wrote in 1935 might have been written in 2020: "There seems to be . . . a good deal of chat going on about Liberty, and no wonder." There is "the shadow of the Totalitarian State abroad" as well as "smaller creeping shadows at home . . . at every other street corner we are reminded that we are no longer at liberty to get ourselves run over."[15] In Eliot's moment as in ours, curtailed freedom engendered a sharpened sense of purpose about choices, a renewed deliberation about what freedom is and what it is for. As he wrote in a 1927 "Commentary," writers like himself at the moment are led inevitably from their own subject to others with apparently higher stakes. "Three events in the last ten years" are of particular interest to those whose business is writing: "the Russian revolution . . . , the transformation of Italy" under Mussolini, "and the condemnation of the *Action Francaise* by the Vatican," all of which "compel us to consider the problem of Liberty and Authority, both in politics and in the organization of speculative thought. Politics has become too serious a matter to be left to politicians."[16] So, in essays and commentaries, Eliot sifts through the "chat" that is filling the air and the press and works toward decisions about which terms he will reject, which he will claim, and how he will use them, gathering and ordering the tools he will need to see himself through an anxious and frequently bewildering time. It is, in a way, the same operation I have been trying to perform in this book, only that the "chat" for me is Eliot's own work.

When he writes about freedom in these years preceding and spanning the Second World War, Eliot sounds quite different than he did in the works that had earlier made him famous. As a younger man, his interest in freedom had far more to do with poetic form than with politics. In the 1917 essay "Reflections on *Vers Libre*," Eliot declared with a characteristic boldness, which he would later come to find shy-making, that "there is no freedom in art."[17] Form, a force to counter and set off freedom, is what matters: "Freedom is only truly freedom when it appears against the background of an artificial limitation."[18] Such ideas he shared with and sometimes learned from his friend Ezra Pound. In another 1917 essay, first published anonymously, he quoted approvingly Pound's dictum that "Any work of art is a compound of freedom and order," and he demonstrated how seriously he took the qualification by using "freedom" in quotation marks throughout the rest of the essay.[19] Still earlier, he wrestled with freedom academically as a graduate student in philosophy, as in his 1913 "Report on the Ethics of Kant's *Critique of Practical Reason*" written for Philosophy 15: The Kantian Philosophy. At this early stage and in this scholastic context, freedom is not yet treated as a matter of grave personal or political urgency.

His approach to freedom—like so much else—shifts noticeably around 1927, the year of his Christian conversion and patriation as a British citizen. Here, though, the shift seems to have more to do with political events in Europe—the Russian Revolution, the rise of Italian fascism, and so on—than with his own journey of identity. He begins to focus on how people can get and stay free in a Europe with the walls hardening and closing in. In this later period, he does not ignore the aesthetic questions of freedom and form that dominate his early writing. But aesthetics and poetics, along with purely philosophical formulations, recede noticeably from his prose reflections. He does engage emphatically and consistently with freedom as a matter of urgent existential and theological importance. There is in the end no way to read Eliot's sense of freedom objectively as tending toward anything other than religious conviction, that is, as anything other than theological, however much one might want to enlist him for a secular cause. Yet his interventions in contemporaneous discussions on the meaning, purpose, and limitations of freedom reveal some perhaps surprising ways such a theology could serve a broader, more worldly praxis of freeing, or, in his preferred term, of liberation.[20]

The first such intervention comes in an April 1930 *Criterion* "Commentary" in which Eliot used the occasion of a debate on censorship to articulate an integral principle of his own conception of freedom. There are those, he wrote, "for whom Freedom, for anything and from anything, is an innate idea;" and there are the "timorous folk who defend, or accept, the actual state of things because the only alternative generally presented to them seems very much worse."[21] Throughout the 1930s, Eliot was at pains to distinguish an abstract "Freedom" from particular choices, actions, and capabilities through which freedom is expressed. He made the same distinction between an abstract "Liberty" and the liberty to *do* particular things.[22] For example, in "Christianity and Communism" (1932), he asks "If we have liberty, what is it that we have liberty to do?"[23] And in "Notes on the Way III" (1935), he writes, "I am likely to be on the side of liberty in particular instances, while unable to attach any meaning to liberty in the abstract."[24] Is abstract Liberty, he asks, "anything but a phantom[?]"

One unmistakable result of the COVID-19 pandemic is to have made freedom concrete to an entire generation. To give only one example, there has been great anxiety about keeping the virus out of US prisons, where more people are incarcerated than anywhere in the world and among whose confined populations the coronavirus is likely to do the most damage. Those who became newly mindful of these populations did so in an environment that is simultaneously inviting—or enforcing—confinement of the un-incarcerated as a means of saving lives. On a purely practical level, people suddenly restricted to their homes looked to prisoners for models of how to cope with the loss of freedom. In April 2020, anarchist prisoner Sean Swain recorded an instructive segment for The Final Straw Radio in which he recommended that people isolated and quarantined for COVID-19 do things like establish a regular routine and stick to it, practice good personal grooming, set and meet small goals, and get sunlight and exercise, so that "you are now doing your time; your time is not doing you." Crucially, he adds that "you have to synthesize your routine with the lives of those around you" and "focus on the struggle of someone else." These practices will not only lessen your anxiety, "keep the peace," and help you survive, they will also require you to conceive of your freedom (and constraint) in relation to that of others, making it real.[25]

Such reciprocity was one of Eliot's constant concerns in the matter of freedom. He concludes that 1930 "Commentary" with a passing—but, as I see it, both devastating and vexing—reference to a contemporary sociopolitical issue with stakes somewhat lower than life-and-death but nonetheless pressing. He writes: "The most conspicuous and most monstrous recent example of humanitarian tyranny is the Canal Boat [*sic*] Bill, a measure which in the name of health and education would destroy the family life of its victims. Such are the fruits of Liberty."[26] The Canal Boats Bill proposed to take canal boat children—that is, the children of the people who operated boats ferrying cargo up and down English canals—into state protection in order to educate them. The difficulty these children faced, which the bill proposed to ameliorate, was, according to Mr. Harry Gosling who argued for the bill in the House of Commons, that "it is impossible to get these children into school because they never remain long enough in one place." Moreover, "removing the children from the boats" would aid in "the prevention of child labour." If the bill were to fail, Gosling warned, "these children . . . will be educated only among themselves. Nothing could be worse. You want to lift these children out of that environment."[27]

Despite such good intentions, the new Canal Boats Bill represented a violation of two other principles essential to Eliot's notion of freedom. "Freedom," he wrote, "can only exist in a . . . balance; it is always threatened, not from one side but from both sides," that is, by the forces of both reaction and revolution; "Freedom does not flourish" where "fanaticism" does.[28] But the bill also evinced the "concern with this world alone" which, for Eliot, hollows out secular conceptions of "liberty." The humanitarian, he wrote in 1935, has two options: "(1) you may think you know what is best for people, and you will envisage them only as 'free' when they come round to your view of what is best for them. (2) You may hold the view that no one can know what is best for people, or that 'best' means only what each thinks for himself . . . In the former choice, you are imposing your own opinion; in the latter you are admitting that there is no purpose for existence."[29] The canal boat families are the victims of "an excessive love of created beings, in other words humanitarianism, leading to a genuine oppression of human beings in what is conceived by other human beings to be their interest."[30] They are the victims, that is, of a little revolution, the promulgator of which—here, the state—dictates the terms of freedom for small collectivities within it in the name of a conception of the good they may or may not share and that, in any event, the state would struggle to articulate. For Eliot, enforcing an idea of freedom in this way is as wrong as leaving every individual and community to do purely as it wishes.

The 1935 essay "Notes on the Way III," which includes the dual-opinion formula above, is Eliot's most sustained meditation on freedom, liberty, and the ultimate ground and fulfillment of these in religion. Here he states frankly that "Freedom," conceived abstractly or as any number of individual freedoms—financial, political, sexual, verbal, etc.—"is not enough." "If one is going to theorize about liberty," then the political and economic must lead to the moral. "And one cannot stop short of theology. What, in short, is the ultimate nature and reason for liberty?"[31] Two years earlier he had answered his own question: "The conception of individual liberty . . . must be based upon the unique importance of every single soul, the knowledge that every man [sic] is ultimately responsible for his own salvation or damnation, and the consequent obligation of society to allow every individual the opportunity to develop his full humanity. But . . . this humanity [must be] considered always in relation to God."[32] In an earlier essay, he likewise argued: "To the baser minded, in the modern world, liberty . . . tends to be tantamount to mere licence . . . The chief liberty of man . . . is the liberty to choose what master he shall serve."[33] And, in a later essay: "The only freedom of choice is our freedom to choose the ideas by which we shall be led."[34] So this affirmation in 1935 is entirely consistent: "The ultimate meaning of liberty is that each individual should be free to determine his own eternal salvation or damnation. There is no other final meaning, there is no other final value, to liberty than this."[35] At points like these, that portion of Eliot's readers—say, half—who share his religious convictions may nod, feeling confirmed in their vision of the ultimate trajectory of Eliot's work and thought. And they are not wrong. And those disinclined to follow Eliot through to religious conclusions may cordon off such testaments or turn their attention to other aspects of his writing.

I would like to suggest that Eliot's position on the matter of freedom and liberty has the potential to invite and challenge both believer and nonbeliever and to sharpen the commitments of each. Because ultimately Eliot's theology of freedom is not a question of belief but of action. "To me," he writes, "the notion of *liberty* is meaningless without the further notion of *liberation*. One lives, not to be free, but to be freed. And to be *freed from* is meaningless unless one has some notion of what one is to be *freed for*."[36] Almost everyone, Eliot argued throughout the 1930s, can agree on the value of abstractions such as peace and liberty. The abstraction is the invitation, but its formlessness, for Eliot, calls for a stiffening corrective. Insisting in this way on the praxis, the activity, of freedom is at once more grounded in the particulars of living than any theology of pure faith, and more meaningful than any commitment to pure action, if such a thing could exist. It challenges the devoted to make faith real in the world through action. It challenges the skeptic to shore up and defend benevolent interventions.[37] As human beings, Eliot affirmed over and over, we have attachments—to our bodies, to one another, to the material world, to time, to culture, to habit, inclination, education, sensation, etc.—and only in relation to these do we experience freedom or unfreedom. Likewise, only to the extent that our relations to these particulars of living affirm or disconfirm a sense of freedom or unfreedom do we get a hint of the kind of trajectories that could give consistent meaning to a life.

To illustrate the political reach of such a position, consider how surprisingly well Eliot's idea of freedom resonates—right up to the point at which it must necessarily diverge—with that of certain writers whose conception of the divine was diametrically opposed to his own. No less an atheist-anarchist light than Emma Goldman, "Red Emma" herself, declared that "true liberty is not a *negative* thing . . . being free *from* something" but "the freedom *to* something . . . the liberty to be, to do; in short the liberty of actual and active opportunity."[38] Nathan Jun explains that for Goldman, positive freedom "serves as the primary vehicle through which 'all the latent powers of the individual' are expressed and the principal means of satisfying her 'desire to create and act freely.'"[39] Precisely like Eliot, Goldman and other anarchists view negative freedom on its own as insufficient. It is only a precursor, if a necessary one, to the active, positive freedom through which the individual works out the real purposes of a life, which are starkly different for Eliot and Goldman, though they are related.

Most anarchists (and there are exceptions) will not join Eliot in avowing that what is at stake in human freedom is the individual's "eternal salvation or damnation," still less that "humanity [must be] considered always in relation to God." But they do share his conviction that freedom that does not recognize moral obligations is at a minimum incomplete and potentially injurious. Goldman argues that only when humans are "left to act for themselves, to feel responsibility for their own actions in the good or bad that comes from them," can they realize the "consciousness of self" that creates in them the "craving for liberty."[40] That is, for an anarchist, freedom (here, liberty) is necessarily linked to outcomes, which is a form of responsibility. Those "good or bad" consequences are a secularist's approximation of salvation and damnation.

Moreover, the morality of anarchist freedom does have a specific basis outside of the individual. Rather than God, the individual's humanity must be considered always in relation to other humans. Fundamental to the anarchist conception of freedom is the conviction that "individual freedom is a 'collective product.'"[41] This idea is nowhere expressed so forcefully as in Bakunin's famous proclamation: "I am truly free only when all human beings, men and women, are equally free. The freedom of other men [sic], far from negating or limiting my freedom, is, on the contrary, its necessary premise and confirmation."[42] Social anarchists have upheld almost without exception Bakunin's position that "the material, intellectual, and moral powers that are latent in each person" and the "all-around development and full enjoyment of all physical, intellectual, and moral faculties" are impossible "outside of human society or without its cooperation."[43] The equality of each human soul before God has a counterpart in the anarchist commitment to the full equality of each individual before others. As Jun explains, quoting Malatesta and then Bakunin, "the fact that 'the freedom of each' finds its 'necessary *raison d'etre* in . . . the freedom of others' implies that 'equality is an absolutely necessary condition for freedom.'"[44] Human equality and the sovereignty of God are of course not equivalents, but they occupy a similar place—a ground of value outside the self—and serve a commensurate function—to establish a morality—in the freedom schemes of Eliot and the anarchists with whom he would appear to share little, if any, philosophy.

Such a family resemblance could be unmoving to the orthodox religious believer or the diehard atheist anarchist. Perhaps the intervention of a third point of view, a third philosophy, can help to bridge the apparent distance. Walt Whitman never met a human way of being he couldn't imaginatively throw his arms around, and when he writes of freedom his words embrace even Bakunin. It might be said that Whitman's work is an expression of total individual freedom within the context of total human solidarity. In his poem "By the Roadside," for example, he writes:

> Of Equality—as if it harm'd me, giving others the same chances
>   and rights as myself—as if it were not indispensable to my
>   own rights that others possess the same.[45]

As Žiga Vodovnik illustrates, the American Transcendentalists wrote of freedom in terms that look forward to Bakunin and Goldman. They also look forward to Eliot. Henry David Thoreau insisted on both positive freedom and the moral obligation that comes with it. "Do we not call this the land of the free?" he asked. "What is it to be free from King George and continue the slaves of King Prejudice? What is it to be born free and not to live free? What is the value of any political freedom, but as a means to moral freedom?"[46] Eliot and Goldman, or Eliot and Bakunin, are strange bedfellows indeed; the Transcendentalists and Bakunin, Goldman, or Eliot are perhaps slightly less so. Those who would match freedom with equality are not limited to one camp, tradition, or denomination. But they are rare enough that their ideological similarity is worth not only noting but potentially taking advantage of when the circumstances call for the use of every resource available. These days there is too little morally grounded freedom and too little equality, and with so much work to do, strange bedfellows might be nearly as welcome as comrades.

Free As We Can

It is typical of Eliot to have been skeptical of any and every formulation of value sweeping a public to pitches of feeling. At no point in the 1930s could he have been convicted of political or religious "enthusiasm" or "fanaticism" in the uncritical sense in which he used those terms. But it is also typical of Eliot, despite his unending process of refining and revising language, to have adopted a stance from which action is possible. The declaration from the 1935 "Notes on the Way III" is more than an attractive soundbite: "The amount of real 'freedom' in most people's lives is apparently very small—which does not abrogate our obligation to become as free as we can."[47] This is a seed of the commitment expressed in "Little Gidding" to never cease from exploration, to find freedom and again freedom in a perpetual cycle culminating in return. It is a freedom for living in and with, a freedom for human beings with bodies inside of finite cycles of time. Whatever freedom we may realize in the divine, we experience liberty while we live with our limited senses as freedom from and freedom to, as, for instance, what we might be able to do in a day with limited resources: "We live in a world in which true liberty declines. Life becomes more precarious, too, without the freedom which makes precariousness tolerable: I mean the freedom and opportunity for adventure."[48]

It is a striking thought in the midst of a lockdown. If you went hiking within a day's drive of New York City during the first couple of years of the pandemic, you could see how desperate locked-down city folk had become for something approximating adventure. The trailheads overflowed with parked cars, and the trails themselves teemed with New

Yorkers, the eagerness in their eyes easy to perceive above their facemasks (worn even outdoors in the early days of the pandemic). Or consider the quintessentially American adventure of cross-country motorcycle riding. The 2020 Sturgis motorcycle rally in South Dakota, where tens of thousands of people capped theirs with days of largely maskless freedom, thereby infecting countless others nationwide with COVID-19, was a veritable carnival of adventure, adventurism, and defiance. Despite the emblems on their leather jackets, not many of those bikers are anarchists in the classic sense. Far more are what we would call "libertarians," but the desperation of their actions during a pandemic recalls Paul Goodman's assessment of freedom through anarchist eyes:

> Many anarchist philosophers start from a lust for freedom. Where freedom is a metaphysical concept or a moral imperative, it leaves me cold—I cannot think in abstractions. But most often the freedom of anarchists is a deep animal cry or a religious plea like the hymn of the prisoners in *Fidelio*. They feel themselves imprisoned, existentially by the nature of things or by God; or because they have seen or suffered too much economic slavery; or they have been deprived of their liberties; or internally colonized by imperialists. To become human they must shake off restraint.[49]

Given that the 2020 Sturgis rally coincided with a summer of marches and demonstrations on behalf of Americans who have been enslaved and systematically deprived of liberties by the state, it is doubtful just how much restraint the bikers actually had to shake off. But there is no doubt that the recklessness of their gathering expressed something like an "animal cry" against perceived constraints. Motorcycle culture—and the marketing of it—is virtually synonymous with such a cry, however feebly the oppression it defies measures up against that experienced by, for instance, African Americans or the Sioux of South Dakota on whose appropriated land the rally takes place.

You would not have found T. S. Eliot on a motorcycle or, in truth, anywhere near Sturgis, South Dakota, in high summer. Perhaps that is why hearing him speak of adventure in such decisive terms is so surprising—and perhaps inspiring. Like Goodman, he doesn't think in abstractions. He was not a rich man, but he was a highly educated, cultured white man from an important family; he didn't suffer anything like economic slavery, the deprivation of his liberties, or colonization by imperialists. Still, his effort to understand and defend meaningful freedom is intended to cut across classes. "If we have liberty," he asks, "what is it that we have liberty to do? The Russian [under Stalinism] must resign his liberty in favour of the Russian State, or in favour of a phantom world-State; and in return, I understand, he is assigned a certain extent of licence. I should prefer to resign my liberty, if I must, in favour of something better than that; but the Russian at least resigns his liberty in favour of *something*."[50] In the Britain of the 1930s, the economic consolations on offer were not enough, and in any event they were precarious: "A shift in the exchanges, and those of us who should travel can no longer afford to travel; at any moment, in a modern State, your food may cost you more or your wages be worth less. The man with a job is in terror of losing it . . . We have comfort without grandeur, and amusement without recreation," and he stresses that the word means *re-creation*.[51]

It sounds familiar enough in these days when stock markets are soaring and unemployment is historically low but most people feel little real richness or security. Even before Vladimir Putin's new expression of a very old style of tyranny in his invasion of Ukraine, resurrecting a specter of unfreedom that had lain dormant for decades, true freedom had not exactly been infusing life in the West, and I am not speaking of the threadbare complaints of antivaxxers and antimaskers. Because even before the pandemic, living in what was supposed to represent the high point of human progress and development, we nonetheless were subjected to what Eliot in the 1930s called "a tyranny without purpose and meaning, the tyranny of what are called natural forces, or economic laws" which, in our case, have kept whole populations subjugated and come close to extinguishing the conditions for organized human life on earth.[52] And we couldn't even agree to do something about it.

A reading of Eliot's reflections on freedom leads to the realization that, in this era of profound division, we may have been dividing ourselves wrongly. It is easy enough to divide Black Lives Matter supporters from Proud Boys, Antifa from Oath Keepers. All would say they are on the side of freedom. It takes a point of view like Eliot's to perceive that, amid all the uproar, there are those who will happily resign trivial liberties in favor of *something*: equality, public health, the well-being of a neighbor, a functioning natural world, the love of God. And there are those who won't. Images abound from the direst pandemic days in which it is anarchists who are wearing the masks in deference to the common good, while their opponents—sometimes cops, sometimes neo-fascists—are not. T. S. Eliot has been called a fascist far more often than an anarchist. Would he have worn his mask? As surely as he put up his blackout curtains in the Blitz. And in neither case would the calculation have been a particularly difficult one. No lover of the secular state, Eliot could nonetheless clearly perceive when *something*—in this case the immediate safety of ordinary people—was worth the sacrifice of a tiny piece of his freedom. Indeed, he may not have considered such gestures a loss of freedom at all but rather practices of liberation: "not less of love but expanding / Of love beyond desire," including the desire to be the master of one's every trivial choice when the well-being of others is at stake.[53]

Chapter 6

Say It Again

Coriolanus, Coriolan, and Occupy

The weeks following the initial pandemic lockdown of 2020 featured a jarring contrast. At first, as schools and businesses closed and whole populations were ordered to shelter in place, the absence of people in the streets was stunning. A Spanish friend sent me a video of nighttime Logroño streets, normally thronging with proverbially social (and nocturnal) Spaniards, now dark, empty, and quieter than any public place I've ever witnessed in Spain, at any hour. It wasn't long before such vacancy found its way to where I live. My already quiet small town became positively silent, and soon I was receiving images and clips of Manhattan blocks likewise apocalyptically devoid of people, vehicles, and the sounds they make. The pandemic swept people from the streets worldwide like leaves before a strong wind. So when people around the United States and then the world began pouring into those streets only a few weeks later, not because of the lifting of safety precautions but in order to demonstrate on behalf of the value of Black lives and against police brutality after the murder of George Floyd, the sound of their voices had unaccustomed space in which to carry, echo, and amplify.

More people participated in a public demonstration in the summer of 2020 than at any time in world history. Millions marched in support of the Movement for Black Lives. Rallies took place most days of the week. Even my little town saw marches down Main Street instead of the usual Memorial and Independence Day parades. The sudden juxtapositions—empty streets followed by full ones, the deprivation of human mingling and then the purposeful assembly of (mostly mask-wearing) millions—provided a rich context in which to reflect on the political utility of congregating itself. Even two years after the historic summer of protest, when the return to the streets had more to do with simply socializing in groups, filling stadium seats, and dining indoors than with revolution but was filled with poignancy nonetheless, questions of what it can mean when people simply get together in public remained potent and alive. When it comes to changing the world, to using the power of the people to challenge injustice and oppression, the question often takes this form: Is it enough for people simply to gather and create in miniature the world they would like to inhabit, or must they identify and name a program of change which is then turned outward, extending the range of their influence and confronting directly the forces aligned to thwart them but also, crucially, rendering them legible to power and thus susceptible to cooptation? A pair of often overlooked Eliot poems, "Triumphal March" and "Difficulties of a Statesman," suggest that getting together doesn't seem like enough in part because the gatherers' attention is always being directed elsewhere—by the poet, by the state, and by their own mistrust of themselves.

Mass uprisings and assemblies since 2011, the year of Occupy Wall Street, provide compelling support for both positions, the inward and the outward facing. During the 2020 rebellion, Seattle saw the establishment of a "temporary autonomous zone," a term coined by Hakim Bey, in which aims of horizontalism, mutual aid, and autonomy were enacted on the ground. In forming such spaces, Bey explains, "we concentrate our force on temporary 'power surges,' avoiding all entanglements 'with permanent solutions.'"[1] But pure prefiguration can also be a dead-end. "At its threshold," writes Christian Scholl, "this orientation declares the present to be the future," greatly increasing the feeling of autonomy and agency of protestors. "However, if our organization *is* our strategy, then strategy and organization become blurred, and instrumental reckoning about objectives becomes impossible . . . If [prefiguration] comes to mean experiments without goals, it may deprive radical movements of one of their most powerful weapons—the idea that current acts have future consequences."[2] Similarly, a movement stands to lose a great deal if it turns entirely inward. Scholl cites Mark and Paul Engler, who warn, "If the project of building alternative community totally eclipses attempts to communicate with the wider public and win broad support, it risks becoming a very limiting type of self-isolation."[3] Without such scope, prefiguration becomes only figuration. Jacob Blumenfeld argues that it is the radical potentially "permanent solutions" of an event like Occupy that give the action its value: "Revolution is not simply people coming together to self-manage their own exploitation, but people coming together to abolish their own conditions of exploitation. Occupations are the material announcement of this revolutionary horizon, but not yet its accomplishment."[4] A temporary autonomous zone, according to such a view, is no substitute for a permanent one.

On the other hand, consider the legacy of Occupy, which in 2011 momentarily transformed not only Wall Street but countless other public spaces globally in the name of equality. Natasha Lennard acknowledges the element of failure as well as the briefly opened space of freedom and the way the moment's radical energies were re-channeled in the aftermath. She would safeguard an appreciation of the fleeting fact of an alternative organization, "of direct action, taking up space, and the kind of shifts that it did make, and the political bonds built that have remained, and gone into different projects."[5] While celebrating the way the movement shifted mainstream political discourse, making possible the widespread and open discussion of topics such as debt cancellation and radical inequality, she would not want that mainstreaming to be Occupy's primary or only legacy at the expense of the *moment* that was also the movement: "I don't want in that kind of historicization of it to miss that, no, there was also a really important tactical set of interventions and taking up of street space and disruption, and that was really radical, and experiments in direct democracy, so I don't want the entire legacy to be 'we changed the conversation so that we can have better Democratic presidential candidate platforms.' "[6] Such a milquetoast upshot, of course, is not the only possible outcome of a successful direct action, but given the difficulty of systemic change under global capitalism, it usually is the one we get.

It feels hopeful to believe that a revolution can be as small as the encounter between a few people. Perhaps this is what the poet Martín Espada meant when he wrote that "rebellion / is the circle of a lover's hands."[7] But it can also feel like an abdication of responsibility to avoid formulating demands to make of the powers that be, or to avoid trying to mainstream the lessons of the encounter. That strange pair of poems Eliot published in 1931 and 1932, later collectively titled *Coriolan*, maps this ambivalence across two other time periods that rhyme with our own. In "Triumphal March" and "Difficulties of a Statesman," Eliot made creative use of Shakespeare's great play of public assembly and raised voices, *Coriolanus*, adapting it to suit the needs of another historical moment full of popular uproar. The period between the two world wars seemed to re-create the political atmosphere of Coriolanus's Rome, and the association is unmistakable in the *Coriolan* poems. Eliot, following Shakespeare, dramatizes the way voices can become noise when politics are taken to the street. The advantage of reading them now is that the poems seem a good deal less strange during times of upheaval and contending voices. In the context of post-Occupy resistance culture, *Coriolan* can help us see the limitations and potentials of unscripted assembly under the deadening influence of the state.

Occupy

The 2009 inauguration of Barack Obama, the first Black president of the United States, briefly stood for a new era of possibility and equality in the United States as well as globally. Under the banner of "hope," Obama won the Nobel Peace Prize (only to double down on US drone strikes and to keep the military prison at Guantánamo Bay open and active) and made broadly affordable healthcare his top priority. It was a reaction to Obama policy, however, that came to signify a new era of activism. After the global financial meltdown during which he was elected, President Obama affirmed the national commitment to the financial sector at the expense of all other classes by bailing out big banks instead of working people, thus providing the cue for a new movement of resistance and hope to take the stage. In Tunisia, on December 17, 2010, a street vendor named Mohammed Bouazizi lit himself on fire to protest economic injustice and political corruption in his own country, and his death initiated the Tunisian Revolution that grew into what became the Arab Spring. In New York the following September, inspired by the courage of the dispossessed in North Africa and elsewhere, and sharing their outrage at continuing "injustice and invisibility," Occupy Wall Street set up in Zuccotti Park and stayed there until November.[8]

So the year 2011 began and ended with raised voices. *Time* magazine named "the Protestor" its Person of the Year. The year bracketed by the Arab Spring and the Occupy movement was characterized by the sound of the human voice—or more accurately human voices—raised in protest.

It took not long at all for those voices and the promise they seemed to represent to fade out. Once Tahrir Square and Zuccotti Park were cleared, both the Arab Spring and Occupy were excoriated by the sympathetic and mocked by the antipathetic for their lack of efficacy, their sound and fury having failed to signify much if anything. Lennard recalls feeling "a little embarrassed" by certain aspects of the Occupy spectacle.[9] Proponents of Occupy bemoaned the anticlimactic end of the 2011 chapter but claimed that the whimpering sound was actually that of a movement finding its way into other expressive channels, like dammed water going underground. Once people did take to the streets again five years later, it was not difficult to conceive of the linkages between the past and the present, between Occupy and #NoDAPL and the Women's March, then #MeToo and Black Lives Matter. As a new era of reaction began—neoliberal economics having made a grim pair with proto-fascist politics—so did a new era of resistance, and suddenly Occupy seemed indeed to have just been waiting to reemerge.

Some intriguing ideas about resistance and causes that seem to be lost were crystalized in 2011, the Year of the Protestor. And some of these ideas find rich expression in an artistic lineage, linking Shakespeare, Eliot, and, of all people, British actor Ralph Fiennes. Just as 2011 was giving way to 2012, and the delirious promise of Tahrir Square and Zuccotti Park was giving way to state and capitalist forces of order, there was a serendipitous but significantly less earth-shaking occurrence in the literary world. The year 2012 began with a new film adaptation, directed by Fiennes, of the Shakespearean tragedy most explicitly concerned with voices, *Coriolanus*. This film made the setting of the story a modern-day European capital (it was filmed in Serbia and Montenegro) and dressed the characters—with Fiennes himself in the leading role—in twenty-first-century clothing, including military uniforms, the suits of bankers and bureaucrats, and the rough but functional garb of an urban working class under stress. Some key dialogue was transferred to television news reports and talk shows and the screens on which they are viewed. This *Coriolanus* looked every bit like a story from the era of Occupy and the Arab Spring.

The release of the film was perfectly timed to pick up and set moving on the screen the energies of a moment in history. In that sense it was adding to a long tradition of looking to the figure and story of Coriolanus for insight about what happens when people get together and raise their voices. Intervening between Shakespeare and Fiennes, unexpectedly but unmistakably, is T. S. Eliot. And mediating in intriguing and instructive ways between the voices of *Coriolanus* and the voices of Occupy are the voices of those unusual and often overlooked *Coriolan* poems. They are overlooked at least in part because they are unfinished. They are unfinished, it seems to me, because they are unfinishable.

Voices

You would never have found T. S. Eliot at a group protest. He was not one for taking his politics to the streets. But he was certainly not indifferent to collective causes or to adding his own voice to them, most often in writing. Few poets of the twentieth century thought more or wrote with such care about the ways human voices interact with one another, or fail to, or about the effects of this interaction not only for aesthetic but also social experience.

From the publication of his first poems, and definitively since the appearance of *The Waste Land* in 1922, Eliot was the poet of voices. The working title of *The Waste Land* was "He Do the Police in Different Voices," a quote from Charles Dickens's novel *Our Mutual Friend* and, as an allusion to another work of literature, itself a demonstration of Eliot's obsession with sampling and juxtaposing voices. It was there from the start in the epigraphs, sometimes in other languages, that he habitually appended to his poems and books. To read Eliot's early poetry is to be introduced not so much to the distinctive voice of one poet as to encounter a whole cast of voices—from different eras, nations, and traditions, from waking life and from the pages of books—piping up in succession, speaking to and often interrupting one another.

But for all the difficulty of reading poems with such a variety of speaking personas—and some of Eliot's early poems are among his most challenging—it is not the difficulty of trying to hear in a crowd. For all their speakers, Eliot's early poems aren't really noisy poems. The voices aren't so many or so overlapping that they can't hear themselves speak or think. Even in *The Waste Land*, the only crowds are those that flowed over London Bridge and swarmed over endless plains, viewed from a distance. The difficulty presented by the voices of *The Waste Land* is that of deeply individuated speakers sharing the same stage, without useful transitions between them. Considered a century later, the more pressing problem with the voices in *The Waste Land* seems to be not that there are too many, but that there aren't enough: the poem's silencing of women has in the era of #MeToo become painfully apparent.[10] And, if the poem has something to do with empires teetering and drying up, where are any of the voices of the subject people with the most to lose when empires rise and fall? These Eliot largely relegated to the obscene private poems he shared with a small group of close friends.

It wasn't until the 1930s that Eliot, through his poetry, truly tried to grapple with the sounds of crowds as well as the meaning of their utterances. He wrote plays with Greek-style choruses; a pageant, *The Rock*, with most of the dialogue spoken by groups; and the two *Coriolan* poems, which follow the model of *Coriolanus* in attempting to represent the voices of people in a crowd but deviate crucially from that model in choosing not to represent those voices challenging institutional power. They are, as one might expect in poems dealing with crowds, noisy poems, which is why they make good guides to reading *Coriolanus* as well as the massed and raised voices of historical moments like the end of 2011; the middle of 2020; January 6, 2021; or whatever is surely coming next.

Initially Eliot had conceived of the *Coriolan* project as a four-part sequence, an idea that he instead went on to realize in *Four Quartets*. The pair of *Coriolan* poems he did complete has perplexed readers from their initial publication and done so to a degree surprising even for the poet of difficulty. As ever in Eliot, the poems' allusiveness and obscurity is partly to blame for this perplexity, but the even more essential difficulty they have always presented is the matter of voice, of sorting out the various voices that seem not so much to contend, as they do in *The Waste Land*, as to pile onto one another, to abolish meaningful distinction and needful attribution. As Grover Smith wrote, crankily, in 1950:

> Both sections [of *Coriolan*] suffer from obfuscation. In 'Triumphal March' the monologue is spoken by a spectator of the triumph who possesses some unusual powers of sight. It is not precisely clear, however, which of the remarks are his own and which come from other people, especially from young Cyril, unable to peer over the heads of the crowd. It is unclear also whether the speaker gives a running account of the proceedings or simply his vivid recollection of them, for he is careless with the tenses of his verbs. All this difficulty could have been moderated by the judicious insertion of quotation marks.[11]

Smith may be grouchy here, but he is accurate. One is rarely sure in the *Coriolan* poems not only who is talking but when, where, and about what.

An earlier observer than Smith, F. O. Matthiessen, had the advantage of sharing with Eliot the lived experience of the era that gave rise to the *Coriolan* poems. In his reading, Matthiessen points out that not only the era but much of Eliot's prose in the preceding few years had been obsessed with the two competing European movements clamoring most noisily for supremacy in solving "the problem of the relation of the individual to the social organism": fascism and communism.¹² The 1930s were a uniquely noisy time, and most of the noise had to do with politics, which is ever and always the business of relating the individual voice to that of a populace. "'Triumphal March,' Matthiessen writes, "is not a Fascist poem any more than Shakespeare's play"¹³ (that is, *Coriolanus*), but it and its partner are poems of their moment, occupied with the idea that the individual must find a meaningful way to be part of a public, a society, a state. Such an idea convinced Harry Levin, like Eliot, that "if certain of Shakespeare's great tragedies have a special significance for certain periods . . . *Coriolanus* is the play that should have the richest meaning in our time."¹⁴ Why then, and why again some eighty years later?

Coriolanus and the Power of the People

One answer is that *Coriolanus* is Shakespeare's great play of voices. The words "voice" and "voices" appear constantly in the dialogue, and the hero Caius Marcius Coriolanus himself is defined as much by his inability to modulate his voice as by his feats in battle. There are proper battles in the play, with swords and bloodshed, but the real focus is the wars of words that shape a war between classes. Shakespeare dramatizes the play of voices within each class designation as well as between them, giving audiences a view into how people talk among their own class as well as across classes.

Four hundred years before Occupy, *Coriolanus* represents what have become familiar formal dynamics of raising voices in group protest. From its opening lines, the play speaks with the fractured, swelling energy of group political resistance. Indeed, the first line foregrounds the tense fusion of action and utterance common among activists: "First Citizen. Before we proceed any further, hear me speak." The group is entirely amenable: "Citizens. Speak, speak." For the moment, unanimity is all:

First Citizen. You are all resolved rather to die than to famish?

Citizens. Resolved, resolved.

First Citizen. First, you know Caius Marcius is chief enemy to the people.

CITIZENS. We know't, we know't.

FIRST CITIZEN. Let us kill him, and we'll have corn at our own price. Is't a verdict?

CITIZENS. No more talking on't; let it be done: away, away![15]

The word *further* in the first line indicates these citizens are already on their way somewhere, and although they pause in their movement to hear an individual speaker, they are anxious to carry on, and so they would if it were not for the intervention of one more voice:

SECOND CITIZEN. One word, good citizens.

This citizen goes on to critique the plan to kill Marcius, to try to fine tune the tactics of the group in support of their common aim, which is food justice. (These citizens seem to exist in what today we might call a food desert, a zone of nutritional scarcity inside a metropolis characterized by abundance.) Both the ends (a just distribution of resources) and the possible means (violence or moderation) are familiar from any number of mass actions to undo systemic inequality, as is the push and pull between the individual speaker and the voice of the collective. But there is an important distinction to be made. In this opening scene, the citizens are speaking not to an audience but to one another. They are not demonstrating, they are, we might say, remonstrating. In their inward-facing arrangement, their insistence on consensus decision-making, and their democratic commitment to allowing individuals a voice, they most resemble the General Assembly at the center of Occupy, however much other aspects of their activity resemble the outward-facing posture that typifies public demonstrations like the 2017 Women's March or the processions and symbolic reenactments of Black Lives Matter. As long as they are still talking to one another, and indeed as long as their ultimate goal is still being debated, the ephemeral, unpredictable, but crucially ungovernable energy produced in the unmediated encounter itself between people thrives. As the Invisible Committee argued of Occupy and other uprisings, the truth of liberation exists in the "encounter," the occupation, itself, not in its articulate expression for an audience: "There is where the *event* resides: not in the media phenomenon fabricated to exploit the rebellion through external celebration of it, but in the encounters actually produced within it. This is something much less spectacular than 'the movement' or 'the revolution,' but more decisive. No one can say what an encounter is capable of generating."[16] Once power, or even representation, intervenes, then lots of people can and do say what the encounter has generated and might go on to generate, and the possibilities narrow accordingly. In the Fiennes film, the citizens' rebellion appears partly on screens in televised news reports, underscoring how easily and automatically a potentially revolutionary encounter between people can become material for cooptation, commodification, and management.

In the play, only upon the arrival of Menenius followed by Marcius—representing the patricians, or what was called in the days of Occupy the 1%—does the citizens' project take on a demonstrative, performative quality. Now it has an audience, and everything changes. The patricians' strategies for dealing with this simmering rebellion are familiar from countless examples where institutional power responds to the unruly energy of a people gathered together. Menenius, "one who has always loved the people," attempts to assuage and redirect them: "I tell you, friends, most charitable care / Have the patricians of you"; "for the dearth, / The gods, not the patricians, make it."[17] He treats them to a long disquisition about the Roman state as a human body, each class with its part to play in the functioning of the whole, and it seems to mollify them. But Marcius confronts them outright: "What's the matter, you dissentious rogues, / That, rubbing the poor itch of your opinion / Make yourselves scabs?" "Hang ye!" "Go, get you home, you fragments!"[18] After a brief initial exchange with Marcius, the citizens are heard no more in this scene. Speech passes from them to the patricians, as Menenius and Marcius engage in their own debate on how to respond to the citizens' challenge.

The major story of the play, the rise and fall of Caius Marcius, is of course not over at this point. But from a structural point of view, the story of the citizens, the play's 99%, is. What is lost in the turn is, again, mirrored in the trajectory of Occupy, "the true content" of which, according to the Invisible Committee,

> was not the demand, tacked onto the movement a posteriori like a post-it stuck on a hippopotamus, for better wages, decent housing, or a more generous social security, but *disgust with the life we're forced to live*. Disgust with a life in which we're all *alone* . . . The life in common that was attempted in Zuccotti park, in tents, in the cold, in the rain, surrounded by police

in the dreariest of Manhattan's squares, was definitely not a full rollout of the *vita nova*—it was just the point where the sadness of metropolitan existence began to be flagrant. At last it was possible to grasp our shared condition *together*, our equal reduction to the status of entrepreneurs of the self. That existential epiphany was the pulsing heart of Occupy Wall Street, for as long as it was fresh and lively.[19]

In Manhattan in 2011 as in *Coriolanus*, genuine revolution could not withstand much contact with power, for two distinct reasons, both of which have to do with representation. First, in terms of resistance, once the people's own process of deliberation is interrupted by power, once they engage in discussion with Menenius and Marcius and allow themselves to be redirected, the possibility of a genuine rebellion is squelched. Their "pulsing heart" is no longer "fresh and lively." Although the Citizens will again raise their voices to effect change in Act II, they will do so within the framework set out by the patricians and the Roman system of governance: they become voters. At the play's outset, they were pursuing what anarchists call direct action: not an appeal to power to ameliorate their situation but the taking of matters into their own hands. After the intervention of the patricians, they opt for the path of representation, in the governmental sense. In the formulation of James C. Scott, they become "legible" to power and thus more easily contained.[20]

The second reason for the citizens' relegation to the sidelines is a matter of representation in the literary sense. A shift in focus occurs that is analogous to the tendency of contemporary media to follow the movement of political speech from radical or grassroots-level expression to its adoption by power in the form of political elites. "The Democratic Party is where radical ideas go to die," radical leftists like to say, but the party commands the overwhelming share of the attention the media gives to leftwing activity. Media coverage of Zuccotti Park and Tahrir Square soon shifted from the raucous street scenes to the debates between those in the ruling classes: mayors, presidents of banks and nations, leaders of armies. Their concerns, not those of the people in the streets, became the focus. Just so, the attention of the playwright and the audience moves from the citizens to the patricians. And in *Coriolanus* the means by which the elites push aside the citizens' demands is what it tends to be in every age: a war. A messenger arrives "hastily," and what mattered a moment before is forgotten. He tells Coriolanus "the Volsces are in arms," and after this, the matter of food justice is closed.[21]

But of course the matter of food justice was not the real story of the citizens' appearance in the Roman street. The citizens marching to kill Marcius and price their own corn are not best understood as the sharp end of a revolutionary program or people already formed. Rather, viewed from the perspective of the Invisible Committee, they had only been in the process of finding their own purpose, indeed of finding themselves, as they marched and talked: "There's no new revolutionary subject whose emergence had eluded observers. So if it's said that the 'people' are in the streets it's not a people that existed previously, but rather the people that previously *were lacking*. It's not the people that produce an uprising, it's the uprising that produces its people, by re-engendering the shared experience and understanding, the human fabric and the real-life language that had disappeared."[22] In other words, it was the getting together, not the plan of action, that gave the citizens the best chance of really shaking up Rome and the possibilities within it for full human realization. "Inside of a protest space," writes Shane Burley, "even the most outwardly disruptive, there is a social fabric, a way of relating between people."[23] What was true in ancient Rome is truer still in the modern world of endless crisis: "This new 'resistance society' is built as much by utility as it is by circumstance, but it offers people something more than the sum of its parts. Our struggle to simply survive is a kind of revolution of its own because, as the State and the old mechanisms of support dissipate under years of privatization, the only thing we can rely [on] is each other. This type of relationship is new to us because togetherness was so alien before."[24] The citizens do have one more opportunity to engage face-to-face with power. Only this time it will be on patrician turf and according to patrician rules. The Roman elites, as Menenius demonstrated, pride themselves on the benevolent care for the people secured by the system of representative government. But Marcius exposes the system's inherent inequity as well as the current of disdain that runs just below the official attitudes of the unequal classes. At the heart of the play is Marcius's deep-seated contempt for the common people of Rome. Later he will be challenged to ingratiate himself to them to win a seat as Consul, but those comments bookending his initial interaction with the citizens—*rogues, scabs, fragments*—tell the whole story.

Within the Roman system, the people have a voice, but it is a voice rigidly circumscribed by institutions. In Act II, Coriolanus must secure the support, the "voices"—what we would call the *votes*—of the people to win his consulship. When he asks them individually for "your voice," it isn't *your* voice, it is the approved voice for participation in an established power structure. *Their* voice was expressed in Act I, Scene 1, before the intervention of the state. The elevation of "your voice" in a system of governance may sound deeply democratic, even liberating, but viewed from the perspective of the citizens it is a neutered voice whose value and parameters the state determines. The voices of the street are co-opted by the tribunes and henceforth used as a weapon in a fight that is not the citizens' own. It all raises the old question of activism: Is the vote or the street the best way to use a voice?

The citizens themselves are doubtful of their own efficacy as an ungoverned collective and seem to feel an innate need to be ruled. They remember Marcius (and others) calling them "the many-headed multitude" and perceive the logic of the appellation: "not that our heads are some brown, some black, some abram, some bald, but that our wits are so diversely colour'd: and truly I think, if all our wits were to issue out of one skull, they would fly east, west, north, south; and their consent of one direct way [the closest they could come to agreement] should be at once to all the points o'th'compass."[25] Just as Marcius approaches, they hover for a moment over the question of consent, consensus, and representation before acceding to the consulship election procedure. "Are you all resolved to give your voices? But that's no matter, the greater part [i.e., the majority] carries it. I say, if he would incline to the people, there was never a worthier man."[26] In this procedure, what Marcius requires is not their anonymous votes but their "own" voices. The format individualizes them to a degree. They become small grounds of individuals, rather than a crowd: "We are not to stay all together, but to come by him where he stands, by ones, by twos, and by threes. He's to make his requests by particulars; wherein every one of us has a single honour, in giving him our own voices with our own tongues."[27] This degree of individuation is enough to secure their participation in the pageant of representation, and they willingly surrender their internal deliberations to the approved ritual, the voices of individual citizens giving way to a line spoken by "ALL. Content, content."[28] The state achieves docility and compliance by offering the people a limited voice. Or, viewed from the other side, the people trade their ungovernable condition for a chance to address the state.

Say It Again

A syntactic feature of *Coriolanus* that appears again in Eliot's *Coriolan* and today's politics of the street is repetition. Characters in Shakespeare's play are constantly repeating themselves and one another. At times this repetition is used for rhetorical effect, as when the tribunes debate with Coriolanus's wife and mother. When Coriolanus and his great enemy, Tullus Aufidius, have their final stand-off, they trade one another's words like sword strikes. Sometimes the repetition of words takes the form of a crowd shouting to be heard and echoing each other, as when the citizens and their tribunes attempt to seize Coriolanus. And when Coriolanus meets his end, the conspirators cry "Kill, kill, kill, kill, kill him!" while the Lords ineffectually plead "Hold, hold, hold, hold!"[29]

Some of this repetition would sound much different on the stage than it reads on the page, as in this late passage:

> ALL THE PEOPLE. Tear him to pieces!—Do it presently!—He kill'd / My son!—My daughter!—He kill'd my cousin / Marcus!—He kill'd my father!—[30]

These voices seem differentiated as written text, but they might not in performance. Handfuls of exclamations like this are sometimes Shakespeare's way of indicating confused shouting, the unintelligible speech of many people speaking more or less at once.

All of these flavors of repetition—as rhetorical technique, as mockery or interrogation, as brute return of force for force, as amplification or insistence, as frenzy, as noise—can be found wherever a crowd is gathered, especially when the voice is the primary means of communication. Repetition seems to find its greatest utility when the size of the crowd or the emotional stakes are highest. *Coriolanus*, moreover, reveals that speakers from all classes rely on repetition, as opposed to more variegated or ornate forms of speech, in situations of extremity. All such speakers appear driven more by the urgency of the moment than any deliberate choice or even thought. However, a special form of repetition, the human microphone or "people's mic" technique used extensively during Occupy Wall Street and other Occupy events, was borne more out of technical than rhetorical urging and to bespeak a commitment to solidarity rather than a poverty of linguistic options. Denied the use of amplification devices or finding them awkward for addressing a crowd of thousands from the center of a "mass circle," the General Assembly turned to the patient repetition of spoken words at increasing distances from their source. The speaker says a phrase, which those closest repeat for the benefit of those behind them, and so on, until the words reach those farthest away. Although spoken by a large group, this kind of speech is anything but unintelligible. As in a poem, it has the effect of binding speaker and audience together, of creating rhythm, and thus of reinforcing memory. The people's mic had an immediate political effect verging on the spiritual:

> Those who spoke at the GA [General Assembly] often did so with barely suppressed emotion. Hearing one's words echoing off the bankers' towers surrounding the park as they were repeated, sometimes up to three times, by expanding concentric circles of the crowd, was evidently an experience both strange and profoundly moving. At the GA on the night following the eviction of the tents from the park, more than one speaker openly expressed love for the assembly, a declaration that would have surely seemed saccharine and disingenuous in more conventional gatherings, but here was received, without embarrassment, as an authentic act of communion.[31]

That communion is a function of a purity and openness that is difficult to maintain and yet central to the ethical truth being embodied in Occupy. "During the first weeks of Occupy Wall Street," the Invisible Committee observes,

> before the usual movement managers instituted their little 'working groups' responsible for preparing the decisions which the assembly would only need to approve, the model for the speeches made to the 1500 persons present was the guy who stepped forward one day and said 'Yo! What up? My name is Mike. I'm just a gangster from Harlem. I hate my life. Fuck my boss! Fuck my girlfriend! Fuck the cops! Just wanted to say, I'm happy to be here, with you all.' And his words were repeated seven times by the chorus of 'human megaphones' that had replaced the microphones prohibited by the police.[32]

It is indeed moving to imagine the experience of hearing those phrases thus repeated and multiplied by a group of strangers being transformed by their utterance into a community.

Yet the form, however liberating and true, was susceptible to the dulling influence of management and could not encompass every need of group communication. When combined with "consensual decision-making" principles, the people's mic could be "clumsy and time-consuming for resolving detailed issues."[33] Unlike in a poem, in order for it to work, the lexical units of the people's mic must be short and easily understood. At the same time, the speakers "bellowing their words in the steady, rhythmic cadence"[34] demanded by the form and having them precisely repeated creates an incantatory aural experience undeniably akin to poetry. The people's mic becomes a collaborative, participatory poem. As the volume and rhythm are for the benefit of the group, not an external audience, it carries a political inflection of autonomy and inwardness. Beyond this basic minimum, all manner of complication, co-optation, and frustration, but also a nearly infinite variety of content, can intervene. Some would argue that beyond that threshold the insurrection should not go, others that that is precisely where an insurrection shifts into the higher gear of revolution.

What we can say with certainty is that once state power interrupts the conversation of the citizens in *Coriolanus*, the play wants little more to do with them, and the little world briefly created by their interaction with one another vanishes from the stage. And that the discourse of "better Democratic presidential candidate platforms" superseding the raw, experimental, experiential discourse of Occupy Wall Street coincided with the forcible clearing of the tent city in Zuccotti Park. Ruling powers seem to know that the electric charge of crowd speech contains the truth of society but also the greatest threat to the ruling order. Thus it must be heard and acknowledged but just as quickly managed, channeled, and silenced. In *Coriolanus*, it is the ungovernability of the people's speech, their voices, that most vexes the patricians and gives substance to their most damning criticism of the people as political actors. Ultimately the play vindicates Caius Marcius's view of the people as dangerously fickle. The bit of efficacy and self-determination glimpsed in their private exchanges is overwhelmed by the ease with which they are manipulated by the tribunes, who get the citizens to change their minds as soon as their endorsement of Marcius is finished. Their inconstancy is as hateful to Marcius as was his having to condescend to appeal to them, and the thin veneer of his civility shatters immediately upon learning of their betrayal. Such folks do not deserve a say in their governance. "Are these your herd?" he demands of Sicinius, "—Must these have voices, that can yield them now, / And straight disclaim their tongues?"[35] They might be the sentiments of "election integrity" Congresspeople, furiously busy since November 2020 working to silence large swaths of the American populace whose inconvenient votes in a presidential election became the justification for denying them a voice in the process of election at all.

Coriolan

In its contests of voices, Shakespeare's *Coriolanus* thus anticipates both the promise of Occupy and the limitations of its forms in the face of state power. Similarly, in the 1930s, the play seemed keyed to the fractious politics of the moment, but with a notably rightward emphasis. "In 1933–1934," writes Warren Chernaik, "a production of the play at the Comédie Française occasioned riots by rival groups of socialists and fascists, each of whom saw the play as right-wing polemic." Moreover, "translations published in Nazi Germany described Coriolanus as 'the true hero and Führer,' opposed to 'a misled people, a false democracy . . . weaklings.' "[36] However, Eliot's appropriation of the play, which, like the play itself, is not much interested in the revolutionary potential of an unscripted gathering of citizens, is likewise skeptical of the potency of a Coriolanus who would presume to rule them.

How did Eliot handle the contests of voices at the heart of *Coriolanus*? In a way, he didn't. Here it is important to recall that Eliot used the *Coriolanus* model to write not a play but rather a sequence of poems. Between the voices of people and power he interposed a third, the voice of lyric poetry. In doing so, he evaded almost all of the class conflict that drives the play, but he also hinted at a way around the stark antagonism enforced by the available rhetoric of class warfare. Eliot was keenly alive to the aural energy and challenges of "Triumphal March," which, he wrote in 1937, "is very much better aloud than when read to oneself. I do not quite see in what way it is susceptible of choral treatment in the ordinary sense, but it obviously could profit by being apportioned between several voices."[37] He spoke further of his own difficulty reading the poem aloud when he did so at Harvard in 1947, introducing it as "one of the most difficult of my poems for me or anyone else to read aloud, but for that reason, if for that reason only, I think one of those best worth trying to read."[38] These were poems to be performed. And yet, as poems, they are different from stage drama in crucial ways. For instance, they are not prone to the kind of blurring or erasure of individual words that frequently occurs, by design, in a play. The lines "Now come the virgins bearing urns, urns containing / Dust / Dust / Dust of dust, and now" must be read as well as heard distinctly. "Please, will you / Give us a light? / Light / Light" is something other than noise.[39]

Moreover, as lyric poems—that is, not epic or explicitly dramatic (even with the familiar Eliotic dramatic inflection)—they are relieved of the burden of narrative and can function as moments nearly out of time. Yet the context of the framing Coriolanus story makes clear precisely what of narrative Eliot has chosen to omit, and the absence sets one limit on the terms of political possibility. Eliot skirts the economic inequality that frames the play's opening act and the rancor between classes that drives Coriolanus from Rome by beginning *Coriolan* after war and spectacle have rendered the citizens' direct action an afterthought. The setting of "Triumphal March" equates to Act II, Scene 1 of Shakespeare's play, when Caius Marcius—now Coriolanus, for his victory at Corioli—returns to Rome like Christ to Jerusalem. Menenius describes the scene thus: "I have seen the dumb men throng to see him, and / The blind to hear him speak: matrons flung gloves, / Ladies and maids their scarfs and handkerchers, / Upon him as he past: the nobles bended, / As to Jove's statue; and the commons made / A shower and thunder with their caps and shouts: / I never saw the like."[40] The people's voices thus employed signal joy and approbation, nothing of dissent. Eliot, in turn, leaves out economics but retains the joyous spectacle, or at least the occasion for it.

It follows that in the first poem, "Triumphal March," the voices are anything but politically efficacious. Onlookers strain to see a passing parade but can't make out much. They wait endlessly with their stools and sausages and smokes, hoping to glimpse the returning Coriolanus, home from victory over the Volsces. But first come the weapons of war, displayed on a scale that would make any dictator salivate. However, in an update akin to the modern setting of the Fiennes film, they are the armaments seized from Germany at the conclusion of the First World War. When Coriolanus finally does come into view, he is something of a disappointment. He is "indifferent," his hands "quiet," his expression and posture indeterminate.[41] An onlooker recounts how the procession then moved to the temple for the requisite sacrifice. All in all, the spectacle has been a matter of "Stone, bronze, stone, steel, stone, oakleaves, horses' heels / Over the paving. // That is all we could see."[42]

The poem's estimation of the political dignity or potential of the masses seems to be not much higher than Coriolanus's. Eliot includes nothing of either the people's direct challenges to Coriolanus over food access or of their demands for his civility in seeking their approval. The gazes of the people of "Triumphal March" are directed outward, at the spectacle of a military parade, but their voices, although directed inward, toward one another, are concerned only with trivialities. They are spectators only. It is little wonder that in recollection they would feel "We hardly knew ourselves that day," as the spectacle of a military parade and an arcane ritual do nothing to enlighten or unite them.⁴³ They engage in desultory gestures of mutual aid, helping one another see ("Are they coming? No not yet [. . .] Here they come. Is he coming? [. . .] What comes first? Can you see? Tell us. It is [. . .]"), managing their food ("We can wait with our stools and our sausages." "Don't throw away that sausage, / It'll come in handy"), and lighting each other's cigarettes ("Please, will you / Give us a light? / Light / Light"⁴⁴). But such hints at solidarity do not add up to anything of consequence. They hardly know themselves because they are not thinking about themselves.

Viewed from that perspective, the apparent lack of a political program overshadows the true revolutionary content of the day. Consider how Sarah Jaffe describes the indelible aspect of a non-state-sponsored commemoration of Bloody Sunday on its fiftieth anniversary in 2022. Programs and positions were not what meant the most: "In Derry, the people marched in the rain and took care of one another as they went, sharing umbrellas and passing out free hot food and drinks at local pubs at the day's end."⁴⁵ Mitchell Cowen Verter writes that "according to Kropotkin, the problem of satisfying needs is the most essential problem of all revolutionary problems, and the question of how we nurture each other is the most important of all revolutionary questions."⁴⁶ Whatever questions it left unresolved, this is a question Occupy answered. For the brief spell when they have the stage to themselves, Shakespeare's citizens likewise seem to be on their way to such an answer. In between the distractions of state pageantry, even the citizens in "Triumphal March" do command the rudiments of mutual aid, speaking and acting instinctively to satisfy one another's needs. It may be a failure of revolutionary potential that they don't do more than this, but it is also the secret to a brief experience of true revolution. In the event, their utterances are largely drowned out by the more memorable language of an unseen narrator: "O hidden under the dove's wing [. . .] O hidden" and by the jarringly specific, enormous, and anachronistic litany of war machinery, from "5,800,000 rifles and carbines" down to "1,150 field blankets."⁴⁷ Under these pronouncements, the voices of the people amount to little more than chatter. And, just as in Shakespeare's play, they promptly give way to the speech of the ruling class.

But the patrician voices of the next poem, "Difficulties of a Statesman," are not efficacious either, which is why Eliot's Coriolanus makes a very poor "true hero and Führer." These voices speak only of committees and commissions and are put to shame by the poetic flights of a meditative narrator. On the one hand: "Where the dove's foot rested and locked for a moment / A still moment, repose of noon, set under the upper branches of noon's widest tree / Under the breast feather stirred by the small wind after noon / There the cyclamen spreads its wings."[48] On the other: "The first thing to do is to form the committees: / The consultative councils, the standing committees, select committees and sub-committees. / One secretary will do for several committees."[49] This is an altogether different kind of repetition: the dead and deadening rhythm of the office. The voice of the individual, the statesman, is surrendered to the voices of useless collectivities and bureaucracies. "Cry what shall I cry?"[50] is Coriolanus's lament. The man of action is nowhere in this scene; there is only a man without words drowning in a lagoon of committee-speak and banality.

In both *Coriolanus* and *Coriolan* the speech of the people is interrupted by that of elites, with predictably stifling results. But whereas both Shakespeare and Eliot stayed with the patricians, the former stayed with them all the way through to the requisite dramatic conclusion, while Eliot resigned, as it were, with the project unfinished. Even with the whole sequence in mind, he had foreseen the real possibility of incompletion. After publishing "Triumphal March" in October 1931, he wrote to his friend John Middleton Murry: "This is part of a much longer piece, of which the second part is already written, of which the third part is I think writable, and of which I doubt whether I am able to write the fourth part—which must be largely derivative from S. John of the Cross—at all."[51] He seems to be suggesting that a sociopolitical agon such as the one he had begun would require a religious resolution. That he ultimately decided not to provide one, leaving the envisioned four-part sequence only half-finished, is in a way the truest reflection of Hannah Arendt's idea that political speech is open-ended.[52] To conclude *Coriolanus* as Shakespeare does is in effect to "unshout the noise" that animated its early scenes.[53] The conservatism of its ending—in the way that all classical tragic endings are conservative—does nothing to address the citizens' demands that unsettled matters at its outset, but it does end with the citizens silent, indeed silenced by authority.

Eliot is likewise conservative in simply not engaging with those demands in his "Triumphal March" before shifting his focus to Coriolanus and the bureaucracy. Would the envisioned four-part poem have included a representation of citizens' voices raised deliberately and meaningfully in support of action? It seems unlikely, and in any event the need to pursue this representation was apparently obviated by the ecclesiastically directed voices of his next project, *The Rock*. Finding himself at a kind of dead end after "Difficulties of a Statesman," Eliot got no further with the sequence, but the work to which he turned next shows that his interest in the vox populi had abated not at all. "Triumphal March" was only Eliot's first foray into crowdspeak, and he had clearly not found it satisfactory. Throughout the 1930s, he experimented with the use of dramatic choruses as a means of representing the sound of a public. And in every case, the voices of his choruses, following their Greek models, are those of the masses. It is no surprise that the choruses in *Murder in the Cathedral* and *The Rock* comprise the poor and working class. In his Greek forebears, as in Eliot's plays, individuation is reserved for those of position, privilege, or power. In *The Rock*, a pageant play written in 1933 to raise funds for the building of new churches in the London suburbs, Eliot comes as close as he ever would to expressing a plea for social change in the voice of the dispossessed. Certain lines in *The Rock* might be drawn from Occupy, Black Lives Matter, or a NoDAPL demonstration:

> Though you have shelters and institutions,
> Precarious lodgings while the rent is paid,
> Subsiding basements where the rat breeds
> Or sanitary dwellings with numbered doors
> Or a house a little better than your neighbour's;
> When the Stranger says: 'What is the meaning of this city?
> Do you huddle together because you love each other?'
> What will you answer? 'We all dwell together
> To make money from each other'? or "This is a community'?[54]

This is an appeal for what the contemporary movements call *systemic change*, for a reimagining of the logic of the city itself, not merely a new round of superficial improvements.

In *The Rock*, Eliot has created a crowd whose voice matters, and it matters precisely because its appeal is grounded in religion: "We build in vain unless the LORD build with us. / Can you keep the City that the LORD keeps not with you?"[55] For Eliot, Christianity was the only foundation upon which to justify and sustain meaningful social interventions; he was skeptical in the extreme of the solidity of any such interventions motivated by liberal humanism, economic rationalism, or appeals to abstract justice. The phrase "the people" occurs several times in *The Rock*, but apart from the Church, the "people" have no meaning. As the people of God, they have their only meaning. *The Rock* thus makes a case for the programming and institutionalization of a social movement and against the efficacy of unscripted assembly: those who want to oppose a killing materialistic culture but disinclined to share the keeping of their city with the Lord will not find success. A secular audience of activists will obviously not follow Eliot here, if indeed they have followed him even to this point. Any encouragement they find in these texts, though, is not so different from that identified in mass actions by those like Kropotkin, the Invisible Committee, or Sarah Jaffe, who see the true revolution in what occurs *prior to* any public formulation of a program: the folks with their sausages and smokes enacting in miniature a different world right under the nose of the old one.

Scott argues that "huge disparities in wealth, property, and status make a mockery of freedom," that "democracy is a cruel hoax without *relative* equality."[56] A pertinent question to ask of our own moment is: in a system that has denied or is working to deny the poor any meaningful leverage or role in the life of society, how efficacious can their appeals be apart from their expression through, on the one hand, an institutional force like the Church or, on the other, a violent uprising? Even the power they might wield as voters is uncertain in this era of voter suppression and the predominance of corporate voices over those of citizens in the electoral and legislative processes. (Interestingly, the original demand of Occupy Wall Street was to be "that Barack Obama ordain a Presidential Commission tasked with ending the influence money has over our representatives in Washington.")[57] In its heterogeneity and comparative lack of religiosity, the present movement for change resembles that of the people of Coriolanus's Rome more than that of the church builders of Eliot's London.

The extremity of the times may finally be making inescapable the fact that the gestures and forms that seemed futile because they skirt institutional entanglement may be the only real way forward, for the left as well as the right. Despite all the horrors of the day, the US Capitol invasion of January 6, 2021, was comparatively easy to put down once its intentions became monological and fully legible: to overthrow the government by force. Moreover, although the insurrectionists were trying to overthrow an institution, they were already well represented within institutional power by a political party and a president. Still more recently, the "white-paper protests" in China and elsewhere seemed promisingly illegible because of their refusal to articulate grievances or demands, but at the same time their message was all too well understood. "Its power," writes Jody Rosen, "rests in a shared understanding, by both the public and the authorities, of the unwritten message," a protest against censorship.[58] Even a sign with nothing written on it is still a sign and as such is directed outward, toward power. Michael Robbins holds out some hope for a way through to a future for the people that circumvents the seemingly inescapable structure that binds them. "We can still demolish this structure—though the hour is getting late—but instead we search within it (not very hard, it must be said) for ways to ameliorate its effects. I don't know how to demolish it," he writes, "I just know that we can't look to the state to save us . . . The state is nothing if not the guarantor of the very property relations that got us into this mess in the first place."[59] So the people are just the people, without even the weight of the Church to counteract the twin structures of state and capital that rule them.

Absent religious clarity or sanction, and often doubtful of their own efficacy, the people only keep getting together and trying. The rhetoric of popular uprising has long stressed repetition and persistence, saying the thing over and over again until it wears away the walls of oppression at which it is directed. Today's social rebellions are characterized far less by one grand gesture than by indefatigability, by showing up in the streets day after day. This is why the final words of "Difficulties of a Statesman," which in the 1930s might have signaled the wrong kind of resignation, can also sound with the relentless clarity of a drumbeat: "RESIGN. RESIGN. RESIGN."[60] Repeated long and loudly enough, and by a large enough collection of voices, they might even bring a head of state, at least one with the capacity to hear the voices of others, to step down. Coriolanus himself in both Shakespeare and Eliot seems tempted to give up the office for the outdoors, the tedium of governing for the earlier life that brought him fame and purpose. The contemporary evidence is notably mixed: "Resign, resign" was precisely the chant at the end of the 2014 Maidan uprising in Ukraine. President Yanukovych resigned the next day. But it was the votes, not the voices, that got a US president who wouldn't accept those votes out of office. Nor could the voices (and blunt instruments) of his supporters keep him in.

Tear gas might momentarily silence protestors, but insofar as the people retain the will to occupy space and hear one another, neither gas nor combat-armed police nor federal forces in unmarked cars can unshout the noise the protestors make. In the collectively amplified voices of a peaceful rebellion, as in a poem (finished or otherwise) the words go on working. The answers to questions of impact—whether a program or an encounter is more powerful, whether a word spoken to a comrade or a vote addressed to a government is louder—may ultimately come down to choices about attention. In their works based on the story of Coriolanus, Shakespeare and Eliot spent a little time with the people before moving on to the voices of state power. Writing that chooses to stay longer in the midst of those ungoverned voices and that resists the urge to turn the noise they make into an expression legible to the state might reveal that resistance can be the same thing as liberation for as long as it lasts.

Postscript

I have largely avoided talking about the Washington, DC insurrection on January 6, 2021, even though it is (as of this writing) the most vivid recent example of a mass uprising in the United States.[61] This is because I have chosen to focus on movements that aren't directed from above. The signal finding of the congressional investigation into January 6 was that the forty-fifth president inspired, choreographed, and led (however ineptly) that day's attack on the Capitol, to say nothing of the movement that led up to it. Rather than devote more space to this eruption of reaction, I will end only by noting the crucial fact that the tools of encounter and reiteration are not only available or attractive to those who would use them to make people free. Expression and repetition are not enough on their own. To Joseph Goebbels is usually attributed the insight that simply repeating a lie frequently enough can give it a credibility and a currency having nothing to do with reality, a lesson we have relearned over the past eight years or so. We have witnessed the sinister utility of repeating "alternative facts" and words like "terrorist," "hoax," "woke," "fake news," "stolen election," "communist," "groomer," etc., etc., like a spell until they erode the power of the truth to restore order. And Walter Benjamin observed long ago that fascism, perhaps more than any other politics, loves the sound of raised voices. "Fascism sees its salvation," he wrote, in giving the people "not their right, but instead a chance to express themselves."[62] It offers them not freedom or justice or truth but simply the sense of having a voice. What do fascists love most? A rally.

Chapter 7

Eliot and Radical Hope, 1939

> So, I answer the question: why resist, why persist in seeking autonomy from power? Where is the hope? The hope is in the limits of my knowledge and understanding. My knowledge and understanding don't see how any development of the social catastrophe could cultivate social well-being. But the catastrophe . . . is exactly the point where a new landscape is going to be revealed.
>
> —Franco "Bifo" Berardi, *After the Future*

One unusual thing (among many, many others) about the year 2020 is that as it lurched to a close, expressions of the desire for that impossible year to end were frequently undercut with misgivings about what 2021 would bring. There is no doubt that for most people, the end of 2020 couldn't come soon enough. Yet there was doubt detectable in the way people longed for 2021, a sense that even on New Year's Day, 2020 wouldn't really be over. The feeling was well expressed in a two-panel meme sent to me by my friend in Spain. In the first panel, a man's beaming, joyful gaze is directed at the numbers 31.12.2020 23:59:59, the last second of the year 2020. In the second, his jaw is slack and the light has vanished from his eyes as he contemplates the numbers 31.12.2020 23:59:61, not the first second of 2021 but an incomprehensible next second of 2020, the year that threatened never to end, despite the laws of God and humans, like (it once appeared and millions still believe) the forty-fifth US presidency. Not even two years on had 2020 ended. The same gallows humor informed another meme, after the year turned over again, observing that

2022 is pronounced the same as "2020, too." The decade ahead offers no relief: 2020 III, 2020 IV . . .

From one perspective, the grim joke is how unbearable it would be for 2020 to go on after midnight on December 31. From another, it captures the vertiginous feeling that we are being ushered into the future on currents that it will take much more than a turn of the calendar page to alter. Even as reasons for optimism solidified in late 2020 and early 2021 (in the United States)—the arrival of a COVID-19 vaccine, the (comparatively unremarked) end of the never-ending US war in Afghanistan, the likelihood of a renewed US commitment to international climate partnerships, measurable progress in the battle for racial justice, the impending installation of a new set of political leaders—Americans could not seem to give themselves entirely to that optimism. We seemed too aware that the catastrophes that defined 2020 began well before that year and that they were unlikely to recede in any permanent way in the next one. The positive changes are welcome, but we know, for example, that global climate change is only accelerating at a rate beyond what capitalism and liberal democracy seem capable of halting. The wildfires of 2020 would burn again in 2021 (and in 2022). We have seen how determined the backlash against the movement for racial justice has been, with new laws criminalizing protest and restricting voting access, and at least as many Blue Lives Matter as Black Lives Matter flags flying. We know that the forces fueling the rise of fascism are not going anywhere, and we fear that the democratic institutions designed to safeguard a power like the United States from collapse have been warped and undermined too deeply to recover. When people yearn for the end of a year, they are often expressing a desire to return to a state of things that preexisted it, to return to familiar, consoling patterns that promised not only security but a way into a better future. But at the end of 2020 they seemed to know that that state and those patterns were unlikely to reemerge anytime soon, and that even if they did they would be unlikely to save us.

And yet this chapter is about hope. The conception of hope I want to develop is as different from ordinary optimism or confidence as climate crisis is from one warm December. The kind of hope I want to describe, radical hope, is not only capable of withstanding the scale of affronts to hope mentioned above but finds its conditions of possibility within them. Radical hope is activated by precisely the level of catastrophic loss capable of ending a world, by the degree of disorientation that can make it difficult to see what makes a life worth living. It is as far removed from merely looking at the bright side or gritting one's teeth and hanging on as genuine justice is from taking down a statue or flying a different flag. And it is detectable, if not quite realized, in T. S. Eliot's writing of his own impossible year, 1939.

I borrow the term "radical hope" from Jonathan Lear, whose 2006 book of that title builds the concept upon the example of Plenty Coups, the Crow chief who had a prophetic dream which became the basis for what Lear calls an "ethics in the face of cultural devastation." With the buffalo herds destroyed that were the foundation of the Crow system of values, Plenty Coups and his people faced a future in which the terms of a meaningful life would no longer apply. The choice they made, based on interpretation of a dream Plenty Coups had, entailed not simply identifying a new object at which to aim but the choice to *refrain* from choosing, or, in other words, to choose hope itself. Radical hope involves a profound level of openness in the face of uncertainty, of an acceptance of unknowns. "What makes this hope *radical*," writes Lear, "is that it is directed toward a future goodness that transcends the current ability to understand what it is. Radical hope anticipates a good for which those who have the hope as yet lack the appropriate concepts with which to understand it."[1] It is a hope that can commit to moving forward into a world in which not only are the buffalo gone but there is also nothing, yet, to replace them. I want to argue that something approaching this kind of hope enabled Eliot in 1939 to make two of the most consequential choices of his life, and two of the hardest for his audiences to live with: to cease writing major poetry and to refuse to marry Emily Hale, to whom he was passionately, singularly devoted for nearly four decades. I echo of Eliot what Lear says of Plenty Coups: "The point is not to establish the historical claim that [he] actually did manifest such radical hope . . . I am not in a position to plumb the depths of his soul . . . The aim is to establish what *we* might legitimately hope at a time when the sense of purpose and meaning that has been bequeathed to us by our culture has collapsed."[2] The aim is to equip ourselves better for the challenge before us by borrowing imaginatively but responsibly from the available evidence of Eliot's life and work as a culture collapsed and yet life went on.

A kind of land acknowledgment before proceeding. As multigenerational St. Louisans, with family as far west as Oregon, the Eliots were deeply enmeshed in the settler-colonial project that was synonymous with the collapse of Crow culture. Although the Crow were not the inhabitants forced out of what became Missouri, they were pushed farther and farther west by other displaced Native peoples who had been, and by the slaughter of the buffalo. The choices made by white settlers resulted in an American West full of choices for their descendants but offering vanishingly few to the original inhabitants of the land. In this way the stories of Eliot and Plenty Coups are not (even in the limited terms in which I propose to compare them) simply parallels; they are linked within histories of causation. The forced removal and eradication of Native Americans made the stories of people like T. S. Eliot possible; the presence of people like the Eliots foreclosed most of the possible stories for the Crow. And as will become apparent, the power to take up and take away possibilities can be as unbalanced in individual relationships as in racist programs of conquest. In such cases, stories don't simply end. Someone ends them. Or they don't.

"East Coker," written in 1939 and published early in 1940, was not the end of Eliot's poetic career, but it was the beginning of the end, as with its composition Eliot first scried the larger structure that would constitute *Four Quartets*, the last significant poems he would ever write. Nor was 1939 the end of his relationship with Emily Hale, but it was the last of what had become annual visits and the last time he saw her with the prospect of a life together still in the air; in hindsight it is possible to see that her departure from England as World War II began effectively closed a door of possibility that would not reopen. As Frances Dickey observes, "The emotional high point of 1939 occurs, ironically, in the days following the outbreak of the war that will separate them for six years" as they put up blackout curtains at Stamford House.[3] The decision to abandon poetry for verse drama has confounded and disappointed readers ever since. And even before the revelations in the Hale letters, the choice not to pursue a romantic relationship with her has long stood as a baffling disappointment to a most promising love story, a rejection, as Dickey describes it, of "the kind of denouement that readers might wish for."[4]

Why renounce two streams of meaning that have nourished one's whole adult life, just when both seem to be in full flow? What is hopeful about such endings? One answer is that, for believers like Eliot, renunciation is a form of hope. To surrender one's own desires to those of God is to believe that there are wider or more important horizons than the ones we set for ourselves. The problem is that the consolations of Eliot's great renunciations seem to have been available only to him—and perhaps, years later, to Valerie Fletcher, whom he married in 1957. The crucial difference between the visions of Plenty Coups and Eliot is that the Crow leader dreamed for the tribe. The Crow "used dreams co-operatively," writes Lear. "The young men were sent out to dream; and at a later ceremonial occasion the old men interpreted the young men's dreams. The tribe relied on what it took to be the young men's capacity to receive the world's imaginative messages; it relied on the old men to say what these messages meant."⁵ While Eliot, ever the skeptic of individual genius or purely personal revelation, consistently argued for the social function of poets and poetry, his creative writing of 1939 indicates a dreaming not so much for the tribe as for himself. As for the wisdom of elders or the virtue of tribal solidarity, "East Coker" expresses profound skepticism, albeit a skepticism mixed with its own kind of hope:

> Do not let me hear
> Of the wisdom of old men, but rather of their folly,
> Their fear of fear and frenzy, their fear of possession,
> Of belonging to another, or to others, or to God.
> The only wisdom we can hope to acquire
> Is the wisdom of humility: humility is endless.⁶

One effect of the opening of the Hale letters has been to show—to confirm, really—just how much Eliot's published work represents the working out of his personal struggles. The choices he made based on the lessons, the vision, of 1939 are personal choices. From the point of view of poetry readers and believers in the love between Eliot and Hale—including, it must be inferred, Hale herself—they are choices that resulted in devastating and nearly inexplicable loss. The plays he wrote after *Four Quartets*, let us admit it frankly, feel like an inadequate substitute for the poems he might still have written. However great the personal fulfillment he found in turning to drama, there is no indication that the public, or any tribe that included Eliot, was served half as well by the plays. And the evidence of the letters makes plain that Eliot renounced Hale not on her behalf but in his own interest, all of which suggests a position less inspiring than radical hope for facing an uncertain future. Eliot's refusal to account adequately for, or to allow himself to be limited by, the present needs or desires of another human being contrasts with the deeply communal character of radical hope. Renunciation can help liberate a spirit from desire, but Eliot's choice of what Dickey calls "a pattern of renunciation imposed both on himself and on Hale" appears to have liberated his spirit at the expense of hers.⁷ Without a deep commitment to solidarity, bold, even hopeful renunciations may not indicate radical hope but rather, as a colleague put it when I tried to explain all this, only charitable (or not so charitable) egotism.

Another possibility is that Eliot's choices weren't renunciations at all. As for Plenty Coups and the Crow, you can't renounce what has been taken from you. But you can choose something besides going down fighting. You can, if you can find the right vision, go on thriving under new but still acceptable terms, which is what Plenty Coups did and what, more importantly, he inspired the Crow people to do. Eliot's personal writings suggest that two frameworks that had ordered his life weren't so much renounced around 1939 as taken away: the coherent idea of Europe on which he had built his poetic career, and the romantic, idealized love of Emily Hale that had taught him both what it is to desire and what it is to deny the satisfaction of desire. The choices he made in response were his own.

Whether renunciation or surrender, one way to make sense of Eliot's unexpected choices is to see in them the seeds of radical hope, involving not a choice of a new medium or a new love, but a choice of a new perspective: open, indeterminate, and resulting in all kinds of unexpected things, including in Eliot's case the late happy marriage to Valerie and all that it entailed for his legacy, the life of poetry, and the lives of generations of readers. The prospect of what might *not* have been were it not for Valerie's stewardship of Eliot's work is at least as alarming as the alternate world in which he marries Hale or goes on writing poems is tantalizing. From this perspective, we must consider ourselves the beneficiaries of Eliot's choices in and after 1939, however agonizing their costs.

Even the brief sketches above begin to suggest how much radical hope has to do with loss. It also has to do, for Plenty Coups as for Eliot, with faith in an extra-personal force of good: for Plenty Coups the Great Spirit, *Ah-badt-dadt-deah*; for Eliot the Christian God. But its working out is not synonymous with the kind of trust or surrender familiar in religious devotion. Both men found the necessary encouragement to radical hope inside the framework of their religion, but the scripture, as it were, the text of their revelation is more Talmud than Torah. Both men were the recipients of a vision, and their elaboration of that vision became the basis for its use, its employment in practical decision-making. This participation in the vision—this working out, passing on, and putting in action—is not only a visible proof of hope, it is where radical hope finds its purchase for changing worlds. I increasingly think of *Four Quartets*, especially "East

Coker," as the working-out of a vision that would see Eliot into the final stage of his life and career. Along with the play he finished in 1939, *The Family Reunion*, "East Coker" charts a path approaching radical hope, a path of unknowing, relinquishing the security of the familiar in favor of risk, exposure, and the possibility of another life worth living.

Visions

That Plenty Coups was the recipient of a vision at age eleven is explicit in the history of the Crow people and in his own autobiographical recollections. In this vision, which at first was only a dream, Plenty Coups foresees the disappearance of the buffalo herds: "All were gone, *all!* There was not one in sight anywhere, even out on the plains. I saw a few antelope on a hillside, but no buffalo—not a bull, not a cow, not one calf, was anywhere on the plains."[8] They are replaced by domesticated cattle. Then he is shown "a very old man sitting in the shade of a particular tree . . . 'This old man is yourself, Plenty-coups,'" he is told by a "Man-person," his guide, who had begun as a buffalo.[9] Then:

> There is a tremendous storm in which the Four Winds begin a war against the forest. All the trees are knocked down, but one. 'Listen Plenty-Coups,' said a voice. 'In that tree is the lodge of the Chickadee. He is least in strength but strongest of mind among his kind. He is willing to work for wisdom. The Chickadee-person is a good listener. Nothing escapes his ears, which he has sharpened by constant use. Whenever others are talking together of their successes and failures, there you will find the Chickadee-person listening to their words. But in all his listening he tends to his own business. He never intrudes, never speaks in strange company, and yet never misses a chance to learn from others. He gains successes and avoids failure by learning how others succeeded or failed, and without great trouble to himself . . . The lodges of countless Bird-people were in the forest when the Four Winds charged it. Only one person is left unharmed, the lodge of the Chickadee-person. Develop your body, but do not neglect your mind, Plenty-coups. It is the mind that leads a man to power, not strength of body.'[10]

The elders of the tribe interpret the dream to mean that white men will "take and hold this country," displacing the buffalo as well as any tribes who choose to fight them. The Crow must cultivate the nimble intelligence of the Chickadee and become adaptable, situational, and receptive to new information. In an ensuing council meeting, "they explicitly recognized . . . that their buffalo-hunting way of life was coming to an end, and they decided to ally with the white man against their traditional enemies. This is the way they hoped to weather the oncoming storm and hold onto their land," a decision broadly vindicated by subsequent Crow history.[11] "Plenty Coups was told in the dream," writes Lear, "that, to survive, he must follow the example of the Chickadee. The Chickadee is a bird that learns from others. But exactly what he needed to learn was left unclear."[12] Thus, the elders identified the first thing the Crow, following the Chickadee, needed to learn: to say goodbye to buffalo hunting and to embrace an alliance with white men. At the same time, they built the lack of clarity, the perpetual openness to new learning, into their new ethic.

I have suggested how far the estimation of the wisdom of old men in "East Coker" differs from that of the Crow. However, in choosing the way of the Chickadee, the Crow elders have anticipated and become the very model of Eliot's declaration in the final lines of "East Coker": "Old men ought to be explorers."[13] They do not settle into the bogus "serenity" of age but instead choose "a willing, almost reckless exposure to the unknown," as Lyndall Gordon argues Eliot is trying in "East Coker" to embolden himself to do.[14] "He imagines," she writes, ". . . a perpetual frontier, a perpetual mystery on the borders of the known world," and a voyage for which the familiar means of locomotion will not do. For Eliot, it is also a voyage on which he can have no company.

Given the mystical qualities of *Four Quartets*, not to mention Eliot's devotion to Dante, St. John of the Cross, and the whole system of Christian revelation, it is no stretch to say that he, too, received a vision. Indeed, "Little Gidding" includes a climactic account of a vision, whether received or invented, a walk with a "familiar compound ghost." It is this "dead master" who gives Eliot permission to bid farewell to poetry: "These things have served their purpose: let them be."[15] It is perhaps enough to say, for now, that the major literary texts he created in 1939, "East Coker" and *The Family Reunion*, function like the articulation of a vision—a coded message responding to present needs, containing prophetic elements, and hinting at a salutary path into the future—if we are open to reading them that way. "For the Crow," writes Lear, "dream-interpretation consisted in showing how the vision embodied in a dream applied—or would come to apply—to reality . . . Because of their general understanding of dreams, the Crow would have received Plenty Coups's dream *as oracular*."[16] In order to understand a puzzling period in Eliot's life, it helps to think a bit like the Crow. Eliot's strange post-1939 trajectories—a series of verse plays almost no one loves as much as his poems, a life of solitude even when marriage to Hale becomes possible—take on a new meaning if we work backwards from them, reading them as the application of the 1939 dream. "East Coker" and *The Family Reunion* make good oracles for what was to come. As Gordon observes, "In a curious way, his work foretold the events of his life."[17] One doesn't need to be convinced of the reality of divine revelation or prophetic vision to identify in the texts of both Plenty Coups and Eliot the translation of mystery into practical wisdom, of the spiritual into the sensible. Plenty Coups had a dream, which in the telling and collective interpretation of it became a plan. If Eliot had a dream, we do not know, but the imaginative processes visible in "East Coker" and *The Family Reunion* may be called visionary in light of what came after.

For Plenty Coups, the disappearance from view of the Crow mind was precipitated by the disappearance of the buffalo herds that, in their relationship with the Crow people, provided the very terms in which Crow life had meaning. This loss outstripped any available frameworks for conceiving of a future. It culminated in their relocation in the 1880s to a reservation. "Plenty Coups" can be translated as "Many Achievements," and the loss of the buffalo represented a level of cultural devastation in which achievements would not simply be different or fewer, but the very conditions for achieving anything would no longer exist. Recounting his life to an interlocutor named Linderman, Plenty Coups said: "I can think back and tell you much more of war and horse-stealing. But when the buffalo went away the hearts of my people fell to the ground, and they could not lift them up again. After this nothing happened."[18] Lear takes this final phrase—"After this nothing happened"—as the adequate expression of the magnitude of Crow cultural devastation. Things didn't change, good things happening weren't replaced by bad things happening; the very conditions in which and by which things could happen vanished. *Happening-ness* vanished. History had exhausted itself, and a true cultural waste land had set in.

These are the conditions within which, through an imaginative process Lear describes with impressive deliberation, Plenty Coups fashioned for the Crow the radical hope that would guarantee them a future. After his dream, and in consultation with the tribe, Plenty Coups decides, in Lear's paraphrase:[19]

1. My dream tells us all that our traditional way of life is coming to an end. It has been so interpreted by the wisest men of the tribe—and the tribe as a whole agrees that this is its meaning. There is nothing we can do to change that.

2. Our conception of goods is intimately tied up with our way of life . . . But that is a nomadic life of hunting plentiful buffalo—and that life is about to disappear.

Thus

3. I recognize that in an important sense we do not know what to hope for or what to aim for. Things are going to change in ways beyond which we can currently imagine. We certainly do know that we cannot face the future in the same way that we have been doing. It is no longer a matter of planning another buffalo hunt or another raid on the Sioux. We must do what we can to open our imaginations up to a radically different set of future possibilities.

Still,

4. There is more to hope for than mere biological survival. It is not enough for me simply to survive . . . If I am going to go on living, I need to be able to see a genuine, positive, and honorable way of going forward . . .

5. . . . My commitment to God's transcendence and goodness is manifested in my commitment to the idea that something good will emerge even if it outstrips my present limited capacity for understanding what the good is.

6. . . . while we Crow must abandon . . . the conception of the good life that our tribe has worked out over centuries, *We shall get the good back*, though at the moment we can have no more than a glimmer of what that might mean.[20]

"This reasoning," writes Lear, "acknowledges that one is at some kind of practical horizon *without* thereby trying to peek over it."[21]

I quote at such length from Lear because the Crow predicament in the nineteenth century illuminates Eliot's struggle in the year 1939 in two ways: first, that the nomadic Crow life is akin to the idea of Europe in which Eliot had invested twenty years of concentrated labor, likewise "worked out over centuries," likewise coming to an end. It is not a familiar form of loss. It has, Eliot wrote, "induced in me a depression of spirits so different from any other experience of fifty years as to be a new emotion."[22] Second, that the indeterminacy, openness, and belief in a positive future that characterizes Crow hope is everywhere present in the language Eliot begins to employ in "East Coker" and *The Family Reunion*. There is no reason to think Eliot was aware of the story of Plenty Coups or the Crow transformation, but within his own cultural cataclysm, he accessed and made use of a strikingly similar ethic.

In "Last Words" (January 1939), in which he announces his resignation as editor of the *Criterion*, Eliot laments that "the 'European mind,' which one mistakenly thought might be renewed and fortified, disappeared from view" in the 1930s.[23] "Enforced insularity" has taken the place of international exchange. Nor has the ending ended: "It will perhaps need more severe affliction than anything we have yet experienced, before life can be renewed."[24] His words bespeak far more than disappointment at the shriveling up of the *Criterion* project. Nothing less than the very ground upon which he had pursued his life's work—the interrelation of European thought—was, as he saw it, coming to a decisive end. From his earliest poetic overtures and critical formulations, the idea of Europe as a living whole had been the condition that made evaluation of poetic production possible. A sense of the shared European tradition had provided Eliot with his terms for poetic meaning and underwritten every poem he published.

His conception of the future articulated in the *Criterion* and in the prose altogether for 1939 contains at best a provisional and limited kind of hope. One can watch Eliot's horizons contracting in "Last Words": "Of the international attempt," only "vestiges" remained in recent *Criterion* numbers, he writes.[25] He suspects that for the "immediate future, perhaps for a long way ahead, the continuity of culture may have to be maintained by a very small number of people indeed," in "small and obscure papers and reviews."[26] Meanwhile, "authors who are concerned with that small part of 'literature' which is really creative . . . should apply themselves sedulously to their work, without abatement or sacrifice of their artistic standards." Sentiments like these provide some measure of how far the British stiff upper lip is from radical hope. Resolve, bucking up, keeping calm and carrying on are strategies, often good ones, of endurance, but they don't renew life.

His 1939 letters to Hale underscore the sense of an ending he conveyed in "Last Words," an ending of which the demise of the *Criterion* is only one symptom. He mourns

> the disappearance of the criterion as a *symbol* . . . I *think* that what I should have liked [readers] to feel, was the seriousness of the collapse of the civilization of the last four hundred years . . . I should have liked people to feel . . . that my stopping the *Criterion* meant that I wanted people to face the fact that if people wanted civilisation they must do something more about it than support a literary review.[27]

The year piled one ending on another. On February 3 he writes of the death of "Willie Yeats," the familiarity of the nomenclature belying the gravity of the loss, actual as well as symbolic, of the century's greatest poet to that point as well as the one, with Eliot, most invested in a unified idea of Europe. "That is the kind of occasion," he wrote, "on which I miss the *Criterion* as a vehicle."[28] Beneath the layers of loss, a note of hope does periodically sound in these 1939 letters. On February 10 he writes, "The only attitude that I think should be called 'defeatist' is that which accepts surrender and refuses to go on struggling; which believes that nothing we can do will make any difference: I hope no one has ever got that impression from *my* writing."[29] This combination of optimism and resolution forms the basis of what Eliot would elevate and transmute into an approximation of radical hope in *Four Quartets*, beginning with "East Coker."

"East Coker"

Lyndall Gordon argues that "for all its rigour, *East Coker* is the most optimistic of the *Quartets*."[30] It begins with the line "In my beginning is my end" and concludes "In my end is my beginning," the phrase which has perhaps most famously signaled optimism to readers, not least during "the darkest moment of the war," as Helen Gardner remembered.[31] Though profound, the line has sometimes seemed to me to wear its profundity too easily. I have often settled for reading it as a mildly reassuring play with paradox, a warm but safe piece of encouragement. But in light of the fact that "East Coker" is the beginning of the end of Eliot's poetic career, *In my end is my beginning* gains some explanatory power.

The concept of radical hope, moreover, charges the line and the entire poem with the energy of cataclysm and renewal, especially considering how Eliot layers (vision-like) meaning on meaning. The poem "seem[s] to speak directly to [its] times," writes Gordon, "yet . . . draw[s] on private, sometimes strange experience, to generalize for all time. In *East Coker* private turmoil is reflected in a world war, which is reflected in turn in cosmic disorder."[32] In key passages, Eliot speaks the Crow language of a hidden path to the future: "In order to arrive at what you do not know / You must go by a way which is the way of ignorance. / In order to possess what you do not possess / You must go by the way of dispossession. / In order to arrive at what you are not / You must go through the way in which you are not."[33] The theme of unknowing is invested with both terror and possibility, as inherited knowledge proves inadequate to present challenges, but stepping out from the precipice where precedent ends makes the present ultimately consequential. The "quiet-voiced elders" have passed on a "wisdom" which is "only the knowledge of dead secrets

> Useless in the darkness into which they peered
> Or from which they turned their eyes. There is, it seems to us,
> At best, only a limited value
> In the knowledge derived from experience.
> The knowledge imposes a pattern, and falsifies,
> For the pattern is new in every moment
> And every moment is a new and shocking
> Valuation of all we have been.[34]

Again, the wisdom of elders does not fare well in "East Coker." If radical hope is equal parts perpetual newness and solidarity, Eliot's speaker (whose vision does appear limited) celebrates one and rejects the other. In the poem's third section, another difference between ordinary hope, which is directed at a desired end, and radical hope becomes nearly explicit. The former kind must be renounced in favor of the latter, a condition of total openness, which here gets the name of "waiting":

> I said to my soul, be still, and wait without hope
> For hope would be hope for the wrong thing; wait without love
> For love would be love of the wrong thing; there is yet faith
> But the faith and the hope and the love are all in the waiting.³⁵

Here is the acknowledgment of a horizon and the acceptance of being unable to peek over it. As the war was caving in one familiar piece of Eliot's life after another, to hope for a simple return to normalcy would be delusory and, moreover, a betrayal of the spirit of true "waiting." The great challenge is to refrain from wishing either for things to go back to the way they were or to become something one can envision. By the end of the first month of 1939, Yeats is dead, as are the *Criterion* and the world that nourished it. By the end of the year, Emily Hale is back in the United States, probably for good. The horizon of the end of *Four Quartets* is visible, but as yet Eliot does not know what lies beyond it. In "East Coker" Eliot settles into such unknowing, not in the "deliberate hebetude" of an assumed "serenity," but as the electric edge where the present is always becoming the future.³⁶ The poem, however, suggests that he is going it alone.

Costs

As for *The Family Reunion*, it presents a protagonist likewise bent on going it alone. Harry, Lord Monchensey, is all out of joint as he stands at a horizon he can't see over. The initial source of his disturbance is guilt. He is a woman killer. Or, if he isn't, he believes himself to be, confessing to Mary that he pushed his wife off a ship in the Atlantic. Critics have long seen Harry's guilt and desperation as reflective of Eliot's own tortured relationship with his first wife, Vivien, and his feelings of responsibility for her psychological deterioration and, in 1938, institutionalization. Indeed, some observers have laid Vivien's 1947 death in an asylum at Eliot's feet. And as he wrote *The Family Reunion*, Eliot was on the brink of putting another woman away: Emily Hale, who was even then helping him with the play and inspiring him to new ecstasies of happiness. On March 10, 1939, he wrote to her of his disappointment "that the first performance of this play (which you have had so much to do with, and have in such important particulars, moreover, modified) should be without you."³⁷ At the end of the year, he was dilating on their love in terms that gave every indication of a future together but also hinted that he was not looking to satisfy their feelings for one another in a bond such as marriage.

One of the greatest questions about Eliot's relationship with Hale has always been why, given their obvious love for one another, they did not marry after Vivien's death. One answer from the perspective of radical hope is that such a marriage would have represented a desired end, whereas hope is an end in itself and unfulfillable, or, rather, fulfillable only in perpetual openness to new ends. Dickey reports that as early as 1936 Eliot "abruptly reminds her that they may not have a future to look forward to and ought to act as if they will never be united in marriage. Instead, they should turn their minds to things of the spirit."[38] While they live, though, human beings open some doors and not others. Even the truly ascetic are subject to the limitations represented by the needs and choices of others and must accept these as part of the structure within which hope can be experienced on earth. Even Crow ethics required the taking of decisions in the present as part of the unfolding of a radical hope over the timescales of generations and centuries. In Eliot's relationship with Hale, at least as expressed in the surviving correspondence, the perpetual denial of ends begins to sour the more the pair move toward and then beyond a point at which one person, Hale, is in need of, is perhaps even entitled to, the fulfillment of a desire.

She could not forever be what Eliot needed her to be. Dickey writes: "As long as Hale remained inaccessible, she fit the Beatrician model that Eliot's imagination demanded or craved," but she would remain unfulfilled.[39] "She does not automatically accept her role as muse and stand-in for the Blessed Virgin Mary (in 1947, trying to explain why they cannot marry, he writes that she has been, for him, 'a B.V.M.'). In fact, she never embraces this role, long hoping for love physically consummated and socially recognized through marriage."[40] For Eliot, "the role of unrequited lover seems to unlock his own creative powers . . . Writing assuages his feelings of longing and loneliness and, conversely, these emotions are also the spur to poetic creation."[41] Later in life, he wrote that marrying Hale "would have killed the poet in me; Vivienne nearly was the death of *me*, but she kept the poet alive."[42] And Dickey agrees, "*not* marrying the woman he loved *did* keep the poet alive in him. Unsatisfied longing for Hale"—however eagerly Hale might have satisfied it—"motivated and directed his poetic creativity throughout his career."[43] So "the waiting to which he has consigned himself and Hale as they grow older" bore bountiful fruit for Eliot the writer and the world of poetry but deprived another soul of her desired happiness and perhaps—who can know?—even a leap in the progress of her own hope.[44]

There is a fearful symmetry between Eliot at the end of 1939, with a wife all but dead and another woman soon to be abandoned, and Harry, with a murdered wife behind him and walking out on his mother as well as a love from childhood. In both cases, leaving women behind seems a nearly constitutive part of "follow[ing] the bright angels" of a personal vision.[45] Agatha reassures Harry that "Love compels cruelty / To those who do not understand love," a handy imprimatur for anyone who needs to hurt others to be true to his own calling.[46]

Eliot's letters to Hale in 1939 are full of suggestions that they were together on a course that would culminate in some kind of consummation of their love. Yet his most powerful articulations of emotion tend to emphasize two sides of a triangle—himself and the intervention of an unnamed outside force—while conspicuously omitting the third: Hale herself. On September 4, following a magical summer spent with her, he confesses, "It seems now as if I had done nothing and deserved nothing, and that this strange happiness had come to me quite in spite of myself,"[47] and a few days later again speaks of "my new happiness, which I think can never leave me."[48] His expansion on the theme of this unaccountable joy stresses his own contentment while also affirming a future reunion. On 13 September he writes of "the greater happiness which, as I said, persists on a plane inaccessible to separation and vicissitude: the acceptance in humble wonder of a certainty which I have never experienced before." He has enjoyed "an assurance of strength to carry me through until we meet again. I have something that very few men can ever have had."[49]

The one-sided nature of the surviving correspondence certainly accounts for some of the impression of one-sidedness these letters give. Even so, Eliot's reluctance to focus entirely on Hale herself is unmistakable. In the passages of greatest intensity, there is always an *I* and a *we* and a story of a developing relationship, but rarely a *you*. He concludes the year with such a passage, one that feelingly describes a way into a future together even when separated by distance, one in which *I*, *one*, and *we* can find a great deal of hope and comfort, but in which *you*, Hale, is absent. The salutation is "Dear Love,":

> We can and do go on growing together. Last summer was very lovely in itself; but I should feel it a kind of impiety to regard anything as an 'episode': therefore it can only hold its

beauty in the light of a further growing relationship of which all that can be asked is, that it should at every period be the best possible under those conditions, and that it should be—not always, of course, proceeding at the same pace or even quite in a straight line—always progressing so that *something* new and precious in the way of mutual understanding and devotion is always developing; something that one could not surrender even in order to get back to a golden phase. We shall certainly be maturing in the interval, and surely maturing towards each other more and more.[50]

In its embrace of imprecision, of a *something* as yet unknown, it is a language full of hope. If its intent is to reassure a lover troubled by the prospect of a long separation, it is also well suited to that. But in its insistence on terms of satisfaction other than those preferred, chosen, by the other party, it seems better suited to console the writer than the reader. Were we able to see Hale's side of the correspondence, to find, for instance, that Eliot was directly addressing ideas or concerns of hers or following her lead to the conclusions he expresses, such impressions might well be significantly altered. On the basis of what is available, and making no further claims for the archaeological truth of Eliot's and Hale's relationship but only for what is useful in the surviving record for readers today, Eliot's management of expectations and desires in his letters to Hale reflects the outlook of a visionary in love, an outlook that stands in need of more mutuality, self-sacrifice, surrender, and solidarity to become radical hope.

Radical hope doesn't end, but its effects can be hidden. We may be able to check in on the work of later years—for Eliot, several verse plays and a small handful of occasional and love poems—and see its operations, but we may not. The Crow without buffalo and consigned to a reservation look little like they did in the glorious centuries before, but, if Lear is correct about radical hope, they are not defeated. In Eliot's case, even the presence of literary disappointments can provide further evidence that he has been animated by hope; as Christopher Castiglia writes, hope "relies on disappointment and failure."[51] Years like 1939 reveal that at certain moments everything can change, including the conditions for things happening, the frameworks for evaluating what constitutes a good life, and the possibilities for an ethical way into the future. The play between endings and beginnings figured in his writing of 1939 captures

Eliot's wrestling with the upheaval of such a year, after which everything would be different for him in life, love, and literature. And *we* might be living through, or at the beginning of, a similar transformation. With our own litany of major upheavals growing—climate crisis, pandemic, plastic-filled lifeless oceans, the fracturing and decay of liberal-democratic ideals and systems, capitalism overheating and collapsing, mass shootings, school shootings—we may be witnessing the loss of the very terms by which things have been able to happen for several centuries. A return to normality is hardly in the offing. We probably require something like radical hope to see us into the next stage of human existence.

As Ben Ehrenreich reflected in a November 2020 essay for the *New York Times*, maybe collapse is not possible for enduring peoples—like the Crow—in the same way it is for cultures in shallower relationships with the earth, the old, and the life of dreams. He quotes Michael V. Wilcox, who points out that indigenous peoples who are "still here after the story of failure has already been written" challenge the very idea of total societal collapse.[52] It isn't difficult to hear something of this spirit in those other famous lines from "East Coker"—"There is only the fight to recover what has been lost / And found and lost again and again: and now, under conditions / That seem unpropitious. But perhaps neither gain nor loss. / For us, there is only the trying. The rest is not our business."[53]

Insofar as they express radical hope, they are genuinely inspiring lines. We should not be lulled into tranquility by Eliot's words, though, because there is trying and then there is trying. There is losing, and there is losing. Eliot's ability to pursue this hopeful course, and to have his expression of it enshrined as a literary monument, is a product of one culture whose flourishing is predicated on the near annihilation of others. It is also the privilege of a powerful, visionary man who can afford to overleap what to a woman who loves him might be a loss unredeemed by any amount of "trying." Lear's account makes no mention of the place of Crow women in the discernment process. Nor does it mention those Crow who dissented—surely there were some?—from the Chickadee ethic, who would choose death over the new dispensation. What is the proper valuation of their lives when radical hope is leading the rest into a bright future? Some losses like that surely ought to be our business and theirs, even when weighed against the pursuit of a worthy ideal. Perhaps the heart of even one person is too high a price to pay for radicalism.

Conclusion

"Every Poem an Epitaph"

> You are not those who saw the harbour
> Receding, or those who will disembark.
> Here between the hither and the farther shore
> While time is withdrawn, consider the future
> And the past with an equal mind.
>
> "The Dry Salvages"

Two streams converge to create the space where this conclusion might fit. The first is the deluge of new biographical material on T. S. Eliot. Since I started writing this book, the following new works have appeared: *Eliot After* The Waste Land, the second volume of a massive Eliot biography by Robert Crawford; *The Hyacinth Girl*, a biography of Emily Hale by Lyndall Gordon; *The Fall of a Sparrow*, the authorized biography of Vivien Haigh-Wood Eliot, by Ann Pasternak Slater; "T. S. Eliot: Into *The Waste Land*," a documentary directed by Susanna White; Volume 9 of Eliot's *Letters*, bringing the correspondence up to 1941; and, of course, the letters from Eliot to Hale. And these follow hard upon the publication of the final volume of Eliot's *Complete Prose*, the eight volumes of which amount to some 6,500 pages of text. It will be a generation at least before such resources are fully explored, before the new story of T. S. Eliot is told with reasonable fullness.

And speaking of deluges, the pace and variety of upheavals brought on by anthropogenic global warming have only increased. Local atmospheric catastrophes brought on by the big climate catastrophe have only intensified, as it has been known for decades they would. During a recent November in the northeastern United States, where I live, temperatures typical of June were frequent. The autumn leaves were unusually vibrant that year, but then whole swaths of forest in the area were brown in August due to a long drought, as though fall had come early. The same summer, drought was so extreme in Europe that normally submerged "hunger stones" were exposed in the river Elbe, bearing four-hundred-year-old inscriptions including: "See me and weep." Meanwhile, Pakistan was devastated by flooding. One upside-down season leads into another. There was no snow at all last winter. My children will probably outlive most of the glaciers and coral reefs on Earth.

This is, of course, not really a book about the Anthropocene (or whatever it is to be called now), and the litany of disasters not explicitly related to the climate crisis has kept pace with those that are. There is no still point from which to take stock of the cascading cataclysms of our day. Elections are not over once winners are chosen. It is now easier to buy an AR-15 than birth control in a large part of the United States. The Russian invasion of Ukraine is now two years old, and as I revised the book, Hamas attacked Israel, and Israel invaded Gaza, initiating a catastrophic siege killing Palestinians in the tens of thousands. Legal protections of voting rights, individual choice, and equality of opportunity are falling in rapid succession. Freedom of inquiry and representation in primary, secondary, and higher education systems is being methodically curtailed in the same US states where books are disappearing from public library shelves as fast as reactionary boards and local governments can ban and burn them. There were six mass shootings in one thirteen-day stretch last year in California alone, but every sentence I write could begin with a reference to the most recent mass shooting, as these are now daily in the United States.

I recognize a feeling of automatism in opening this conclusion with an update on the signs of apocalypse that have emerged since I began writing: new instances of crisis related to climate, government, disease, violence, and so on. Indeed, such rehearsals have become de rigeur in much contemporary nonfiction and essayistic writing. Not only do they provide a handy way to situate any new critical intervention within an immediate context of catastrophe, but they also seem responsible, like land acknowledgments. If the world as we know it is ending, it seems the most relevant context in which to conceive some attempt at writing. The trouble with these litanies is that they age poorly. New signs of the end supersede the old ones as soon as they happen, which presents a difficult challenge for writing that tries to address things as they are *right now*. Eliot meditated on a similar temporal conundrum in "The Dry Salvages," mixing a tone of admonishment with one of reassurance:

> You cannot face it steadily, but this thing is sure,
> That time is no healer: the patient is no longer here.
> [. . .]
> Fare forward, travellers! not escaping from the past
> Into different lives, or into any future;
> You are not the same people who left that station
> Or who will arrive at any terminus[.][1]

There is frustration in the present constantly and immediately becoming the past, but there is also liberation, these lines suggest, in the perpetual newness that is every moment. If such a prospect is too dizzying, there is also the grounding effect of the way the present keeps repeating itself. The video of the police murder of Tyre Nichols was released since I began writing this conclusion, now there has been a mass shooting in Prague, and authorities have already begun to clear the encampments of American university protestors of Israel's demolition of Gaza.

Better than a hasty catalogue trying and failing to stay current is a broad characterization of the problem, and for that I will invoke Bifo Berardi one more time. "Fundamentally," he writes in *Futurability*, "I think we have to . . . acknowledge that democracy is over, that political hope is dead. Forever."[2] Of course, "political hope" is something far narrower than hope itself and certainly more so than radical hope. But before working to restore the note of hope that will be the one this book ends on, I want to look at the situation directly, as Berardi does. He continues:

> Expecting the revivification of democracy and fighting for such a goal would be futile because the very conditions for the effectiveness of political reason (and particularly of democratic politics) have since dissolved. I'm not talking here of a political or military defeat, or a battle that was lost. Many times in the course of modern history the good guys have been defeated; they have resisted, have recovered and, in the end, have achieved what they needed by playing and winning the democratic game. But I think this will not happen again.

> The systemic conditions for democracy have been cancelled by prevailing irreversible processes. Irreversible is the enslavement of immaterial labour because the global labour market requires boundless competition among workers and pre-emption of any social solidarity. Irreversible is the moral and psychological misery of a generation of children who have learned more words from an electronic screen than from a human voice. Irreversible is the melting of the Arctic ice, and irreversible is the spiral of economic competition and military aggression.
>
> The conditions for democracy are two (at least): freedom and effectiveness of political volition. Both have been dismantled. Since language has been subjected to the rule of the technic, and techno-linguistic automatism has taken hold of social relations, freedom has become an empty word, and political action has grown ineffective and inconsequential. Hoping for the revivification of the values, principles and expectations of democracy is therefore a self-deception because true decision has been absorbed by the connective machine, and popular rage has been organized instead by nationalist and racist parties.[3]

This is one of the best descriptions I have found of the condition that, as suggested in the introduction, informs almost every thought I have about the work of literary analysis today and to which I felt I had to relate any writing I would do on T. S. Eliot, however remote the relation might appear at first. Eliot was of course no champion of democracy or of the solidarity of workers. Still, given Berardi's concerns with the degradation of language and a humanity losing or having lost its capacity for "conjunction," and his description of the rise of militarism and "nationalist and racist parties," the world he addresses seems not so far removed from Eliot's.[4] Indeed, Eliot might have agreed, for very different reasons, that "democracy is over, that political hope is dead." Yet neither Eliot nor Bifo, who uses a stanza from "Prufrock" as the epigraph to the first chapter of *Futurability*, settles on despair.

The centenary year of *The Waste Land* has recently passed. What are the paragraphs above but a description of the twenty-first century wasteland? The new biographies and documentary have made clearer than ever that Eliot's most famous poem is neither "a personal and wholly insignificant grouse against life" nor a piece of "social criticism," whatever he may have said about it.⁵ It is, rather, the sound made by a poet racked by a series of crises in his personal life *and* by the annihilation of the social landscape that has given meaning and a measure of predictability to the work of living. And after that, he went on writing poems and plays for another forty years. As for Berardi: "In recent years, I have published a book about the end of the future and another about suicide in the connective generation. Now I write a book about impotence. Some friends worry for me and suggest I take a vacation as they think I'm depressed. The truth is different."⁶ Whatever else we need to do with Eliot, surely this is no time to leave him alone. As I have said in several ways throughout this book, in times of such extremity we need every alliance we can find.

That is one way presentism can sound. But besides the fact that the present is always becoming the past, the past seems to matter less and less, and the pressure the future places on the present is becoming more and more relentless. Recent events in the United States highlight the limitations of the presentist approach. The bulk of this book was written in 2020–2021, in the months when the COVID pandemic and the death throes of the Trump regime combined to create an atmosphere of dread and alarm. But as I argued in the last chapter, no decisive ending to that period came. Nor has it come. For close to 50 percent of the US population, the Trump presidency continues. As I began to write this conclusion, the country seemed poised to elect a host of new political and judicial leaders committed to ensuring that it never really ends. But then the midterm elections produced a resounding defeat for Trumpism. Election deniers and white nationalists did get elected but not in the numbers most had predicted. The forces of reaction—at least on the national level—appeared to have stalled to a degree not at all evident in the months following the US Presidential Election of 2020.⁷ Things did appear to have changed somewhat, and the changes reveal the difference between an intervention aimed at resistance to immediate pressures and one that attempts to prefigure a way of being in the world. They also highlight the difference between reform and radicalism.

A satirical *New Yorker* headline immediately after the 2022 midterm election trumpeted: U.S.A. THE ENVY OF WORLD AFTER TEN BILLION DOLLARS IN CAMPAIGN ADS CHANGES ALMOST NOTHING.⁸ The United States appears locked in a perverse stasis wherein as the threats to human dignity and freedom rise, the possibility of enacting substantive change through existing institutional mechanisms recedes. The structure of the government ensures that forces of reaction will always have a disproportionate influence and that revolutionary energies will find at most a muted expression in the institutionally sanctioned voices of "progress." The greatest victory for those who seek greater equality and liberation is usually a holding operation against further subjugation, whereas when reaction gains the upper hand change can be swift and comparatively sweeping.

This is not to suggest that the immediate gains and losses experienced by individuals within such a system are inconsequential. When rights and opportunities arrive or (as is more often the case) are nullified, it can mean everything. It is, however, to say that those who aspire to more than a temporary victory in the game of giving or taking away this or that freedom are bound to be disappointed by the results of activism within such a system. This is the point at which the paths of reformism and radicalism diverge. And it is one more way to try to justify the approach I have taken in this book. Every chapter is informed by an obvious ethical commitment. Every chapter has been an exercise in using literature not to advocate for or against a discrete position but to enact that ethical commitment within a consideration of T. S. Eliot's work and life—to stay with Eliot and with the ethics, to dwell there, to see things as clearly as possible from that vantage point, and in doing so to demonstrate a way of reading and using Eliot that if it can lead to greater liberation and hope in the future it is because it is prefiguring those values now. There is, again, both reproval and consolation in the deployment of the Bhagavad Gita in "The Dry Salvages":

> At the moment which is not of action or inaction
> You can receive this: 'on whatever sphere of being
> The mind of a man may be intent
> At the time of death'—that is the one action
> (And the time of death is every moment)
> Which shall fructify in the lives of others:
> And do not think of the fruit of action.
> Fare forward.[9]

Getting somewhere ("you who think that you are voyaging"), making some meaningful intervention on behalf of the future, is impossible if the world is new in every moment. However, the poem also instructs "You shall not think 'the past is finished' / Or 'the future is before us,'"[10] which brings back the eternally important present of "Burnt Norton." What matters is what we are about in "every moment," which is a good argument for prefiguration, for making ends and means equivalent. The end of the same section of "The Dry Salvages" no longer refers to "you who think that you are voyaging" but to "voyagers": "Not fare well, / But fare forward, voyagers,"[11] which may mean that because we are probably deluded about time or teleology, about where we have been or where we are going, our charge is to act as though the voyage is our destination.

Moreover, every chapter has been an attempt to show the capacity of not only T. S. Eliot but also literature and, to dilate still further, the humanities to help us understand what we want to do and be. I hope the greatest claim made by this book is not for my method but for the ability of literary study itself, in politically perilous times, to provide an arena in which it is possible to practice values threatened, discounted, or viewed with suspicion by the forces contending for power—capital, the state, technology. Literature and literary study can and do create anarchic cooperative spaces in which people may happily assemble without having to buy or sell anything, spaces in which the nonviolent exchange of intellectual resources models the opposite of war. Anyone who has taught literature in a prison can affirm that literary study can make people free from what oppresses them as well as free to take new actions and think new thoughts. It opens imaginative pathways to distant and unfamiliar places, pathways that frequently lead to literal journeys across borders. Because it treasures ideas, variety, and complexity, it creates zones inhospitable to fascism. Literary study is a temporary autonomous zone in which one never knows just what will happen but trusts that something will, even (or especially) if it means learning an entirely new language for imagining what that could be.

Which brings me to ChatGPT. In the current academic year, most conversations in my discipline bend eventually toward this new Artificial Intelligence capable of generating (reasonably) high-quality college-level essays in response to almost any prompt typically given in humanities courses (and much, much else besides). And ChatGPT can turn these essays out in seconds. One of the besieged values of the academic humanities, and perhaps of literary study in particular, is slowness. The rise of ChatGPT is only the latest assault on slowness, but at least on the front pertaining to the production of traditional college essays, it seems destined to win, however quickly AI-detection programs and other defensive measures are developed. Speed and the absence of reflection win in the present dispensation. As Berardi writes, for the current generation, "thought is a self-defeating act because thinking slows one's reactions, and slowness makes you prey in the game in which every other player is also trying to eliminate you."[12] Writing a book on the work of T. S. Eliot will soon (if it doesn't already) require no more thought or time than it takes to enter a prompt into an AI window. The same may well be true of poetry. Given this reality—a world in which writing poems or writing about them no longer even requires human beings—simply carrying on writing about T. S. Eliot seems preposterous. I have invoked Eliot's inspirational line "For us there is only the trying" twice already, but I will resist the temptation to do so here. Not because repetition is the problem (indeed, it is nearly the point of the line) but because there are times when people have to refuse the usual terms of the challenge and create something new, as Eliot tried to do in many of the cases I have described. I don't have a ready answer to the challenge of ChatGPT, but I suspect its advent is one of those times. If it doesn't already constitute the moment when writing, and writing about writing, can be done by a robot as well as or better than by humans, that capacity is just around the corner, the experts say. That is a situation more severe than the long, slow grinding away of the status of the humanities in the face of mounting technical and financial supremacy; it sounds more like what Berardi says of the transformation of the political face of Europe: "What we in the European Union are facing is not merely provisional suspension of democracy, but the final replacement of politics with a system of techno-financial automatism."[13] In which case, working through ordinary political forms becomes a farce, as does trying to use literature as a political tool.

If literary study as we know it is finally replaced or simply run out by a regime of code, there will be no choices to make about how to proceed. At present, I could not describe how people who live by literature would continue to engage with such a world. Perhaps someone at this moment is having the necessary dream to be translated into a way forward. In the meantime, certain ends, certain ideals, could persist, including the ones on which the essays in this book are based: peace, equality, friendship, nondomination, freedom, solidarity, care, hope. Such a statement may sound like an evasion, but the same is often true of deliberately refusing the terms of a fight one is destined to lose. In the short term it might sound like losing, but it keeps the voyagers faring forward. Doing so in the face of power that reduces the number of possibilities to one or zero is itself a kind of radical thinking.

David Graeber, with whose ideas about idealism I ended my introduction, died during the time I was writing this book, which I mention not to be sentimental but rather because it provides such a vivid illustration of the way the world is always exceeding our attempts to get our intellectual arms around it. Graeber died just as the world was being subsumed in a pandemic hugely exacerbated if not caused outright by the forces of capitalist and state domination and competition he had spent his career elaborating and criticizing—a pandemic, that is, of which he would have been a uniquely valuable observer and through which he would have been a special guide. The world is so rapidly demolishing the terms on which we pursue our scholarly—or artistic or activist—projects that as soon as we arrive at some provisional account of reality, a new one is already needed. It was Eliot, after all, who wrote: "Every poem an epitaph."[14] With a world so indifferent to the descriptions we make of it, and yet always needing something to go on with, the ideals underpinning our projects are probably the best means we have to link the best of ourselves to those who will inhabit the world that will leave us behind. Such a world is a good reason to keep things open-ended, as Graeber did, especially in the aptly named *Possibilities*. "One common feature of the essays collected in this book," he wrote, "is that they are meant to keep possibilities open. They are not, in any sense, an attempt to create a single grand theory of anything—let alone, a single grand theory of everything."[15] Incompleteness, like slowness, is probably a virtue worth fighting for amid the systems of totalization and instantaneity that surround us.

    Such a position doesn't excuse all omissions, of course. The big themes I admitted to leaving out—gender, race, climate, religion—remain there at the end of this book, pointing accusing fingers. I offer the book as a tool that might be used by those who take on the challenges represented by those themes—or that might be left alone by them if it doesn't serve. No matter how much Eliot has meant to me or how much I want readers to keep encountering his work anew, I believe we stand to lose much more than just Eliot if we lose the big fights over ideals. I would rather use what I can of Eliot to help win those fights rather than to defend Eliot himself. I don't want to fight *for* T. S. Eliot. I want to fight *with* him.

Notes

Introduction

1. For his part, Eliot contributed a handful of essays, letters, and reviews to the *Spectator* from 1932 to 1940. The first was a contribution to a series, "Studies in Sanctity." Another, in 1934, was a response to the question, "What Does the Church Stand For?"
2. *Prose 5*, 169.
3. *Prose 6*, 503.
4. *Poems 1*, 179.
5. Cunningham, 51.
6. *Prose 5*, 20.
7. *Prose 6*, 664.
8. *Prose 3*, 513.
9. Atkins, 265.
10. Lowe, 913.
11. Matthews, 44.
12. https://en.oxforddictionaries.com/definition/presentism.
13. *Poems 1*, 208.
14. Berger, 11.
15. Seybold, 6.
16. Seybold, 6.
17. Seybold, 12.
18. Felski, 186.
19. Felski, 186.
20. North, 11–12.
21. North, 12 (my emphasis).
22. North, 15.
23. Castiglia, 2–3.
24. North, 7.

25. In Victorian studies, the V21 Collective has embraced presentism and idealism explicitly, as against "positivist historicism," in its manifesto. http://v21collective.org/manifesto-of-the-v21-collective-ten-theses/
26. Lagalisse, 14.
27. Lagalisse, 15.
28. North, 20.
29. Lagalisse, 11.
30. Ramnath, 5–6.
31. *Prose 4*, 163.
32. Halberstam, "The Wild."
33. *Poems 1*, 179.
34. *Prose 2*, 112.
35. *Prose 4*, 161.
36. Graeber, 2.

Chapter 1

1. *Poems 1*, 5.
2. For a detailed analysis of the poem's prehistory, inception, and development, see Jayme Stayer's astonishing book *Becoming T. S. Eliot* (2021).
3. Dorfman, 49.
4. Dorfman, 49.
5. Read "T. S. E.," 35.
6. Gordon, 96.
7. *Letters 1*, 52.
8. Crawford, 205.
9. *Letters 1*, 53.
10. *Letters 1*, 53.
11. *Poems 1*, 32.
12. *World Migration Report* 21. These figures of course predate the invasions of Ukraine by Russia (2022) and Gaza by Israel (2023), which have created huge new populations of migrants.
13. Institute on Migration, 132.
14. Crawford, 271. For more on Eliot's immersion in European finances and markets via his work at Lloyds—and the political implications of this work—see Matthew Seybold's "Astride the Dark Horse: T. S. Eliot and the Lloyds Bank Intelligence Department" and Beci Carver's "Death by Capitalism in Eliot's *The Waste Land*."
15. Abrahamian, 50.
16. The definitive work on this subject remains Jed Esty's *A Shrinking Island* (2004).
17. *Prose 6*, 714.

18. Abrahamian, 50.
19. Balibar, "Can Europe Make It?"
20. Agamben, 10.
21. Taylor, 7.
22. Scott, *Two Cheers for Anarchism* 87.
23. Taylor, 7.
24. Taylor, 9.
25. Taylor, 13.
26. Taylor, 9.
27. Deleuze and Guattari, 380.
28. Balibar, "Can Europe Make It?"
29. *Poems 1*, 5.
30. *Poems 1*, 7.
31. Ellermann, "Undocumented Migrants and Resistance."
32. *Poems 1*, 5.
33. *Poems 1*, 68.
34. *Poems 1*, 55.
35. *Poems 1*, 57.
36. *Poems 1*, 69.
37. *Poems 1*, 33, 31.
38. *Poems 1*, 31.
39. James, 75–76.
40. *Poems 1*, 760.
41. *Poems 1*, 760.
42. *Poems 1*, 101.
43. *Poems 1*, 101.
44. Those who smuggle people across borders, akin to *coyotes* in North America. I thank Rajaa Chouairi, Scott Harris, and Khanna Mandzha for directing me to the correct Arabic term.
45. *Poems 1*, 102.
46. *Poems 1*, 208.
47. *Poems 1*, 181.
48. *Poems 1*, 191.
49. *Poems 1*, 191–92.
50. Read, "T. S. E.," 48.
51. *Poems 1*, 197.
52. *Poems 1*, 197.
53. *Poems 1*, 198.
54. *Poems 1*, 201.
55. *Poems 1*, 202.
56. *Poems 1* 208–209.
57. Anzaldúa, 26, 33.

58. In a November 2023 review-essay, Marina Warner writes: "Many, many have drowned in 'the liquid cemetery' of the Mediterranean" trying to reach Europe. "The current official register puts the number at around 28,192 in the past nine years—but these are the known deaths. There are many more missing whose bodies were not found" ("No Freedom to Move").

Chapter 2

1. Gordon, 511.
2. Gordon, 513.
3. Gordon, 458.
4. May, 71–72.
5. May, 62.
6. Wallace, 162.
7. Wallace, 162.
8. May, 70.
9. Wallace, 162.
10. Wallace, 163.
11. Read, *Anarchy and Order*, 61.
12. Ward, 20.
13. Read, *Anarchy and Order*, 107–108.
14. Ward, 26.
15. Marshall, 16.
16. Bakunin, "Man, Society, and Freedom."
17. Vodovnik, 101.
18. Vodovnik, 101.
19. *Poems 1*, 191.
20. *Prose 2*, 478.
21. Unpublished letter.
22. Harding, 227.
23. Harding, 228.
24. Harding, 113, 109.
25. Harding, 123.
26. King, 220.
27. King, 221.
28. Woodcock, 242.
29. King, 218.
30. Read, *Anarchy and Order*, 57.
31. Read, "Pragmatic Anarchism," 76.
32. Goodway, 190.
33. Harding, 124.
34. Read, "T. S. E.," 33.

35. Read, "T. S. E.," 42.
36. King, 79.
37. Read, "T. S. E.," 54.
38. Read, "T. S. E.," 52–53.
39. Read, "T. S. E.," 52.
40. Read, "T. S. E.," 43.
41. Read, "T. S. E.," 51.
42. Read, "T. S. E.," 38.
43. Read, "T. S. E.," 46–47.
44. Cunningham, 51.
45. Read, *Anarchy and Order*, 86.
46. Cunningham, 55.
47. Cunningham, 56.
48. *Prose 5*, 410.
49. King, 203.
50. *Prose 6*, 820.
51. *Prose 6*, 821.
52. *Prose 6*, 820.
53. Woodcock, 212.
54. May, 66.
55. King, 254.
56. King, 276.
57. Qtd. in May, 65.
58. Ward, 29.
59. Read, *Anarchy and Order*, 108.
60. Qtd. in Gordon, 73.
61. Qtd. in Cohn, 116.
62. Cohn, 117.
63. May, 68–69.
64. Wallace, 164.
65. Wallace, 165.
66. Invisible Committee, *To Our Friends*, 16.
67. Scholl, 319.
68. May, 72.
69. Vodovnik, 121.
70. *Poems 1*, 200.
71. Read, "What Is There Left to Say?," 30.

Chapter 3

1. As for anarchists as antifascists, I am of course not referring to such recent appropriators of the term *anarchist* as "anarcho-capitalists" and "national

anarchists," who under even the most limited scrutiny are seen to be at least fascism-friendly when not espousing outright fascist positions and beliefs of their own.

2. *Eliot–Hale* March 22, 1935; April 7, 1938; January 11, 1940; January 30, 1935; December 31, 1935.

3. Gordon, 467.

4. In 2003, Ronald Schuchard memorably took "the liberty" of playfully designating Eliot a "philo-Semite" at the conclusion of an essay arguing for a reconsideration of Eliot's anti-Semitism. Controversy predictably ensued. See Schuchard, "Burbank with a Baedeker, Eliot with a Cigar: American Intellectuals, Anti-Semitism, and the Idea of Culture."

5. *Poems 1*, 207.

6. Lennard, "Fighting Fascism."

7. Murray, 10.

8. Sontag, "Fascinating Fascism."

9. Paxton, 218.

10. More detailed still is Umberto Eco's fourteen-point characterization of "Ur-Fascism." See Eco, *How to Spot a Fascist*.

11. Griffin, 26.

12. Burley, 50.

13. Burley, 48–49.

14. *Prose 3*, 545.

15. *Prose 3*, 542.

16. *Prose 3*, 544.

17. *Prose 3*, 543.

18. *Prose 3*, 334.

19. *Prose 3*, 333.

20. *Prose 3*, 660, 663.

21. *Prose 3*, 664.

22. *Prose 5*, 187, 190.

23. *Prose 5*, 425.

24. *Prose 5*, 426.

25. But then he follows by saying "there would be no excuse for violent anti-semitism here [i.e., in London], though there might be some cause, if not justification, for it in New York" (*Eliot–Hale*, February 6, 1934).

26. *Eliot–Hale*, April 27, 1934.

27. *Eliot–Hale*, March 3, 1936.

28. Surprising because it contains more criticism of Franco and the Nationalists than he ever uttered publicly: "My feelings, on the whole, are against the Rebels . . . I certainly sympathise with the people of Catalonia, and with the Basques" (*Eliot–Hale*, November 23, 1936).

29. *Prose 6*, 584. As David Chinitz points out, "*Roll Call* . . . highlights Polish rather than Jewish suffering; the incident it recounts took place before the mass

extermination of Jews in Auschwitz began. Prior to 1942, the camp held mainly Polish political prisoners, with as many as 150,000 of these interned there during the war, together with religious, ethnic, and other minorities" (*Prose* 6, 581).

30. *Prose 6*, 584.
31. *Prose 6*, 584.
32. *Prose 8*, 550.
33. *Prose 5*, 426.
34. West, 69.
35. West, 72.
36. Two English executioners, William Marwood in 1871 and later James Berry, calculated the length of rope and height of fall relative to the weight of the executed person needed to break the neck and achieve the quickest death (West, 71).
37. West, 72.
38. Orwell, 18.
39. Orwell, 900.
40. Orwell, 901.
41. Orwell, 902.
42. West, 246.
43. West, 246.
44. Arendt, 370.
45. Arendt, 373.
46. Arendt, 379.
47. Bayoumy.
48. West opens "Greenhouse with Cylamens III" saying, "It seemed a pity we were there [the Lake of Lucerne] because one of our party was attending a congress of economists. For economists are the fortune-tellers of our age . . . and though their claims are extravagant, or the world would not be as it is, they are not quite baseless" (233).
49. These Western Germans are exemplified by the "one-legged man and the child of twelve" who work in the titular greenhouse growing cyclamens: "Here in this greenhouse the trading genius of the Germans was reasserting itself in what was probably an amusing and impudent way. For it seemed likely that this greenhouse had been kept going during the war in defiance of Hitler's rules and regulations, and that it was now defying the Allies' rules and regulations" (West, 28).
50. West earlier describes the way that workers, especially women, in occupied Berlin "had to rebuild the whole organization from the ground up . . . To say [to them], 'I was at the Nuremberg trial,' would have meant nothing to any of these women, and, indeed, it would have presented them with an argument less developed than their own. There men had made a formal attack on the police state. But here these women had incarnated the argument. They were discussing the matter with their bodies as well as their minds" (159).

51. "Hans Fritzsche, Goebbels' radio chief, one of the three Nazi leaders who were acquitted at Nuremberg, had given his account of the trial in a book named *The Sword in the Scales*" (West, 234).
52. West, 250.
53. *Poems 1*, 191.

Chapter 4

1. *Poems 1*, 71.
2. Filkins, 8.
3. *Prose 5*, 184.
4. *Eliot–Hale*, 3 Mar. 1936.
5. *Prose 5*, 183.
6. *Prose 5*, 186.
7. *Eliot–Hale*, 23 Nov. 1936.
8. *Prose 5*, 380.
9. *Prose 5*, 163.
10. *Prose 5*, 187.
11. *Prose 5*, 680.
12. *Prose 5*, 398.
13. *Prose 5*, 722.
14. *Prose 5*, 722.
15. Wheatley, "Posturing for Peace."
16. Wheatley, "Posturing for Peace."
17. Wheatley, "Posturing for Peace."
18. *Prose 2*, 395.
19. Wheatley, "Posturing for Peace."
20. White, 4.
21. White, 4.
22. *Poems 1*, 56.
23. *Letters 4*, 573.
24. *Letters 4*, 573.
25. Levenson, 172.
26. Krockel, 121.
27. *Poems 1*, 70.
28. *Poems 1*, 71.
29. *Poems 1*, 59, 632.
30. *Poems 1*, 60.
31. *Poems 1*, 70–71.
32. Krockel, 119. The unsealed letters reveal that Eliot had Emily Hale consciously in mind in several of these *Waste Land* passages, especially the "hyacinth

garden" and the "friend, blood shaking my heart," revelations that decenter the war and the Verdenal story without necessarily diminishing them.
33. Cole, 81.
34. Black, 15.
35. Black, 11.
36. Krockel, 119.
37. Lockerd, 11.
38. Lockerd, 11.
39. Dudley, 116.
40. Dudley, 112.
41. Dudley, 115.
42. *Poems 1*, 59.
43. *Poems 1*, 66; Jones, 87; Pound, 816.
44. Chandran, 683.
45. Chandran, 683.
46. Berardi, *After the Future*, 31.
47. *Prose 5*, 680.

Chapter 5

1. Nelson, 4.
2. Nelson, 4.
3. Nelson, 6.
4. Nelson, 4.
5. *Poems 1*, 204.
6. Eliot, *Murder in the Cathedral*, 49.
7. Eliot, *Murder in the Cathedral*, 33, 75.
8. *Poems 1*, 199.
9. *Poems 1*, 200.
10. See Arendt, 178–79.
11. *Poems 1*, 206.
12. Eliot, *The Family Reunion*, 31, 53.
13. Eliot, *The Family Reunion*, 103.
14. Eliot, *The Family Reunion*, 98.
15. *Prose 5*, 166.
16. *Prose 3*, 286–87.
17. *Prose 1*, 512.
18. *Prose 1*, 514.
19. *Prose 1*, 634.
20. In intriguing ways, Eliot's thought anticipates the *liberation theology* that emerged in Latin America after the Second Vatican Council, which ended the same

year Eliot died, 1965. As Gustavo Gutiérrez wrote, for the Christian, "*liberation* can be applied to an understanding of history. Humankind is seen as assuming conscious responsibility for its own destiny. This understanding provides a dynamic context and broadens the horizons of the desired social changes" (Gutiérrez, 24). A fuller consideration of this linkage beckons, but it is outside my scope for now.

21. *Prose 4*, 91.

22. While he at times used *freedom* and *liberty* interchangeably, he also utilized a conceptual scheme in which liberty is the synthesis or totality of individual freedoms. Thus: "We cannot justify liberty simply in the political field, because the word means so very much more than that. Assuming that the individual has political and economic freedom, is that enough to guarantee his liberty? Liberty for the individual means, and must mean, a great deal more than that. There is freedom from the influence of environment, of heredity, of public opinion, of mass-made thought . . ." (*Prose 5*, 168).

23. *Prose 4*, 426.
24. *Prose 5*, 166.
25. Swain, "You Are the Resistance."
26. *Prose 4*, 92.
27. "Canal Boats Bill."
28. *Prose 4*, 92.
29. *Prose 5*, 170.
30. *Prose 4*, 537.
31. *Prose 5*, 169.
32. *Prose 4*, 537.
33. *Prose 4*, 427.
34. *Prose 5*, 681.
35. *Prose 5*, 170.
36. *Prose 5*, 170.

37. Gustavo Gutiérrez again echoes and extends such ideas. Liberation theology has the capacity, he writes, to avoid "two pitfalls . . . first, *idealist* or *spiritualist* approaches, which are nothing but ways of evading a harsh and demanding reality, and second, shallow analyses and programs of short-term effect initiated under the pretext of meeting immediate needs" (Gutiérrez, 25).

38. Qtd. in Jun 52. Both Eliot and Goldman thus anticipate Gutiérrez and another principle of liberation theology: "St. Paul," wrote Gutiérrez, "asserts not only that Christ liberated us; he also tells us that he did it in order that we might be free. Free for what? Free to love" (Gutiérrez, 24).

39. Jun, 52.
40. Qtd. in Jun, 54.
41. Jun, 52.

42. Bakunin, "Man, Society, and Freedom." It is worth noting how much Bakunin here sounds like the Lutheran anti-Nazi dissident Dietrich Bonhoeffer,

who wrote that "in the language of the Bible, freedom is not something man has for himself but something he has for others. . . . It is not a possession, a presence, an object, . . . but a relationship and nothing else. In truth, freedom is a relationship between two persons. Being free means 'being free for the other,' because the other has bound me to him. Only in relationship with the other am I free" (Gutiérrez, 24).

43. Jun, 52.
44. Jun, 53.
45. Whitman, 414.
46. Thoreau, 765.
47. *Prose 5*, 170.
48. *Prose 4*, 426.
49. Goodman, 57.
50. *Prose 4*, 426.
51. *Prose 4*, 426.
52. *Prose 4*, 427.
53. *Poems 1*, 206.

Chapter 6

1. Qtd. in Scholl, 325.
2. Scholl, 325.
3. Qtd. in Scholl, 324.
4. Blumenfeld, 245.
5. Lennard, "Fighting Fascism."
6. Lennard, "Fighting Fascism."
7. Espada, 26.
8. Slaughter, "Occupy Wall Street."
9. Lennard, "Fighting Fascism."
10. Thanks in large part to the work of Megan Quigley, who organized a cluster called "Reading *The Waste Land* with the #MeToo Generation," for the journal *Modernism/modernity*.
11. Smith, 160.
12. Matthiessen, 141.
13. Matthiessen, 141.
14. Qtd. in Matthiessen, 141.
15. Shakespeare, *Coriolanus*, 1.1.4–11.
16. Invisible Committee, 45.
17. *Coriolanus*, 1.1.49, 61–62, 68–69.
18. *Coriolanus*, 1.1.159–61.
19. Invisible Committee, 49.

20. See, for instance, the Introduction to Scott's *Seeing Like a State*.
21. *Coriolanus*, 1.2.221.
22. Invisible Committee, 44.
23. Burley, 25.
24. Burley, 25.
25. *Coriolanus*, 2.3.15–22.
26. *Coriolanus*, 2.3.34–37.
27. *Coriolanus*, 2.3.39–43.
28. *Coriolanus*, 2.3.45.
29. *Coriolanus*, 5.6.128–129.
30. *Coriolanus*, 5.6.119–121.
31. Writers for the 99%, 26–27.
32. Invisible Committee, 48.
33. Writers for the 99%, 27.
34. Writers for the 99%, 25.
35. *Coriolanus*, 3.1.33–35.
36. Chernaik, "I Banish You."
37. *Poems 1*, 818.
38. *Poems 1*, 819.
39. *Poems 1*, 132.
40. *Coriolanus*, 2.1.251–57.
41. Aakanksha Virkar identified how much Eliot's descriptions of Coriolanus resemble the statue of Beethoven by Max Klinger in her paper "Nietzsche, Max Klinger and Eliot's 'Triumphal March,'" presented at the International T. S. Eliot Society annual meeting, 25 September 2022. Beethoven's Coriolan Overture, Op. 62 was also in Eliot's mind as he composed his own *Coriolan* poems.
42. *Poems 1*, 132.
43. *Poems 1*, 131.
44. *Poems 1*, 131–132.
45. Jaffe, 139.
46. Verter, 107.
47. *Poems 1*, 131–132.
48. *Poems 1*, 134.
49. *Poems 1*, 133.
50. *Poems 1*, 133.
51. *Poems 1*, 818.
52. See, for instance, Arendt, 178–80.
53. *Coriolanus*, 5.5.4.
54. *Poems 1*, 162.
55. *Poems 1*, 162.
56. Scott, *Two Cheers for Anarchism*, xv–xvi.
57. Writers for the 99%, 11.

58. Rosen, 8.
59. Robbins, 30.
60. *Poems 1*, 135.
61. That is, until protests at an increasing number of US universities against the Israeli invasion of Gaza. These seemed to be reaching their maximum size and intensity and meeting with a wave of state suppression as I reviewed the manuscript.
62. Benjamin, 193.

Chapter 7

1. Lear, 103.
2. Lear, 104.
3. Dickey, 452.
4. Dickey, 451.
5. Lear, 71.
6. *Poems 1*, 188.
7. Dickey, 434.
8. Lear, 69.
9. Lear, 70.
10. Lear, 71.
11. Lear, 73.
12. Lear, 74.
13. *Poems 1*, 191.
14. Gordon, 356.
15. *Poems 1*, 204.
16. Lear, 73, 75.
17. Gordon, 398.
18. Lear, 2.
19. Here I quote directly from the numbered list in Lear's book.
20. Lear, 93–94.
21. Lear, 94.
22. *Prose 5*, 663.
23. *Prose 5*, 661.
24. *Prose 5*, 663.
25. *Prose 5*, 661.
26. *Prose 5*, 663.
27. *Eliot–Hale,* January 13, 1939.
28. *Eliot–Hale* February 3, 1939.
29. *Eliot–Hale,* February 10, 1939.
30. Gordon, 353.

31. Gordon, 353.
32. Gordon, 355.
33. *Poems 1*, 189.
34. *Poems 1*, 187.
35. *Poems 1*, 189.
36. *Poems 1*, 187.
37. *Eliot–Hale*, March 10, 1939.
38. Dickey, 447.
39. Dickey, 445.
40. Dickey, 435.
41. Dickey, 438.
42. *Eliot–Hale*, Eliot's statement November 25, 1960.
43. Dickey, 439.
44. Dickey, 441.
45. Eliot, *The Family Reunion*, 111.
46. Eliot, *The Family Reunion*, 107.
47. *Eliot–Hale*, September 4, 1939.
48. *Eliot–Hale*, September 8, 1939.
49. *Eliot–Hale*, September 13, 1939.
50. *Eliot–Hale*, December 28, 1939.
51. Castiglia, 4.
52. Ehrenreich, "How Do You Know When Society Is about to Fall Apart?"
53. *Poems 1*, 191.

Conclusion

1. *Poems 1*, 197.
2. Berardi, *Futurability*, 39.
3. Berardi, *Futurability*, 42–43.
4. *Conjunction* is the freer and less manageable counterpart of the superficial *connection*, for Berardi: "Conjunction is the meeting and fusion of rounded and irregular forms that infuse in a manner that is imprecise, unrepeatable, imperfect, and continuous. Connection is the punctual and repeatable interaction of algorithmic functions, straight lines and points that juxtapose perfectly and are inserted and removed in discrete modes of interaction" (*After the Future* 40).
5. Eliot, *The Waste Land*, 1.
6. Berardi, *Futurability*, 61.
7. Of course, since then Trump has quoted Hitler multiple times in his campaign speeches, promising to root out the "vermin" of dissent and to close the door on immigrants "poisoning the blood of our country," and affirmed that

he would rule as a dictator, and his approval has only increased (Kim, Layne, Sherman).
    8. Borowitz.
    9. *Poems 1,* 198.
    10. *Poems 1,* 197–98.
    11. *Poems 1,* 198.
    12. Berardi, *Futurability,* 46.
    13. Berardi, *Futurability,* 42.
    14. *Poems,* 208.
    15. Graeber, 1.

Bibliography

Abrahamian, Atossa Araxia. "The Right to Belong," *New York Review of Books*, December 17, 2020.
Agamben, Giorgio. *Homo Sacer: Sovereign Power and Bare Life*, trans. Daniel Heller-Roazen. Stanford, CA: Stanford University Press, 1998.
Andrews, Charles. *Writing against War: Literature, Activism, and the British Peace Movement*. Evanston, IL: Northwestern University Press, 2017.
Arendt, Hannah. *The Portable Hannah Arendt*. Edited by Peter Baehr. New York: Penguin, 2000.
Atkins, Hazel. "Raising *The Rock*: The Importance of T. S. Eliot's Pageant-Play." *Christianity and Literature* 62, no. 2 (Winter 2013): 261–82.
Bakunin, Mikhail. "Man, Society, and Freedom." 1871. https://www.marxists.org/reference/archive/bakunin/works/1871/man-society.htm.
Balibar, Etienne. "Can Europe Make It? Borderland Europe and the Challenge of Migration." *Open Democracy*, September 8, 2015, https://www.opendemocracy.net/en/can-europe-make-it/borderland-europe-and-challenge-of-migration/.
Bayoumy, Yara, and Kathy Gilsinan. "A Reformed White Nationalist Says the Worst Is Yet to Come," *The Atlantic*, August 6, 2019. https://www.theatlantic.com/politics/archive/2019/08/conversation-christian-picciolini/595543/.
Benjamin, Walter. *Illuminations: Essays and Reflections*, edited by Hannah Arendt. Translated by Harry Zohn. New York: Schocken Books, 1969.
Berardi, Franco "Bifo." *After the Future*. Edited by Gary Genosko and Nicholas Thoburn. Translated by Arianna Bove, Melinda Cooper, Erik Empson, Enrico Giuseppina Mecchia, and Tiziana Terranova. Oakland, CA: AK Press, 2001.
Berardi, Franco "Bifo." *Futurability: The Age of Impotence and the Horizon of Possibility*. New York: Verso, 2019.
Berger, John. *Ways of Seeing*. London: British Broadcasting Corporation and Penguin, 1972.
Black, Ezekiel. "Mouthlessness and Ineffability in World War I Poetry and *The Waste Land*." *War, Literature, and the Arts* 26, no. 1: 1–17.

Blumenfeld, Jacob. "Postface," *The Anarchist Turn*, edited by Jacob Blumenfeld, Chiara Bottici, and Simon Critchley, 235–45. London: Pluto, 2013.

Borowitz, Andy. "U.S.A. the Envy of World after Ten Billion Dollars in Campaign Ads Changes Almost Nothing." *The New Yorker*, November 9, 2022. https://www.newyorker.com/humor/borowitz-report/usa-the-envy-of-world-after-ten-billion-dollars-in-campaign-ads-changes-almost-nothing.

Burley, Shane. *Fascism Today: What It Is and How to End It*. Oakland, CA: AK Press, 2017.

Burley, Shane. *Why We Fight: Essays on Fascism, Resistance, and Surviving the Apocalypse*. Oakland, CA: AK Press, 2021.

"Canal Boats Bill," *HC Deb 31 January 1930 vol 234 cc1385-463* https://api.parliament.uk/historic-hansard/commons/1930/jan/31/canal-boats-bill.

Carver, Beci. "Death by Capitalism in Eliot's *The Waste Land*," *Textual Practice* 36, no. 5 (2022): 831–49.

Castiglia, Christopher. *The Practices of Hope: Literary Criticism in Disenchanted Times*. New York: New York University Press, 2017.

Chandran, K. Narayana. "'Shantih' in The Waste Land," *American Literature* 61, no. 4 (1989): 681–83.

Chernaik, Warren. "'I Banish You': Shakespeare's *Coriolanus*," Shakespeare Theatre Company, https://www.shakespearetheatre.org/watch-listen/i-banish-you-shakespeares-coriolanus/.

Cohn, Jesse. "What Is Anarchist Literary Theory?" *Anarchist Studies* 15, no. 2 (2007): 115–31.

Cole, Sarah. *At the Violet Hour: Modernism and Violence in England and Ireland*. Oxford: Oxford University Press, 2012.

Cosgrove, Shady E. "Reading for Peace? Literature as Activism—an Investigation into New Literary Ethics and the Novel." *Activating Human Rights and Peace*, Centre for Peace and Social Justice, Southern Cross University, 2008. https://ro.uow.edu.au/creartspapers/82/.

Crawford, Robert. *Young Eliot: From St. Louis to* The Waste Land. New York: Farrar, Straus, and Giroux, 2015.

Cunningham, Valentine. *Spanish Front: Writers on the Civil War*. Oxford: Oxford University Press, 1986.

Deleuze, Gilles and Guattari, Félix. *A Thousand Plateaus: Capitalism and Schizophrenia*. Translated by Brian Massumi. Minneapolis, MN: University of Minnesota Press, 1987.

Dickey, Frances. "May the Record Speak: The Correspondence of T. S. Eliot and Emily Hale," *Twentieth-Century Literature* 66, no. 4 (December 2020): 431–62.

Dorfman, Ariel. "Songs of Loss and Revolution," Review of *The Penguin Book of Migration Literature: Departures, Arrivals, Generations, Returns*. New York Review of Books, December 3, 2020. https://www.nybooks.com/articles/2020/12/03/songs-of-loss-and-reinvention/.

Dudley, Jack. "Transcendence and the End of Modernist Aesthetics: David Jones's *In Parenthesis*," *Renascence* 65, no. 2 (2013): 103–24.
Eco, Umberto. *How to Spot a Fascist*. 1997. London: Harvill Secker, 2020.
Ehrenreich, Ben. "How Do You Know When Society Is About to Fall Apart? Meet the Scholars Who Study Civilizational Collapse." https://www.nytimes.com/2020/11/04/magazine/societal-collapse.html.
Eliot, T. S. *The Complete Prose: The Critical Edition*. Vols. 1–8: 1905–1965. Edited by Ronald Schuchard, Jewel Spears Brooker, David E. Chinitz, Anthony Cuda, Frances Dickey, Jennifer Formichelli, Jason Harding, Iman Javadi, and Jayme Stayer. Baltimore: Johns Hopkins University Press, 2014–2019.
Eliot, T. S. *The Family Reunion*. 1939. New York: Harvest-Harcourt, 1967.
Eliot, T. S. *Letters*. Vols. 1–9: 1898–1941. Edited by Valerie Eliot, John Haffenden, and Hugh Haughton. London: Faber, 2009–2021.
Eliot, T. S. *The Letters of T. S. Eliot to Emily Hale*. Edited by John Haffenden. Estate of T. S. Eliot. https://tseliot.com/the-eliot-hale-letters.
Eliot, T. S. *Murder in the Cathedral*. New York: Harcourt, Brace, 1963.
Eliot, T. S. *Poems: The Annotated Text*. Volume I: Collected & Uncollected Poems. Edited by Christopher Ricks and Jim McCue. Baltimore: Johns Hopkins University Press, 2015.
Eliot, T. S. *The Waste Land*. Edited by Valerie Eliot. Centenary ed. London: Faber, 2022.
Ellerman, Antje. "Undocumented Migrants and Resistance in the Liberal State," *Politics and Society* 38, no. 3 (2010), https://doi.org/10.1177/0032329210373072.
Espada, Martín. *Rebellion Is the Circle of a Lover's Hands*. Willimantic, CT: Curbstone Books, 1995.
Felski, Rita. *The Limits of Critique*. Chicago: University of Chicago Press, 2015.
Filkins, Dexter. "What Is It Good For?" Review of *War: How Conflict Shaped Us*, by Margaret MacMillan. *New York Times Book Review*, November 29, 2020.
Goodman, Paul. *Drawing the Line Once Again: Paul Goodman's Anarchist Writings*. Oakland, CA: PM Press, 2010.
Goodway, David. *Anarchist Seeds Beneath the Snow: Left-Libertarian Thought and British Writers from William Morris to Colin Ward*. Oakland, CA: PM Press, 2011.
Gordon, Lyndall. *T. S. Eliot: An Imperfect Life*. New York: W. W. Norton, 1998.
Graeber, David. *Possibilities: Essays on Hierarchy, Rebellion, and Desire*. Oakland, CA: AK Press, 2007.
Griffin, Roger. *The Nature of Fascism*. London: Routledge, 1991.
Gutiérrez, Gustavo. *A Theology of Liberation*. Maryknoll, NY: Orbis Books, 1988.
Halberstam, Jack. "The Wild: The Aesthetics of Queer Anarchy," https://www.youtube.com/watch?v=ZDP4lcoZ9s4.
Hankins, Gabriel. *Interwar Modernism and the Liberal World Order: Offices, Institutions, and Aesthetics after 1919*. Cambridge: Cambridge University Press, 2019.

Harding, Jason. *The* Criterion: *Cultural Politics and Periodical Networks in Inter-War Britain*. Oxford: Oxford University Press, 2002.

Institute on Migration. *International Migration Law: Glossary on Migration*, no. 34. International Organization for Migration, 2019. https://publications.iom.int/system/files/pdf/iml_34_glossary.pdf.

International Organization for Migration. https://www.iom.int/key-migration-terms.

Invisible Committee, The. *To Our Friends*. Translated by Robert Hurley. South Pasadena, CA: Semiotext(e) Intervention Series, 2014.

Jaffe, Sarah. "Bloody Sunday at Fifty," *Dissent*, Spring 2022, 137–41.

James, Henry. *Portraits of Places*. Boston: Houghton, Mifflin, 1883.

Jones, David. *In Parenthesis*. 1937. New York: New York Review Books, 2003.

Jun, Nathan. "Freedom." *Anarchism: A Conceptual Approach*. Edited by Benjamin Franks, Nathan Jun, and Leonard Williams, 44–59. London: Routledge, 2018.

Killjoy, Margaret. "Margaret Killjoy on an Anarchist Approach to Prepping in an Age of Climate Change." *It's Going Down*. Podcast, July 17, 2021. https://itsgoingdown.org/margaret-killjoy-on-an-anarchist-approach-to-prepping-in-an-age-of-climate-change/.

Kim, Soo Rin, and Lalee Ibssa. "Trump Compares Political Opponents to 'Vermin' Who He Will 'Root Out,' Alarming Historians." ABC News, November 13, 2023. https://abcnews.go.com/Politics/trump-compares-political-opponents-vermin-root-alarming-historians/story?id=104847748.

King, James. *The Last Modern: A Life of Herbert Read*. London: Weidenfeld and Nicolson, 1990.

Krockel, Carl. *War Trauma and English Modernism: T. S. Eliot and D. H. Lawrence*. London: Palgrave Macmillan, 2011.

Lagalisse, Erica. *Occult Features of Anarchism: With Attention to the Conspiracy of Kings and the Conspiracy of the Peoples*. Oakland, CA: PM Press, 2019.

Layne, Nathan. "Trump Repeats 'Poisoning the Blood' Anti-immigrant Remark." Reuters, December 16, 2023. https://www.reuters.com/world/us/trump-repeats-poisoning-blood-anti-immigrant-remark-2023-12-16/.

Lear, Jonathan. *Radical Hope: Ethics in the Face of Cultural Devastation*. Cambridge, MA: Harvard University Press, 2006.

Lennard, Natasha. "Fighting Fascism, Rejecting Liberalism: A Conversation with Natasha Lennard." Podcast audio. *It's Going Down*. Channel Zero, October 22, 2019. https://itsgoingdown.org/fighting-fascism-rejecting-liberalism-a-conversation-with-natasha-lennard/.

Levenson, Michael. *A Genealogy of Modernism: A Study of English Literary Doctrine 1908–1922*. Cambridge: Cambridge University Press, 1984.

Lewis, C. S. "Letter to Paul Elmer More," in *The Collected Letters of C. S. Lewis, Vol. 2: Books, Broadcasts and War 1931–49*, edited by Walter Hooper, 163. New York: HarperCollins 2006.

Lockerd, Benjamin, ed. *T. S. Eliot and the Christian Tradition*. Lanham, MD: Fairleigh Dickinson University Press, 2014.

Lockerd, Martin. "Into Cleanness Leaping: Brooke, Eliot, and the Decadent Body," *Journal of Modern Literature* 36, no. 3 (2013): 1–13.
Lowe, Peter. "Churches Built and Churches Bombed: T. S. Eliot's Vision of National Loss and Spiritual Renewal." *English Studies* 94, no. 8 (2013): 908–30.
Marshall, Peter. *Demanding the Impossible: A History of Anarchism*. Oakland, CA: PM Press, 2010.
Matthews, Steven. "'You Can See Some Eagles. And Hear the Trumpets': The Literary and Political Hinterland of T. S. Eliot's *Coriolan*." *Journal of Modern Literature* 36, no. 2: 44–60.
Matthiessen, F. O. *The Achievement of T. S. Eliot: An Essay on the Nature of Poetry*. 3rd ed. Oxford: Oxford University Press, 1958.
May, Todd. "Friendship as Resistance." *The Anarchist Turn*, edited by Jacob Blumenfeld, Chiara Bottici, and Simon Critchley, 59–79. London: Pluto Press, 2013.
McIntire, Gabrielle. *Modernism, Memory, and Desire: T. S. Eliot and Virginia Woolf*. Cambridge: Cambridge University Press, 2008.
Murray, Douglas. "Far Wrong: If Everyone Is a Fascist, then Nobody Is." *Spectator* (USA), October 2019, 10.
Nelson, Maggie. *On Freedom: Four Songs of Care and Constraint*. Minneapolis: Graywolf Press, 2021.
North, Joseph. *Literary Criticism: A Concise Political History*. Cambridge, MA: Harvard University Press, 2017.
Orwell, George. *Essays*. Edited by John Carey and Peter Davison. London: Everyman, 2002.
Paxton, Robert. *The Anatomy of Fascism*. New York: Vintage Books, 2005.
Pound, Ezra. *Cantos*. New York: New Directions, 1998.
Quigley, Megan. "Reading *The Waste Land* with the #MeToo Generation," *Modernism/modernity* Print Plus, March 4, 2019. https://modernismmodernity.org/forums/reading-waste-land-metoo.
Ramnath, Maia. Foreword. *The Operating System: An Anarchist Theory of the Modern State* by Eric Laursen, 1–7. Oakland, CA: AK Press, 2021.
Read, Herbert. *Anarchy and Order: Essays in Politics*. Boston: Beacon, 1971.
Read, Herbert. "Pragmatic Anarchism," *Encounter* 30, no. 1 (January 1968): 54–61.
Read, Herbert. "T. S. E.—A Memoir," *The Sewanee Review* 74, no. 1 (1966): 31–57.
Read, Herbert. "What Is There Left to Say?" *Encounter*, no. 109 (October 1962): 29–30.
Robbins, Michael. "Apocalypse Nowish: The Sense of an Ending." *Harper's Magazine*, December 2022, 25–30.
Rogers, Gayle. *Modernism and the New Spain: Britain, Cosmopolitan Europe, and Literary History*. Oxford: Oxford University Press, 2014.
Rosen, Jody. "White Noise." *New York Times Magazine*, December 25, 2022, 7–10.
Scholl, Christian. "Prefiguration," *Keywords for Radicals: The Contested Vocabulary of Late-Capitalist Struggle*, edited by Kelly Fritsch, Clare O'Connor, and AK Thompson, 319–25. Oakland, CA: AK Press, 2016.

Schuchard, Ronald. "Burbank with a Baedeker, Eliot with a Cigar: American Intellectuals, Anti-Semitism, and the Idea of Culture." *Modernism/modernity* 10, no. 1 (2003): 1–26.

Scott, James C. *Domination and the Arts of Resistance: Hidden Transcripts*. New Haven, CT: Yale University Press, 1990.

Scott, James C. *Two Cheers for Anarchism: Six Easy Pieces on Autonomy, Dignity, and Meaningful Work and Play*. Princeton, NJ: Princeton University Press, 2012.

Scott, James C. *Seeing Like a State: How Certain Schemes to Improve the Human Condition Have Failed*. New Haven, CT: Yale University Press, 1999. https://theanarchistlibrary.org/library/james-c-scott-seeing-like-a-state.

Seybold, Matthew. "Astride the Dark Horse: T. S. Eliot and the Lloyds Bank Intelligence Department." *T. S. Eliot Studies Annual* 1 (2017): 131–55.

Seybold, Matthew. Review of *Interwar Modernism and the Liberal World Order: Offices, Institutions, and Aesthetics after 1919*, by Gabriel Hankins. *Time Present* 102 (Fall 2020): 6, 12.

Shakespeare, William. *The Tragedy of Coriolanus*, edited by Harry Levin. London: Penguin Books, 1956.

Sherman, Amy. "In Context: Donald Trump Was Asked if He Will Be a Dictator if Reelected. Here's What He Said." *Politifact*. December 7, 2023. https://www.politifact.com/article/2023/dec/07/donald-trump-was-asked-if-he-will-be-a-dictator-if/.

Slaughter, Anne-Marie. "Occupy Wall Street and the Arab Spring." *Atlantic*, October 7, 2011. https://www.theatlantic.com/international/archive/2011/10/occupy-wall-street-and-the-arab-spring/246364/.

Smidt, Kristian. *Poetry and Belief in the Work of T. S. Eliot*. London: Routledge Library Editions, 2017.

Smith, Grover. *T. S. Eliot's Poetry and Plays: A Study in Sources and Meaning*. 3rd Impression. Chicago: University of Chicago Press, 1960.

Sontag, Susan. "Fascinating Fascism." *New York Review of Books*, February 6, 1975. https://www.nybooks.com/articles/1975/02/06/fascinating-fascism/.

Stayer, Jayme. *Becoming T. S. Eliot: The Rhetoric of Voice and Audience in* Inventions of the March Hare. Baltimore: Johns Hopkins University Press, 2021.

Swain, Sean. "You Are the Resistance." Final Straw Radio Podcast, April 5, 2020. https://archive.org/details/youaretheresistance001/youaretheresistance20200405.mp3.

Taylor, Becky. *Another Darkness, Another Dawn: A History of Gypsies, Roma and Travellers*. London: Reaktion Books, 2014.

Thoreau, Henry David. *Walden and Other Writings*. New York: Modern Library, 1992.

V21 Collective. "Manifesto." http://v21collective.org/manifesto-of-the-v21-collective-ten-theses/.

Verter, Mitchell Cowen. "Undoing Patriarchy, Subverting Politics: Anarchism as a Practice of Care." *The Anarchist Turn*, edited by Jacob Blumenfeld, Chiara Bottici, and Simon Critchley, 101–10. London: Pluto Press, 2013.

Virkar, Aakanksha. "Nietzsche, Max Klinger, and Eliot's 'Triumphal March.'" 43rd Annual Meeting of the International T. S. Eliot Society, September 25, 2022.

Vodovnik, Žiga. *A Living Spirit of Revolt: The Infrapolitics of Anarchism*. Oakland, CA: PM Press, 2013.

Wallace, Simon. "Friendship," *Keywords for Radicals: The Contested Vocabulary of Late-Capitalist Struggle*, edited by Kelly Fritsch, Clare O'Connor, and AK Thompson, 159–65. Oakland, CA: AK Press 2016.

Ward, Dana. "Art and Anarchy: Herbert Read's Aesthetic Politics." *Re-Reading Read: New Views on Herbert Read*, edited by Michael Paraskos, 20–33. London: Freedom Press, 2007.

Warner, Marina. "No Freedom to Move." *New York Review of Books*, November 23, 2023. https://www.nybooks.com/articles/2023/11/23/no-freedom-to-move-the-edge-of-the-plain-crawford/.

West, Rebecca. *A Train of Powder: Six Reports on The Problem of Guilt and Punishment in Our Time*. Chicago: Ivan R. Dee, 1955.

Wheatley, David. "Posturing for Peace." Review of *101 Poems Against War*, edited by Paul Keegan and Matthew Hollis. *The Guardian*, May 23, 2003. https://www.theguardian.com/books/2003/may/24/featuresreviews.guardianreview8.

White, R. S. *AUMLA: Journal of the Australian Universities Language and Literature Association*. 2009: 4.

Whitman, Walt. "By the Roadside," *Poetry and Prose*. New York: Library of America, 1982.

Whittier-Ferguson, John. *Mortality and Form in Late Modernist Literature*. Cambridge University Press, 2014.

Woodcock, George. *Herbert Read: The Stream and the Source*. Montreal: Black Rose Books, 1972.

World Migration Report. United Nations. International Organization for Migration. https://migrationnetwork.un.org/resources/world-migration-report-2022.

Writers for the 99%. *Occupying Wall Street: The Inside Story of an Action that Changed America*. New York: OR Books, 2011.

Index

92nd Street Young Men's and Young Women's Hebrew Association, 63
101 Poems Against War (Keegan and Hollis), 76–77, 83

Abrahamian, Atossa Araxia, 25
Action Francaise, 91
activism, 7, 9, 12, 13, 106, 115, 150
After the Future (Berardi), 127
Agamben, Giorgio, 27, 30, 31
Ahmad, Dohra, 20
anarchism/anarchy, 7, 8, 41–48 49–50, 53, 57, 96–97, 99, 113, 151, 159–60n1
anarchists, 6, 47, 55, 99, 100, 159–60n1; *See also* Mikhail Bakunin, Alexander Berkman, Dorothy Day, Emma Goldman, David Graeber, Margaret Killjoy, Maia Ramnath, Herbert Read, Sean Swain, George Woodcock
Anatomy of Fascism, The (Paxton), 57
Andrews, Charles, 76
Anthropocene, 146
Antifa, 58, 100
antifascism, 2, 12, 55–69, 74, 159n1
antisemitism, 5, 6, 32, 48, 55–56, 58, 59, 62–65
Anzaldúa, Gloria, 36
Apel (Roll Call), 63

Arab Spring, 106, 107
Arendt, Hannah, 56–58, 67–70, 84, 89–90, 122
Arnold, Matthew, 43
Art and Letters, 45
Artificial Intelligence, 151–52
Atkins, Hazel, 7
Atwood, Margaret, 71
Auden, W. H., 7, 13, 46
Auschwitz, 63, 161n29

Bakunin, Mikhail, 41, 42, 53, 55, 91, 97–98, 164n42
Balibar, Etienne, 26, 29, 37
Baudelaire, Charles, 13, 16
Becket, Thomas à, 89
Beckett, Samuel, 83
Benjamin, Walter, 57, 126
Berardi, Franco "Bifo," 85, 127, 147–49, 151–52; conjunction, 168n4
Berger, John, 9
Berkman, Alexander, 42, 55
Bey, Hakim, 104
Bhagavad Gita, 150
Black, Ezekiel, 80, 82
Black Lives Matter, 100, 103, 107, 111, 123, 128
Bloody Sunday, 121
Blue Lives Matter, 128
Blumenfeld, Jacob, 104

Borderlands/La Frontera (Anzaldúa), 36
Bouazizi, Mohammed, 106
British Union of Fascists, 64
Brooke, Rupert, 77, 80–81
Browne, E. Martin, 8
Burley, Shane, 58, 114

camps, 20, 24, 27, 36, 37, 63, 68
Canal Boats Bill, 94
Carver, Beci, 156n14
Castiglia, Christopher, 10, 143
Cats, 4
Chandran, K. Narayana, 84
Charlottesville, Virginia, 55
Chernaik, Warren, 119
classicism, 41, 48, 50
ChatGPT, 151–52
Chinitz, David E., 7, 13, 160n29
Christianity, 8, 33, 43, 47, 64, 89, 164n20, 164n38; Eliot's 5, 7, 8, 16, 23, 31, 59, 61, 62, 74–75, 92, 123, 132, 134; Christian pacifism, 75; Christian Socialists, 60
Church of England (Anglicanism), 2, 6, 32, 34, 46, 52
Cohn, Jesse, 49
Cole, Sarah, 80
Colson, Daniel, 49
communism, 43, 46, 48, 59–62, 93, 110, 126
Congress of the United States, 118, 126
conservatism, 1–4, 6–7, 51, 57, 61
Coriolanus (film), 107, 112, 120
Coriolanus (play), 105, 107, 109–16, 118–22, 125–26
Coriolanus, Caius Marcius, 110, 113, 114, 116, 119–22, 124–26; in *The Waste Land*, 80
Cosgrove, Shady, 76
COVID-19, 88, 93, 99, 128, 149

Crawford, Robert, 22, 25, 145
Criterion, The, 8, 24, 26, 43, 45, 46, 60, 71, 137–38, 140. *See also* Eliot, Thomas Stearns: works: *Criterion* Commentaries
Crow people, 129–37, 139, 141, 143, 144
Culture and Anarchy (Arnold), 43
Cunard, Nancy, 46

Dante, 19, 31, 134
Danticat, Edwidge, 20
Day, Dorothy, 42
Deleuze, Gilles, 28, 29
democracy, 59, 63, 69, 70, 119, 124, 128, 144, 147–48, 152; direct, 105
Democratic Party, 105, 113, 118
Dickens, Charles, 108
Dickey, Frances, 130, 131, 141
Dorfman, Ariel, 20–21
Dudley, Jack, 81–82, 83
Dylan, Bob, 6

ecology, 15, 76, 78
Education through Art (Read), 44
Ehrenreich, Ben, 144
Eliot After The Waste Land (Crawford), 145
Eliot Now (Quigley and Chinitz), 7
Eliot, Thomas Stearns, works: "Burnt Norton," 3, 14, 34, 150; "Christianity and Communism," 93; *Confidential Clerk, The*, 48; *Coriolan*, 2, 8, 105–6, 107, 109, 115, 119–22, 166n41. *See also* "Difficulties of a Statesman" and "Triumphal March"; *Criterion* Commentaries, 47, 60–61, 74, 75, 91, 93; "Difficulties of a Statesman," 104, 105, 121–23, 125; "Dry Salvages, The," 35, 53, 145, 147, 150–51; "East Coker," 34, 69,

130, 131, 133–35, 137–40, 144; *Family Reunion, The*, 90, 133–35, 137, 140; *Four Quartets*, 4–5, 20, 34, 36, 49, 89, 109, 130–32, 134, 138, 140. *See also* "Burnt Norton," "Dry Salvages," "East Coker," "Little Gidding"; "Gerontion," 31; "The Hollow Men," 4; *The Idea of a Christian Society*, 74, 75; "Journey of the Magi," 20, 32, 34; "Last Words," 137–38; Letters to Emily Hale. *See* Hale, Emily: Eliot's letters to; "The Literature of Fascism," 59–60; "Little Gidding," 9, 35, 56, 88, 90, 98, 134; "The Love Song of J. Alfred Prufrock," 2, 4, 19–20, 24, 29–30, 31, 148; *Murder in the Cathedral*, 89, 123; "Notes on the Way III," 93, 94, 98; Preface to *Apel (Roll Call)*, 63; *Prufrock and Other Observations*, 19, 80; "Reflections on *Vers Libre*," 92; "Report on the Ethics of Kant's *Critique of Practical Reason*," 92; *The Rock*, 2, 7–8, 109, 123–24; "Tradition and the Individual Talent," 16, 24; "Triumphal March," 104, 105, 109–10, 119–21, 122–23, 166n41; *The Waste Land*, 2, 4, 20, 21, 24, 25, 30–32, 71–85 passim, 108–9, 148, 156n14, 165n10
Eliot, Valerie (née Fletcher), 39, 130, 132
Eliot, Vivien (née Haigh-Wood), 45, 140, 141, 145
Ellermann, Antje, 30
Ellison, Ralph, 6
Engler, Mark and Paul, 104
equality, 4, 7, 15, 16, 17, 39–42, 49, 50, 53, 97–98, 100, 105, 106, 124, 146, 150, 152. *See also* inequality
Espada, Martín, 105

Europe, 43, 46, 48, 57, 58, 60, 62, 84, 92, 107, 109, 146, 152; and migration, 23, 24–29, 31, 33, 36–37, 158n58; in Eliot's imagination, 19, 20, 22–26, 29–32, 34, 60, 92, 132, 137–38, 156n14

Faber and Faber, 45, 47, 76, 81
Facebook, 40
Fall of a Sparrow, The (Pasternak-Slater), 145
fascism, 1, 4, 5–7, 11, 41, 46, 48, 55–70, 92, 101, 107, 110, 119, 126, 128, 151, 160n1, 160n10; *See also* antifascism
Felski, Rita, 40
Fiennes, Ralph, 107, 112, 120
Filkins, Dexter, 73, 78, 84
Final Straw Radio, The, 93
First World War (World War I), 5, 22, 26, 44, 74, 76, 79, 80, 83, 84, 120, 163n32
Floyd, George, 103
Forster, E. M., 79
Foucault, Michel, 87–88
Franco, Francisco, 46, 58, 160n28
freedom, 4, 7, 12, 15, 16, 20, 50, 52, 87–101, 105, 124, 126, 148–49, 152: Eliot's ideas of, 2–3, 6, 41, 49, 62, 74, 87–101, 164n22; Herbert Read on, 41, 49; and anarchism, 41–42, 49, 96–98, 99–100, 165n42; particular freedoms, 48, 94, 95, 150; and COVID-19, 88, 93, 98–99, 100–1
Freedom Press, 47–48
friendship, 1, 12, 39–41, 48–53, 152; Eliot and, 2, 39–41, 44–53, 56, 74, 80, 108
Fritzsche, Hans, 69, 162n51
Fussell, Paul, 5, 81–82
Futurability (Berardi), 147–48

Gallipoli, 80
Gardner, Helen, 138
Gaza, 146, 147, 156n12, 167n61. *See also* Palestine
Germany, 22–23, 25, 64–66, 69, 119, 120, 161n49
Ginsberg, Allen, 6
Godwin, William, 41
Goebbels, Joseph, 126, 162n51
Goering, Hermann, 66
Goldman, Emma, 41, 55, 91, 96–98, 164n38
Goodman, Paul, 91, 99
Goodway, David, 45
Gordon, Lyndall, 22, 39, 134, 135, 138, 139, 145
Gosling, Harry, 94
Graeber, David, 14, 17, 152–53
Green Child, The (Read), 44
Greenhouse with Cyclamens (West), 65, 67, 69, 161n48
Griffin, Roger, 58
Guantánamo Bay prison, 106
Guattari, Félix, 28

Halberstam, Jack, 14
Hale, Emily, 2, 39, 129–30, 132, 135, 140, 141, 145; Eliot's letters to, 2, 13, 53, 55–56, 62, 74, 131, 132, 138, 141–43, 160n28, 162n32
Hamas, 146
Hankins, Gabriel, 9
Harding, Jason, 43, 45
Harvard University, 19, 119
Hayward, John, 39
Hitchens, Christopher, 13
Hitler, Adolf, 58, 59, 64, 161n49, 168n7
Hollis, Matthew, 77
hope, 2, 4, 6, 7, 12, 15, 17, 69, 106, 127–31, 137, 139–44, 147, 148, 150, 152; shared by Eliot and Read, 39, 44, 50, 52–53; radical, 9, 128–44, 147; and literary criticism, 78, 84
Hulme, T. E., 41
humanities, 10, 72–73, 76, 78–79, 82–83, 85, 151–52

idealism, 10–11, 13, 17, 68, 76, 78, 152, 156n25
Imagists, 44
In Parenthesis (Jones), 81, 84
Invisible Committee, 1, 51, 111, 112–13, 114, 117, 124
Israel, 146, 147, 156n12, 167n61
Italy, 60, 92

Jaffe, Sarah, 121, 124
James, Henry, 32
Jerrold, Douglas, 62
Jewish people, 15, 25, 55, 56, 160–61n29
"Jews," 6, 32, 55, 64, 66
Jones, David, 81, 84
Joyce, James, 43
Julian of Norwich, 56
Julius, Anthony, 5
Jun, Nathan, 96, 97

Kallen, Horace M., 32
Keegan, Paul, 77
Killjoy, Margaret, 7
King, James, 44, 47
Kolodney, William, 63
Krockel, Carl, 79, 80
Kropotkin, Peter, 41, 121, 124

Laforgue, Jules, 19
Lagalisse, Erica, 11
Last of the Nuba, The, 57
Lear, Jonathan, 129, 131, 134–37, 143, 144

Lennard, Natasha, 56, 105, 107
Levenson, Michael, 79, 81
Levin, Harry, 110
liberalism, 2, 15, 40, 43, 52, 56, 59, 64, 75, 123, 128, 144
liberation, 4, 6, 10–17 passim, 44, 53, 73, 87, 101, 111, 115, 117, 126, 131, 150; Eliot on, 90–96, 147; Emma Goldman on, 96; theology, 163–64n20, 164nn37–38
libertarian, 42, 45, 99
liberty/liberties, 8, 42, 48, 53, 57, 89, 91, 93–100 passim
Lloyds Bank, 25, 156n14
Lockerd, Benjamin, 16
Lockerd, Martin, 80–81, 82
low theory, 14
Lowe, Peter, 7–8

MAGA ("Make America Great Again"), 12, 60
Mahon, Derek, 78
Malatesta, Errico, 97
Manhattan, 103, 113
Mann, Heinrich, 46
Matthews, Steven, 8
Matthiessen, F. O., 109–10
May, Todd, 39–40, 48, 50
McIntire, Gabrielle, 15
McKay, Claude, 9
MeToo, 7, 107, 108, 165n10
migration, 2, 8, 12, 19–24, 26–36, 73, 89, 156n12, 168n7
Milne, A. A., 73–75
misogyny, 5, 6
Modernism, Memory, and Desire (McIntire), 15
Montenegro, 107
Mosley, Oswald, 64
Murray, Douglas, 57
Murry, John Middleton, 122

Mussolini, Benito, 56, 58–60, 64, 91

Nazis/Nazism, 27, 59, 63–68, 119, 162n51, 164n42
Nelson, Maggie, 87–88
neoliberalism, 40, 51, 107
Neruda, Pablo, 46
Nichols, Tyre, 147
NoDAPL (Dakota Access Pipeline Protests), 107, 123
nomad/nomadism, 28–30, 33, 34, 35, 36, 136–37
North, Joseph, 10, 11
Nuremberg, 65, 67, 69, 161n50, 162n51

Oath Keepers, 100
Obama, Barack, 106, 124
Occupy, 8, 53, 104–24 passim
On Freedom: Four Songs of Care and Constraint (Nelson), 87
Orwell, George, 56, 57, 58, 65–66, 67, 69, 70, 77
Our Mutual Friend (Dickens), 108
Owen, Wilfred, 77

pacifism, 2, 12, 42, 46, 74–78, 82
Pakistan, 146
Palestine, 20, 30, 146. *See also* Gaza
Pasternak-Slater, Ann, 145
Paxton, Robert, 57
Peace News, 48
Picciolini, Christian, 68
Plenty Coups, 129–30, 132, 133–37
Poetry and Anarchism (Read), 45, 46
Poetry and Belief in the Work of T. S. Eliot (Smidt), 16
Possibilities (Graeber), 17
Pound, Ezra, 6, 56, 84, 92
Prague, 147
presentism, 8–9, 149, 156n25

Proud Boys, 100
Proudhon, Pierre Josef, 42
Putin, Vladimir, 100

Quigley, Megan, 7, 165n10

racism, 5, 6, 15, 130, 148
radical hope. *See* hope
Radical Hope (Lear), 129, 133–37
radicalism, 2, 4, 6, 61, 104–5, 113, 129, 144, 149, 150, 152
Ramnath, Maia, 11
Read, Herbert, 2, 21, 35, 39–54, 68, 74; as anarchist, 2, 41–50
renunciation, 39, 130–32, 139
repetition, 115–18, 122, 125, 126
Ribbentrop, Joachim von, 65, 66
Riefenstahl, Leni, 57
Robbins, Michael, 125
Rogers, Gayle, 43
Roma/Romani, 25, 27–28
Rosen, Jody, 124
Russia, 1, 63–64, 91, 92, 100, 146, 156n12
Rutter, Frank, 45

Sakae, Ōsugi, 1
Sassoon, Siegfried, 77
Scholl, Christian, 53, 104
Schuchard, Ronald, 160n4
Scott, James C., 27, 113, 124, 166n20
Seattle, Washington, 104
Second World War (World War II), 27, 35, 40, 47, 58, 62, 66, 67, 69, 74, 76, 92, 130, 138–40, 161n29, 161n49
Serbia, 107
Seybold, Matthew, 9, 156n14
Shakespeare, William, 3, 105–6, 107, 110, 115–16, 119–22, 125, 126
Sioux people, 99, 136
Smidt, Kristian, 16

Smith, Grover, 109
Sontag, Susan, 57
Soviet Union, 64
Spain, 46, 47, 103
Spanish Civil War, 5, 45, 47, 62
Spectator, The, 1–2, 3, 4, 13, 48, 57, 155n1
Spender, Stephen, 7, 43
St. John of the Cross, 122, 134
Stalin, Joseph/Stalinism, 58, 59, 100
Stayer, Jayme, 15, 156n2
Sturgis, South Dakota, 99
Swain, Sean, 91, 93

T. S. Eliot and Christian Tradition (B. Lockerd), 16
"T. S. Eliot: Into *The Waste Land*" (White), 145
Tahrir Square, 106–7, 113
Taylor, Becky, 27
Telfer, Elizabeth, 48
Thoreau, Henry David, 91, 97
Time Magazine, 106
totalitarianism, 8, 25, 48, 51, 58, 75, 88
Transcendentalists, 97–98
Trevelyan, Mary, 39, 56
Triumph of the Will, 57
Trump, Donald, 1, 149, 168n7
Tunisia, 106

Ukraine, 100, 125, 146, 156n12
Unite the Right, 55
US Presidential Election of 2020, 149

Verdenal, Jean, 80, 163n32
Verter, Mitchell Cowen, 121
Vodovnik, Žiga, 42, 53, 87

Wallace, Simon, 40, 50, 51
war, 13, 42, 71–86, 113, 120–21, 128, 135, 151 *See also specific wars*

Ward, Dana, 41, 42, 49
Washington, D. C., 126
Waugh, Evelyn, 57
Ways of Seeing (Berger), 9
West, Rebecca, 56, 57, 58, 65–67, 69, 70, 161n48, 161n50, 162n51
Wheatley, David, 76–78
White, R. S., 78, 83, 85
White, Susannah, 145
Whitman, Walt, 91, 97
Whittier-Ferguson, John, 16
Why Orwell Matters (Hitchens), 13
Wilcox, Michael V., 144
Wittgenstein, Ludwig, 87
Women's March, 107, 111
Woodcock, James, 44, 48
Woolf, Virginia, 6, 9
Writing Against War (Andrews), 76

Zuccotti Park, 106–7, 112, 113, 118

www.ingramcontent.com/pod-product-compliance
Lightning Source LLC
Chambersburg PA
CBHW022028240426
43667CB00042B/1407